An ICD–10–CM
Casebook
and Workbook
for Students

An ICD–10–CM Casebook and Workbook for Students

Psychological and Behavioral Conditions

Edited by
Jack B. Schaffer and **Emil Rodolfa**

American Psychological Association ◆ Washington, DC

Published by
American Psychological Association
750 First Street, NE
Washington, DC 20002
www.apa.org

APA Order Department
P.O. Box 92984
Washington, DC 20090-2984
Phone: (800) 374-2721; Direct: (202) 336-5510
Fax: (202) 336-5502; TDD/TTY: (202) 336-6123
Online: http://www.apa.org/pubs/books
E-mail: order@apa.org

In the U.K., Europe, Africa, and the Middle East, copies may be ordered from
Eurospan Group
c/o Pegasus Drive
Stratton Business Park
Biggleswade Bedfordshire
SG18 8TQ United Kingdom
Phone: +44 (0) 1767 604972
Fax: +44 (0) 1767 601640
Online: https://www.eurospanbookstore.com/apa
E-mail: eurospan@turpin-distribution.com

Typeset in Meridien by Circle Graphics, Inc., Columbia, MD

Printer: Sheridan Books, Chelsea, MI
Cover Designer: Beth Schlenoff Design, Bethesda, MD

Library of Congress Cataloging-in-Publication Data
Names: Schaffer, Jack B., editor. | Rodolfa, Emil, editor. | American
   Psychological Association, issuing body.
Title: An ICD-10-CM casebook and workbook for students : psychological and
   behavioral conditions / edited by Jack B. Schaffer and Emil Rodolfa.
Description: First edition. | Washington, DC : American Psychological
   Association, [2018] | Includes bibliographical references and index.
Identifiers: LCCN 2017038845 | ISBN 9781433828270 (alk. paper) |
   ISBN 1433828278 (alk. paper)
Subjects: | MESH: International statistical classification of diseases and
   related health problems. 10th revision. | Mental Disorders—diagnosis |
   Mental Disorders—classification | International Classification of
   Diseases | Diagnosis, Differential
Classification: LCC RC455.2.C4 | NLM WM 141 | DDC 616.89001/2—dc23 LC record
available at https://lccn.loc.gov/2017038845

British Library Cataloguing-in-Publication Data
A CIP record is available from the British Library.

Printed in the United States of America
First Edition

http://dx.doi.org/10.1037/0000069-000

10 9 8 7 6 5 4 3 2 1

To the memory of my mother. She is responsible for
much of the good around me. I miss her.
—Jack B. Schaffer

To my mom. Thanks.
To my wife. Thanks.
To my kids. Thanks.
To Bob Reilley, my mentor. Thanks.
—Emil Rodolfa

Contents

Contributors

Jeff Baker, PhD, Executive Director, Association of Psychology Postdoctoral and Internship Centers, Houston, TX; Clinical Professor, Department of Anesthesiology, University of Texas Medical Branch, Galveston

Mark S. Barajas, PhD, Assistant Professor, Department of Psychology, Saint Mary's College of California, Moraga

Deborah C. Beidel, PhD, ABPP, Trustee Chair and Pegasus Professor of Psychology and Medical Education, Department of Psychology, University of Central Florida, Orlando

Larry E. Beutler, PhD, Distinguished Professor Emeritus, Pacific Graduate School of Psychology, Palo Alto University, Palo Alto, CA

Lauren Bigham, MS, EdS, Doctoral Student in Counseling Psychology, Department of Counseling and Human Development Services, University of Georgia, Athens

Ryan E. Breshears, PhD, Chief Behavioral Health Officer, Director of Psychology and Integrated Behavioral Health, WellStar Health System, Marietta, GA; Adjunct Assistant Professor, Department of Counseling and Human Development University of Georgia, Athens

Lucia Cavanagh, PhD candidate, Baylor College of Medicine, Houston, TX; psychology intern, Adult Neuropsychology, UCLA Semel Institute for Neuroscience and Human Behavior, Los Angeles, CA

Eli Coleman, PhD, Academic Chair in Sexual Health, Professor and Director, Program in Human Sexuality, Department of Family Medicine and Community Health, University of Minnesota Medical School, Minneapolis

Brooke Davidson, PsyD, California School of Professional Psychology at Alliant International University, Sacramento

Claytie Davis III, PhD, Director of Training, Counseling and Psychological Services, University of California, Berkeley

Katherine Elliott, PhD, Hospitals and Communities Integrated Health Services, Tertiary Mental Health Services, Hillside Centre, Interior Health Authority, Kamloops, British Columbia, Canada

Natacha M. R. Foo Kune, PhD, Director, Counseling Center, University of Washington, Seattle

Gregory A. Hinrichsen, PhD, Assistant Clinical Professor and Consulting Psychologist, Department of Geriatrics and Palliative Medicine, Icahn School of Medicine at Mount Sinai, New York, NY; Associate Clinical Professor of Psychiatry and Behavioral Sciences, Albert Einstein College of Medicine, Bronx, NY

Beth Limberg, PhD, Associate Professor, California School of Professional Psychology at Alliant International University, Sacramento; Family Services Manager, Contra Costa Interfaith Housing, Pleasant Hill, CA

Marsha M. Linehan, PhD, Professor of Psychology and Psychiatry and Behavioral Sciences; Director of the University of Washington Center for Behavioral Technologies, Behavioral Research and Therapy Clinics, Department of Psychology, Seattle

Genny Lou-Barton, LMFT, Doctoral Student in Marriage and Family Therapy, California School of Professional Psychology at Alliant International University, Sacramento

Stephen R. McCutcheon, PhD, Director of Psychology Training, VA Puget Sound Health Care System, Seattle, WA

Staci Leon Morris, PsyD, Research Assistant Professor, Associate Director for Clinical Services and Training, Florida International University Banyan Research Institute on Dissemination, Grants, and Evaluation, Miami

Maryann E. Owens, PhD, Postdoctoral Fellow, VA Pittsburgh Healthcare System, Pittsburgh, PA

Raquel M. Peña, PsyD, California School of Professional Psychology at Alliant International University, Sacramento

Carol B. Peterson, PhD, Associate Professor, Department of Psychiatry, University of Minnesota Medical School, Minneapolis

Emily M. Pisetsky, PhD, Assistant Professor, Department of Psychiatry, University of Minnesota Medical School, Minneapolis

John Preston, PhD, ABPP, Professor, California School of Professional Psychology at Alliant International University, Sacramento

Emil Rodolfa, PhD, Distinguished Professor of Psychology, California School of Professional Psychology at Alliant International University, Sacramento

Aliza Romirowsky, PsyD, Ferkauf Graduate School of Psychology, Yeshiva University, New York, NY

Jack B. Schaffer, PhD, Retired Independent Practitioner and Professor, St. Paul, MN

Jennifer A. Scheurich, Doctoral Student in Clinical Psychology, Department of Psychology, University of Central Florida, Orlando

Martin Sellbom, PhD, Associate Professor, Department of Psychology, University of Otago, Dunedin, New Zealand

Chelsea E. Sleep, Doctoral Student in Clinical Psychology, Department of Psychology, University of Georgia, Athens

Rainey Sealey, MS, Doctoral Student in Clinical Psychology, Department of Psychology, Palo Alto University, Palo Alto, CA

Sinéad Unsworth, PhD, Registered Doctoral Psychologist, Student Counselling Centre, University of Saskatchewan, Saskatoon, Saskatchewan, Canada

Jennifer A. Vencill, PhD, Assistant Professor, Program in Human Sexuality, Department of Family Medicine and Community Health, University of Minnesota Medical School, Minneapolis

Eric F. Wagner, PhD, Professor and Director, Florida International University Banyan Research Institute on Dissemination, Grants, and Evaluation, Miami

Ken C. Winters, PhD, Senior Scientist, Oregon Research Institute, Eugene; Adjunct Faculty, Department of Psychology, University of Minnesota, Minneapolis

Nicola Wright, PhD, CPsych, Schizophrenia Program of the Royal Ottawa Health Care Group (ROHCG); Clinical Professor, Department of Psychology, Faculty of Social Sciences, University of Ottawa, Ontario, Canada

Samantha S. Yard, PhD, Staff Psychologist, VA Puget Sound Health Care System, Seattle, WA

Joyce P. Yang, PhD, Postdoctoral Fellow, National Center for PTSD, VA Palo Alto Health Care System, Palo Alto, CA

Christina B. Yeagley, PsyD, California School of Professional Psychology at Alliant International University, Sacramento

Acknowledgments

Jack and I would like to thank the chapter authors for the enormous work that they put into writing, revising, updating, reviewing, and revising once more. Their goal and ours is to bring you a casebook that will not only provide you knowledge but also challenge you to think critically. We hope you will find this text useful on your path to becoming a competent psychologist. We wish you, the students who read this book, our best as you take each step to become competent.

An ICD-10-CM Casebook and Workbook for Students

Emil Rodolfa and Jack B. Schaffer

Introduction

Competent psychological assessment, including differential diagnosis, is a complex and critically important process. It sets the foundation for the professional relationship with your patient[1] and defines your approach to him or her. Therefore, to ensure competent practice, you need to start with competent assessment and diagnosis. Given your patient's set of symptoms and overall presentation, you must be able to select accurately the most appropriate diagnosis and rule out all other possibilities. This can be a daunting process, especially for budding clinicians who are only just beginning to develop their clinical skills. Thus, our goal in this book is to teach students how to think critically in a professional context and to perform assessments and diagnosis with competence. To achieve that goal, the authors of each chapter present a case that places you, the reader, in the position of the assessing or treating psychologist to provide you with the experience of making clinical decisions.

This casebook is one of several books published by the American Psychological Association (APA) to enhance psychologists' ability to diagnose using the *International Classification of Diseases, 10th Revision—Clinical Modification*

---

[1]In our previous text, we discussed the use of the terms *client* and *patient* by the profession and provided reasons for our use of *patient*. In this casebook, we defer to the chapter authors to use the term they typically use in their clinical settings.

http://dx.doi.org/10.1037/0000069-001
An ICD–10–CM Casebook and Workbook for Students: Psychological and Behavioral Conditions, J. B. Schaffer and E. Rodolfa (Editors)

(ICD–10–CM; World Health Organization [WHO], 2016). In our previous book, *A Student's Guide to Assessment and Diagnosis Using the ICD–10–CM: Psychological and Behavioral Conditions* (Schaffer & Rodolfa, 2016), we provided a framework to assess and diagnose mental health disorders. In this casebook, we have asked well-respected psychologists to work with one (and in some cases, more) of their students to examine and discuss how they go about making a differential diagnosis in specific diagnostic categories.

To accomplish this, we asked the authors of each chapter to use the following format to structure their chapter: Provide a brief overview of the diagnostic classification; present a case, either totally invented or greatly altered from any real case to protect confidentiality; describe the process of assessment, as well as the process of diagnosis using the ICD–10–CM; discuss the ethical issues raised by interacting with this client; summarize how to manage the issues of risk that arise with the case; and consider possible dispositions of the case, including some comments about a possible treatment plan. We are thrilled with the results! Each chapter is filled with thoughtful, helpful comments about the process of assessment and differential diagnosis.

This text comprises chapters covering 16 diagnostic categories. We chose the diagnoses on the basis of the frequency of presentation of people with these diagnoses in clinical settings, as well as the frequency in the literature and in educational settings of discussions about diagnoses, that is, the diagnoses that have the attention of the profession at this time.

We and the chapter authors hoped to make the cases as realistic as possible. Part of what this means is that they are complex, because people in the real world are complex. One consequence is that in a book of this length, every issue cannot be considered or resolved. Just like in the real world! This book is not only a casebook but also a workbook that includes a number of activities for you to consider, perhaps as part of a classroom discussion. We hope these activities, based on the case under consideration, will guide your analysis of the case and, in turn, help you consider the issues related to assessment, diagnosis, and disposition. More on this in a moment.

As you can see from the table of contents, the chapters are ordered in the way they are ordered in the ICD–10–CM; thus, each chapter in this casebook explores one diagnostic category listed in the ICD–10–CM. The only exception to this plan is Chapter 14, which covers the assessment and diagnosis of a personality disorders and provides a cutting-edge discussion of the categorical and dimensional approaches to diagnosis. We believe this discussion is critical to help students look to the future in assessment and, as a result, included this helpful discussion in this casebook.

A word about the diagnostic process that cuts across all of the chapters in this book: As we described in our previous book (Schaffer & Rodolfa, 2016), the process of assessment follows a scientific methodology of hypothesis generation, followed by data collection, resulting in hypothesis testing, leading to a conclusion about the person being assessed. The diagnostic process follows by comparing the data—in particular, in the form of signs and symptoms, and conclusions drawn with the criteria developed for specific diagnostic categories. The *Diagnostic and Statistical Manual of Mental Disorders*

(*DSM*; 5th ed., text rev.; American Psychiatric Association, 2014) system typically lists a series of symptoms representative of a particular diagnosis, with a requirement that a certain number of those symptoms be present for the diagnosis to fit. Although this seems like a precise methodology, as we pointed out in our previous book, given a range of symptoms to choose from, there can be a large number of ways to arrive at a specific diagnosis; for example, 72 combinations of symptoms might arrive at a diagnosis of major depressive disorder. Thus, the diagnostic category itself is not particularly helpful to the psychologist who is trying to understand, "Who is this person that I am working with, and why is this person the way he or she is?" The ICD–10–CM takes a different approach. It uses a kind of best-fit method. Given the data available, including signs and symptoms, but involving all of the information you have about a person, which diagnostic category best fits the particular combination of characteristics and symptoms of this individual? The authors of each of the chapters will lead you through their process of considering, then ruling out, the diagnoses that seem not to fit the data well enough, leaving you with the best remaining diagnosis or diagnoses.

We appreciate each author's hard work and believe that their effort provides you with an outstanding discussion of how to go about making a diagnosis and integrating the ICD–10–CM into the process.

How to Use This Book

As we have already described, this book is a casebook in that each chapter includes the diagnostic, ethical, risk management, and disposition issues involved in a specific case with a specific diagnosis. It is also intended as a workbook. That is, we believe that this book will be most helpful to if you don't simply read it from beginning to end—although we do hope you make it to the end!—but by reading each chapter in conjunction with other resources, such as a diagnostic manual or textbook, and by stopping periodically to think about what you perceive to be the most important issues being raised by the case and the resultant discussion. In particular, as we wrote this book, we had in mind using it in a graduate course in assessment, psychopathology, or treatment. We believe that the more time you spend thinking about how a psychologist goes about assessing and diagnosing a patient, the more useful this book will be for you and the more prepared you will be down the road to function as a competent psychologist.

This book also covers a great deal of ground—namely, 16 diagnostic categories and complex decision-making processes involving data collection and diagnosis. In so short a text, we cannot cover everything that is part of that process. Therefore, this volume is meant to be used in conjunction with other texts on the ICD–10–CM (e.g., Schaffer & Rodolfa, 2016; Goodheart, 2014), as well as texts on psychopathology and psychological treatment (see Chapter 10 in Schaffer & Rodolfa, 2016, for additional resources).

To assist you in this process, the chapter authors provide Activity Boxes to stimulate your thinking about the specific case and the issues it raises for a psychologist. These Activity Boxes will appear five times throughout the chapter. The first activity will appear after you have read the case and typically will ask you to consider issues related to the assessment. The second activity will ask you to apply information learned from the assessment to possible diagnoses. The third activity will raise ethical issues specifically about the case under discussion, the fourth activity will help you examine risk management issues, and the final will raise issues about the disposition of the case.

Many of the issues to consider actually crosscut all of the cases and diagnostic categories. Therefore, rather than repeat the same or very similar activities throughout the chapters, in the activity that follows (Activity 0.1), we provide you with a list of questions you can consult as you read through each chapter. You might dog-ear this page so you can turn back to it easily and often as you read through the following chapters. In addition to these questions, the chapter authors have provided case-specific questions for you to ponder and discuss in class and with colleagues. We hope you will take advantage of all of these questions to stimulate your thinking; we believe that these exercises will help you think like a psychologist.

Once you have read through one of the case descriptions, a number of questions will likely come to your mind. Here is a list of some that we recommend you spend some time thinking about before you continue with the chapter.

ACTIVITY 0.1: General Questions About the Case

- What are your initial impressions of this person?
- What are this person's primary concerns?
- How able is this person to function?
- Do you have any particular worries about this person?
- Based on your theoretical orientation, what are the fundamental psychological issues this person is experiencing?
- Why has this person come in to see you?
- What additional information do you want to know?
- What questions would you plan to ask in your first contact with this person?
- Write some thoughts about how you might phrase your questions to the patient and, perhaps, to other professionals or family members whom you might interview or consult with.

Once you have given these questions some thought, but before you read beyond the case description, we encourage you to turn your focus to diagnostic considerations. Here are some questions you might spend some time considering and researching. We encourage you to find helpful sources to assist you in making an appropriate differential diagnosis. The chapter authors have provided you a number of references they use to help them as they rule out and rule in diagnoses.

ACTIVITY 0.2: General Diagnostic Considerations

▪ Make a list of ICD–10–CM diagnoses that you would want to consider, listing them from most to least likely.
▪ What are the behaviors, emotions, and/or cognitions that lead you to these diagnostic hypotheses?
▪ In addition to the general information you would like, what specific data will you need to rule out diagnoses you have listed?
▪ Would psychological test data be helpful?

This would be a good time to check a diagnostic manual or textbook that describes the particular disorders you are considering. It might also be helpful to create a spreadsheet, listing possible symptoms based on a diagnostic manual and the specific manifestations of those symptoms, if present, in this person.

Before you start the Ethics section of each chapter, here are some issues to consider and think about.

ACTIVITY 0.3: General Ethics Questions

▪ Refer to the APA (2017) and/or Canadian Psychological Association (CPA; 2017) codes of ethics. List any ethical concerns or dilemmas you can identify regarding the case.
▪ Are there any safety, privacy, or competency concerns that you should be aware of?
▪ As you consider where your actions might take you, can you conceive of any "slippery slopes" in dealing with this type of patient? That is, are there behaviors on your part that might seem ethical initially or on the surface but could lead to ethical problems down the road?

Having considered ways to protect the client in the Ethics section, now consider ways of protecting yourself by thinking about these questions.

ACTIVITY 0.4: Risk Management Questions

▪ What risks could you imagine facing when working with this person?
▪ What actions do you need to consider from your first professional contact with this person?
▪ How can you protect yourself without violating the ethical rights of the patient?

Now you have reached the ultimate goal of the psychological assessment process, deciding how you are going to proceed, whether by offering treatment yourself, making a referral to someone else, or offering a recommendation to the referring person. Here are some questions you will need to consider with every person you work with, regardless of what your eventual disposition is.

ACTIVITY 0.5: Disposition Issues

▪ What presenting problems need to be addressed?
▪ How would you prioritize the presenting problems to determine what to do first?
▪ What goals has the patient identified?
▪ What goals do you have for this patient?
▪ What interventions do you think would be most appropriate, and why did you choose them?
▪ What results or trends would you expect to see over time?
▪ How would you evaluate whether your treatment of this person is successful?

The ICD–10–CM: The Foundation for Diagnosis

The ICD–10–CM is a compendium of diagnoses that cover causes of mortality (death) and morbidity (symptoms and illness), not a diagnostic manual that provides criteria for making a diagnosis. The ICD–10–CM assumes that the professional using this system has sufficient expertise and knowledge to apply the best-fit diagnosis to a constellation of symptoms in a reasonably reliable and valid fashion. In other words, the fact that the ICD–10–CM is not a manual provides the practitioner with considerable flexibility, as opposed to a manualized system like the *DSM*. Consult other texts on how to use the ICD–10–CM in your practice, such as Chapter 1 in our previous book (Schaffer & Rodolfa, 2016) or Carol Goodheart's (2014) primer for ICD–10–CM users.

As you enter this profession, it may seem that some diagnoses are not as challenging to make; however, as you read this casebook, you will note that the cluster of symptoms that make up a diagnosis is often not quite so clear-cut. The chapter authors discuss how they make sense of these diagnoses as they discuss their assessments and understanding of their clients' symptom presentation.

The authors use a variety of resources as a foundation to discuss the disorders they present to you. For instance, some have chosen to use the *ICD–10 Classification of Mental and Behavioural Disorders: Clinical Descriptions and Diagnostic Guidelines*, typically referred to as the *Blue Book* (WHO, 1993). They believe the convenience and availability of the *Blue Book* outweigh the disadvantages and that the diagnostic criteria are adequately current for their diagnostic category. We discussed the issues involved in using this particular resource in more detail in our other book in this series (Schaffer & Rodolfa, 2016). Although the *Blue Book* has been in existence for some time, it is easily and inexpensively accessible through the World Health Organization (WHO, 1993). Other authors have chosen to rely on various texts as diagnostic manuals for the diagnosis they make in their chapter because they are more current or complete than the *Blue Book*. In that case they have provided you with references to that text.

In your practice, you should consider these perspectives along with the texts you use in your graduate program's psychopathology course. And, of course, after graduation you should stay current with the literature and decide which diagnostic texts are most appropriate for the individuals with whom you work.

The ICD–10–CM is available in PDF format free of charge from the U.S. government's Centers for Medicare and Medicaid Services (2017) website (https://www.cms.gov/Medicare/Coding/ICD10/2017-ICD-10-CM-and-GEMs.html). The *Blue Book* (WHO, 1993) is available free of charge on the WHO website (http://www.who.int/classifications/icd/en/bluebook.pdf).

Issues That Cut Across Chapters

A number of issues are discussed in more than one chapter. In particular, three issues—competence, suicide assessment, and self-care—are raised by many authors. As a result, we believe that it will be helpful and will prevent simple repetition to discuss briefly these three issues in this introduction, so we have asked the authors who raise them to limit their discussions in their chapters.

As you may be able to intuit from your experiences and classes in psychology, the issues of the therapist's competence, the assessment of the patient's suicidality, and the concern of therapist self-care are encountered regularly during one's training and career. This brief overview will help provide a foundation for your understanding when the chapter authors discuss these issues in the context of the cases they present.

COMPETENT PRACTICE IN PSYCHOLOGY

Competent practice is based on a combination of knowledge, skills and values/attitudes (APA Commission on Accreditation, 2015; Association of State and Provincial Psychology Boards, 2014; Rodolfa et al., 2013). To be competent, a psychologist must have a basic foundation of knowledge; effectively display the skills needed to assess, diagnose, and treat; be open to new perspectives through continued learning and consultation with others as needed; and have a sound understanding of and ability to apply the ethical standards of the profession. Both the APA (2017) *Ethical Principles of Psychologists and Code of Conduct* and the CPA (2017) *Canadian Code of Ethics for Psychologists* emphasize the importance of competency (APA Ethics Code, Standard 2.01, Boundaries of Competence; CPA Code of Ethics, Standard II.6) in the practice of psychology.

The issue of competent practice is raised by each of the authors in this casebook. These authors challenge you to consider what steps you will need to take to develop or enhance your competency in the assessment and treatment of the described disorders. We believe competency is one of the most critical concepts in the practice of psychology. As a student, you are currently going through the process of gaining competency in the profession of psychology. Your classes and your practicum, internship, and postdoctoral fellowship will all greatly enhance your competency. Each of these experiences is created to help you in a sequential, graded, and cumulative way

(APA Commission on Accreditation, 2015) to develop the foundational and functional knowledge, skills, and values (Rodolfa et al., 2005) to practice as a competent psychologist. Yet even after you complete your degree and receive your license to practice psychology independently, it is incumbent on you to continue the process of lifelong learning (see Wise et al., 2010). Your education does not end with your degree. It does not even end at licensure because maintaining competence is a career-long and lifelong process. It is with this mind-set that we encourage you to read this casebook.

SUICIDE ASSESSMENT

Numerous useful articles and books have been written about assessing suicidal ideation and behavior (Kleespies, 2014). There is a reason for that. Suicide assessment is a critically important aspect of the work of a psychologist: 13.4 per 100,000 people in the United States die by suicide each year (Centers for Disease Control and Prevention, National Center for Health Statistics, 2017). This translates to almost 45,000 people each year. That makes the probability of your having to confront the possibility of suicide in your practice at some point in your career very high. In addition, working with a suicidal client is a difficult and stressful endeavor. Kleespies and Dettmer (2000) reported that conducting a suicide assessment is challenging, at times aversive, and perhaps the most stressful activity performed by a psychologist. In Pope and Vasquez's (2016) exploration of psychology ethics, Linehan indicated that one of the difficulties in responding to suicidal clients is that practitioners do not have appropriate training and experience to assess and treat them. Sommers-Flanagan and Shaw (2017) noted that psychologists' graduate curriculum is not consistently infused with training to enhance suicidal competencies. We hope that reading about and discussing the issues of suicidal behavior presented in this casebook will be a first (or second) step to help you become better prepared to respond when a client presents with suicidal ideation or behavior.

The following comments are provided to give you an overview of the assessment and intervention with a client expressing suicidal ideation. Pope and Vasquez (2016) described 22 risk factors that may be useful for a clinician to take into consideration, although there are limitations to these factors discussed by Pope and Vasquez (i.e., factors may interact, factors can change, factors are not comprehensive or conclusive). These factors include a verbal warning, having a plan, prior attempts, communicating intent indirectly, and depressive disorders, among many others. Rogers and Joiner (2017) noted that these risk factors focus primarily on suicidal ideation rather than suicide attempts. In an interesting study, they highlighted the importance that rumination and brooding, rather than problem-solving, play in placing individuals on the path toward suicide attempts instead of considering alternatives to suicide.

Franklin et al. (2017), in a meta-analysis of 50 years of research of suicidal thoughts and behaviors (STB), found that the consideration of STB risk factors as well as protective factors has limited utility because of methodological constraints in the studies they analyzed. They emphasized that STB risk factors are based on rational derivations from expert consensus. However, although they have not been evaluated by the literature, they may be helpful. As all authors agree, the roles of STB risk factors are complex and likely interactive, and using only single risk factors yields limited utility in predicting STBs. Current research is zeroing in on the most important factors in influencing suicidal tendencies (see Witte, Holm-Denoma, Zuromski, Gauthier, & Ruscio, 2017). Such research makes keeping up with the current literature in this area especially crucial.

Sommers-Flanagan and Shaw (2017) underscored the importance of keeping up-to-date with the suicide assessment and intervention literature, documenting the following six shifts in current research:

> (a) acknowledgment that suicide risk factors are not especially helpful to psychologist-practitioners; (b) a movement away from medical model formulations and toward social constructionist and collaborative orientations [i.e., movement away from viewing suicidal behavior as a specific illness and toward a collaborative understanding of the client's suicidal experience]; (c) progress in theoretical knowledge pertaining to suicidal individuals; (d) recognition that the clinical encounter and comprehensive suicide assessment interviews are essential to developing and maintaining a therapeutic relationship; (e) advancements in how clinicians question patients about suicide ideation; and (f) methods for monitoring suicide ideation over time. (p. 98)

Sommers-Flanagan and Shaw emphasized that "psychologists who understand and apply these approaches to suicide risk assessment will be more capable of conducting competent suicide assessment and treatment and thereby contribute to national suicide prevention efforts" (p. 98).

Although critical to practice, competence in suicide assessment will not be achieved by reading this book—or any book, for that matter. We hope that this text and the related resources referenced herein will help you develop the foundational knowledge to enter supervised practice experiences (i.e., practicum and internship) to take additional steps to achieve competence.

SELF-CARE

Acquiring the knowledge and skills necessary for the competent practice of psychology allows one to develop a sense of self-efficacy, the experience and belief that one is able to manage life's challenges effectively (Bandura, 1977, 1997). Part of what self-efficacy means is that a person is able to respond to life's challenges without feeling overwhelmed by them, a process referred to as *resilience* (see Rutter, 2012). Research has demonstrated that support systems, both within the family (Laub & Sampson, 2003) and beyond the family (Masten & Tellegen, 2012), provide important protective factors for the development and maintenance of resilience and in turn competence.

Competence is also developed through gaining experience (skill) in a wide range of experiences. This wide range of skill development may increase a person's adaptability and ability to manage new and challenging situations (Chandra & Leong, 2016). Thus, one of our messages to you, our reader, is this: Develop supportive social networks, both professionally and personally, and accumulate many different kinds of experiences, both as a psychologist and otherwise, and, in the process, seek out consultation and supervision from others who can assist you in managing the new challenges in ways that lead to "steeling" (Rutter, 2012) rather than capitulation.

But this is not the end of the story. We do want to emphasize that the process (the lifelong process) of achieving competence is not easy. The courses you take and the supervised training you are receiving to acquire competence as a psychologist constitute an arduous journey. And once you become a psychologist, the work will continue to be taxing. Guy, Poelstra, and Stark (1989) reported that 75% of psychologists surveyed realized that they experienced significant work-related distress, and 37% acknowledged that their distress was negatively affecting their work. These are striking numbers and ones that you should heed, particularly in light of Richards, Campenni, and Muse-Burke's (2010) study, which suggests that mental health professionals are particularly susceptible to burnout and emotional and functional impairment within their professional roles.

The APA (2017) Ethics Code and the CPA (2017) Code of Ethics that are referred to throughout this casebook provide the foundation for the necessity of self-care. On the basis of the guidance provided by these codes, it is essential that psychologists and psychology trainees take steps to prepare themselves—that is, take care of themselves—for the hard work that lies ahead.

Richards et al. (2010) reported that there is no one definition of self-care, but they described the following possibilities: psychological, physical, and spiritual efforts and support with the goal of enhancing subjective well-being. Richards and coworkers discussed a significant positive relationship among self-care, self-awareness, and well-being.

In a thoughtful discussion of the work of a mental health practitioner, Svokholt (2012) acknowledged the intensity of the therapeutic process as an interpersonal situation with high stakes, high vulnerability, and great potential for personal harm to the client when practiced inadequately. Svokholt asserted that to be successful, the mental health practitioner must be personally and emotionally available throughout his or her clinical work with clients. He suggested that mental health practitioners ensure high levels of personal and emotional functioning by engaging in positive and enjoyable activities (i.e., self-care activities) that stimulate emotional coping and build up emotional reserves so they are more resilient and are able to practice in a consistently competent manner.

Self-care also involves using your best judgment, based on the best evidence available (and, in our field, as in others, the best evidence is gained through using a scientific methodology; see Schaffer & Rodolfa, 2016), thus training yourself to ask questions and make decisions based on the evidence before you. This casebook offers many examples of psychologists using the scientific method to determine a diagnosis and then taking the next step in the process of assessment and treatment.

Although it is a broad topic, when discussing self-care, as when discussing so many important topics in psychology, specificity is important. Myers et al. (2012) found that when self-care is being promoted to graduate students, it is important to emphasize specific behaviors that will be useful in managing stress rather than simply encouraging an ambiguous concept of self-care. Thus, when thinking about self-care, think in specifics: How much sleep am I getting? Am I exercising? When was the last time I had a social contact? What am I doing to manage my emotional responses to the clients I am assessing and treating? How can I help myself live in this moment? Taking specific steps to care for yourself will help you manage your stress and in turn help you acquire the knowledge and skills to competently assess and diagnose your clients.

As we stated at the beginning of this Introduction, competent assessment and diagnosis set the foundation for competent psychological practice. They are critically important processes, yet they are also complex and difficult to master. Our hope is that this casebook, in combination with our previous text, will help you increase your competence in assessing and diagnosing patients using the ICD–10–CM, thus preparing you to practice competently throughout your career as a psychologist.

References

American Psychiatric Association. (2014). *Diagnostic and statistical manual of mental disorders* (5th ed., Text rev.). Washington, DC: Author.

American Psychological Association. (2017). *Ethical principles of psychologists and code of conduct* (2002, Amended June 1, 2010 and January 1, 2017). Retrieved from http://www.apa.org/ethics/code/index.aspx

American Psychological Association Commission on Accreditation. (2015). *Standards for accreditation for health service psychology*. Retrieved from http://c.ymcdn.com/sites/www.asppb.net/resource/resmgr/guidelines/2017_ASPPB_Competencies_Expe.pdf

Association of State and Provincial Psychology Boards. (2014). *Competencies expected of a psychologist at the point of licensure*. Retrieved from http://c.ymcdn.com/sites/www.asppb.net/resource/resmgr/guidelines/2017_ASPPB_Competencies_Expe.pdf

Bandura, A. (1977). Self-efficacy: Toward a unifying theory of behavioral change. *Psychological Review, 84*, 191–215. http://dx.doi.org/10.1037/0033-295X.84.2.191

Bandura, A. (1997). *Self-efficacy: The exercise of control*. New York, NY: Freeman.

Canadian Psychological Association. (2017). *Canadian code of ethics for psychologists* (4th ed.). Retrieved from http://www.cpa.ca/docs/File/Ethics/CPA_Code_2017_4thEd.pdf

Centers for Disease Control and Prevention, National Center for Health Statistics. (2017). *Suicide and self-inflicted injury*. Retrieved from https://www.cdc.gov/nchs/fastats/suicide.htm

Centers for Medicare and Medicaid Services. (2017). *ICD–10–CM*. Retrieved from https://www.cms.gov/Medicare/Coding/ICD10/2017-ICD-10-CM-and-GEMs.html

Chandra, S., & Leong, F. T. L. (2016). A diversified portfolio model of adaptability. *American Psychologist, 71*, 847–862. http://dx.doi.org/10.1037/a0040367

Franklin, J., Ribeiro, J., Fox, K., Bentley, K., Kleiman, E., Huang, X., . . . Nock, M. (2017, February). Risk factors for suicidal thoughts and behaviors: A meta-analysis of 50 years of research. *Psychological Bulletin, 143*, 187–232. http://dx.doi.org/10.1037/bul0000084

Goodheart, C. (2014). *A primer for ICD–10–CM users: Psychological and behavioral conditions.* http://dx.doi.org/10.1037/14379-000

Guy, J., Poelstra, P., & Stark, M. (1989). Personal distress and therapeutic effectiveness: National survey of psychologists practicing psychotherapy. *Professional Psychology: Research and Practice, 20,* 48–50.

Kleespies, P. (2014). *Decision making in behavioral emergencies: Acquiring skill in evaluating and managing high-risk patients.* Washington, DC: American Psychological Association.

Kleespies, P., & Dettmer, E. (2000). An evidence-based approach to evaluating and managing suicidal emergencies. *Journal of Clinical Psychology, 56,* 1109–1130.

Laub, J. H., & Sampson, R. J. (2003). *Shared beginnings, divergent lives: Delinquent boys to age 70.* Cambridge, MA: Harvard University Press.

Masten, A. S., & Tellegen, A. (2012). Resilience in developmental psychopathology: Contributions of the Project Competence Longitudinal Study. *Development and Psychopathology, 24,* 345–361. http://dx.doi.org/10.1017/S095457941200003X

Myers, S., Sweeney, A., Popick, V., Wesley, K., Bordfeld, A., & Fingerhut, R. (2012). Self-care practices and perceived stress levels among psychology graduate students. *Training and Education in Professional Psychology, 6,* 55–66. http://dx.doi.org/10.1037/a0026534

Pope, K., & Vasquez, M. (2016). *Ethics in psychotherapy and counseling: A practical guide* (5th ed.). Hoboken, NJ: Wiley.

Richards, K., Campenni, C., & Muse-Burke, J. (2010). Self-care and well-being in mental health professionals: The mediating effects of self-awareness and mindfulness. *Journal of Mental Health Counseling, 32,* 247–264.

Rodolfa, E., Bent, R., Eisman, E., Nelson, P., Rehm, L., & Ritchie, P. (2005). A cube model for competency development: Implications for psychology educators and regulators. *Professional Psychology: Research and Practice, 36,* 347–354. http://dx.doi.org/10.1037/0735-7028.36.4.347

Rodolfa, E., Greenberg, S., Hunsley, J., Smith-Zoeller, M., Cox, D., Sammons, M., . . . Spivak, H. (2013). A competency model for the practice of psychology. *Training and Education in Professional Psychology, 7,* 71–83. http://dx.doi.org/10.1037/a0032415

Rogers, M., & Joiner, T. (2017, March 13). Rumination, suicidal ideation, and suicide attempts: A meta-analytic review. *Review of General Psychology.* Advance online publication. http://dx.doi.org/10.1037/gpr0000101

Rutter, M. (2012). Resilience as a dynamic concept. *Development and Psychopathology, 24,* 335–344. http://dx.doi.org/10.1017/S0954579412000028

Schaffer, J., & Rodolfa, E. (2016). *A student's guide to assessment and diagnosis using the ICD–10–CM: Psychological and behavioral conditions.* Washington, DC: American Psychological Association.

Sommers-Flanagan, J., & Shaw, S. (2017). Suicide risk assessment: What psychologists should know. *Professional Psychology: Research and Practice, 48,* 98–106.

Svokholt, T. (2012). *Becoming a therapist: On the path to mastery.* Hoboken, NJ: Wiley.

Wise, E. H., Sturm, C. A., Nutt, R. L., Rodolfa, E., Schaffer, J. B., & Webb, C. (2010). Lifelong learning for psychologists: Current status and a vision for the future. *Professional Psychology: Research and Practice, 41,* 288–297. http://dx.doi.org/10.1037/a0020424

Witte, T. K., Holm-Denoma, J. M., Zuromski, K. L., Gauthier, J. M., & Ruscio, J. (2017). Individuals at high risk for suicide are categorically distinct from those at low risk. *Psychological Assessment, 29*, 382–393. http://dx.doi.org/10.1037/pas0000349

World Health Organization. (1993). *ICD–10 classification of mental and behavioural disorders: Clinical descriptions and diagnostic guidelines.* Retrieved from http://www.who.int/classifications/icd/en/bluebook.pdf

World Health Organization. (2016). *International classification of diseases and related health problems—10.* Retrieved from http://apps.who.int/classifications/icd10/browse/2016/en

Jeff Baker and Lucia Cavanagh

F06.03 Mood Disorder Due to Known Medical Condition

1

Affective responses such as sadness or anxiety are typically expected when there is a change in health. Although many emotional reactions that occur in association with medical conditions are normal human reactions, the interference of these affective responses with an individual's daily routine suggests the presence of a mood disorder (Kaptein, 2014). In addition, normal affective reactions to stress are usually experienced for a limited period of time. When they persist, which often occurs in the presence of medical conditions that are chronic (long term), the individual's susceptibility to the development of a mood disorder is heightened (Egede, 2007). A number of factors can affect whether distress from chronic medical conditions develops into a mood disorder, including demographic variables, resiliency, positive affect, cognitive appraisals of the illness (e.g., illness acceptance, internal health locus of control), and availability of social and environmental resources (see Helgeson & Zajdel, 2017).

Any of a wide range of medical conditions can result in a mood disorder that negatively affects emotional well-being, employment, income, relationships, or living arrangements (Brannon, Feist, & Updegraff, 2013). Some medical conditions (and medications used to treat the condition) may directly affect mood by altering levels of key neurotransmitters in the brain associated with emotional states (Patten & Barbui, 2004); other medical conditions can affect

http://dx.doi.org/10.1037/0000069-002
An ICD–10–CM Casebook and Workbook for Students: Psychological and Behavioral Conditions, J. B. Schaffer and E. Rodolfa (Editors)

mood indirectly by limiting physical function or the ability to engage in meaningful tasks or social interactions.

The bidirectional relationship of mental and physical health, with a patient's mood affecting and being affected by health outcomes (Koran et al., 1989), and the variability in both presentation and precipitating conditions make it difficult to estimate reliably the prevalence of mood disorders that are due to medical conditions. Estimates are that about 50% of Parkinson's disease patients, 33% of heart attack survivors, and 25% of patients with cancer may experience depression (National Institute of Mental Health, 2002).

The practice of psychology in medical settings is broadly known as *integrated care psychology*, meaning that the psychologist works as an integral member of a team of health care providers to treat the patient. Each team member knows what the other team members are doing, and the overall care of the patient is at the forefront of the treatment plan (Tauber, 2005). The practice of integrated care psychology is long-standing, but its presence is likely to continue to grow as the medical community becomes more aware of these biopsychosocial interactions (L. Fisher & Dickinson, 2014; Kazak & Noll, 2015). Although considerable heterogeneity exists in the degree that mental health is integrated into medical settings (Ouwens, Wollersheim, Hermens, Hulscher, & Grol, 2005), many medical centers have psychologists on several services or departments who may serve as supervisors for medical fellows so the fellows can better understand the clinical presentations and prevalence of psychological overlays to chronic medical conditions, including managing symptoms and improving quality of life. Psychologists in a department of psychiatry usually focus primarily on mental illness (Feuerstein, Labbé, & Kuczmierczyk, 2013), whereas psychologists located in other units tend to focus on adjustment related to the medical condition and the ways in which psychological factors contribute to health problems, such as the impact of stress on heart disease or the effects of behaviors such as diet and exercise on diabetes.

The Case

Ms. H is a 57-year-old White woman who was seen by you, a psychologist working in the Anesthesiology Pain Clinic. She presented with primary complaints of chronic pain in the lower back, neck, shoulder and knees resulting from prior injuries. Chronic pain syndrome due to injury (G89.21) refers to pain that has not subsided over the normal healing period expected for physical injuries, which is usually 6 to 12 weeks in duration (National Institute of Neurological Disorders, National Institutes of Health, 2009). Additional active medical problems for Ms. H. included Type 2 diabetes mellitus without complications (E11.9), Hypertensive heart disease without heart failure (I11.9), and psychosocial changes marked by sleep and memory difficulties (Z72.821 and Z65.8), in part due to her pain. Last, Ms. H. reported a history of depressive symptoms, anxiety, and relationship difficulties.

During the initial evaluation, Ms. H states that her pain was the result of a motor vehicle accident (MVA) that occurred 25 years ago, with the pain progressively intensifying since then from subsequent accidents, falls, and increasing health problems. Using a standard pain assessment, with 1 as the lowest level of pain and 10 as the highest, Ms. H reports a current pain level of 7 and an average pain rating of 5, with a range between 3 and 10. She reports previous pain management treatment, including relaxation techniques, that she states helped to reduce her pain. Ms. H relates that her pain increases with activity, which is exacerbated even by a minimum of household chores. She reports minimal pain relief with the use of opioids and expresses concern about potential addiction problems, which she has experienced in the past. Behavioral observations during the interview indicate that Ms. H is attentive, cooperative, open to discussing details, and appears to be in mild distress. Beyond her reported memory complaints, Ms. H's cognitive functioning appears within normal limits, and her emotional stability appears fair. She is able to communicate without difficulty.

PSYCHOSOCIAL HISTORY

Ms. H states that she has lived with her partner for 15 years in a nonconflictual but distant relationship. She has two children from a previous relationship, describing a positive relationship with her son (28 years old) but not with her daughter (26 years old). She completed 10 years of school and received her GED at age 42. Following her MVA, Ms. H was diagnosed as medically disabled. She relies on her partner's salary and her Social Security disability insurance to live and expresses considerable worry about her financial resources. She reports sometimes feeling so overwhelmed by her pain, worry, and lack of social support that she withdraws into her room and does not interact with others.

PHYSICAL ABUSE, SUBSTANCE ABUSE, AND ADDITIONAL MENTAL STRESSORS

Ms. H reports a recent decrease in sleep, concentration/memory, and interest in activities, and a recent increase in crying, agitation, depression, withdrawal, and excessive worrying. She denies current suicidal ideation but endorses a past history of a suicidal attempt that involved taking a "handful of black mollies" about 20 years ago when she was married, diagnosed with cancer, and her husband had just left her. She reports problems with alcohol when she was younger but has not used alcohol in the past 5 years. Finally, Ms. H reports that she had been physically abused in the past but denied any current experiences of abuse.

MEDICATIONS AND MEDICAL HISTORY

Ms. H's relevant medical history includes an appendectomy 33 years ago; cancer (now in remission) 24 years ago, with treatment including a radical hysterectomy; open cholecystectomy 22 years ago; and left knee endoscopy 3 years ago. Her medical chart indicated she had a history of 23 medications. Medications she is currently taking include amitriptyline, Cymbalta, Seroquel, and trazodone, which are used to treat depression and pain, plus an additional six medications (Neurontin, Flexeril, Zanaflex, Darvocet, tramadol, propoxyphene) that actively treat pain. Other current medications include albuterol (an inhaler), Synthroid (for hypothyroidism), Lipitor (for high cholesterol), metformin (for diabetes), Boniva (for osteoporosis), and Imitrex (for migraines).

Assessment Using ICD–10–CM

ACTIVITY 1.1:

Given the medical complexities in this case, what are your thoughts about your role in the diagnostic process? Which variables will be most important to consider when assessing Ms. H? Are there any variables not yet specified in your initial evaluation of Ms. H or in her medical history that you will need to consider?

Your initial impressions should highlight that this is a complex case and that there are many variables to prioritize during assessment. Variables of concern may be Ms. H's chronic pain, substance abuse history, and financial situation (particularly as it relates to affording expensive medications). Secondary issues may include availability of social support, physical limitations, and cognitive complaints (especially as they relate to making medical decisions). Your initial impression was that her chronic pain was negatively affecting her emotional state, resulting in depressive and anxious symptoms. The relationship between her mood and her health is a central issue.

In addition to the available information, it would be helpful to know what coping strategies and resources this patient might have available to her, which could highlight a potential area for treatment intervention. Although she indicated she has not used substances in 5 years and is confidently sober, you wonder whether this is in fact true or whether you might need additional information to corroborate this. You might also want to consult with the anesthesiologist to understand better Ms. H's use of narcotics. Last, you will want to know how involved Ms. H was in previous pain management interventions, how successful they were, and how that might affect her motivation to work with you.

Let's assume that you collected data in the form of a clinical interview, review of medical records, and an assessment battery that included self-report questionnaires, personality measures, and cognitive tests. Each data method lends a unique piece of information that is then integrated to develop a comprehensive understanding of the patient.

The patient completed the following measures: (a) Coping Strategies Questionnaire (CSQ; Rosenstiel & Keefe, 1983), (b) Type D Distress Questionnaire (Type D; Denollet, 2005), (c) Beck Depression Inventory FastScreen for Medical Patients (BDI–FMS; Beck, Steer, & Brown, 2000), (d) Brief Pain Inventory (BPI; Cleeland & Ryan, 1994),

(e) Minnesota Multiphasic Personality Inventory—2 (MMPI–2; Butcher, Dahlstrom, Graham, Tellegen, & Kaemmer, 1989; Hathaway, McKinley, & the MMPI Restandardization Committee 1989), and (f) the Repeatable Battery for the Assessment of Neuropsychological Screening (RBANS; Randolph, 1998). General personality measures, such as the MMPI–2 (or MMPI–2—Restructured Form), can be helpful in understanding the patients' personality dynamics and coping style, while a more focused test, such as the BDI–FS, is sensitive to depression that is a result of medical conditions. The data from these tests and the interview indicated that (a) Ms. H had some positive coping strategies in being able to divert her attention from her pain and make positive coping statements to herself; (b) she has a high level of negative cognitions about herself and her life; (c) her chronic medical condition interferes with almost all aspects of her physical and mental functioning, and as a result, she has a poor quality of life; (d) she presents with symptoms of depression, anxiety, and a past history of poor impulse control; (e) she presents with memory deficits that likely contribute to problems in managing her pain and her medication; and (f) her depression appears to be related more to her physical problems than her mental state, an important finding for determining her diagnosis.

ELECTRONIC MEDICAL RECORDS

A review of the medical chart is standard when evaluating a patient in a medical setting. The electronic medical record (EMR) provides a simple method of providing integrated care for patients because notes from other treatment providers are readily available. In a medical record, you will want to look for a problem list, notes concerning the patient's involvement and cooperation with treatment (e.g., keeping appointments, taking medications as prescribed), and a description of what interventions have been attempted and their effectiveness. In this case, the EMR provided support for the symptom timeline that associates Ms. H's mood with her physical condition. The American Psychological Association (APA; 2007b) has guidelines that provide ethical and professional standards of patient records.

ICD–10–CM Diagnosis

A list of differential diagnoses from the *International Classification of Disease, 10th Revision—Clinical Modification* (ICD–10–CM; World Health Organization, 1993) suggested by the symptoms of this patient might include Mood disorder due to known medical condition with mixed features (F06.34), Adjustment disorder with mixed anxiety and depressed mood (F43.23), Dysthymic disorder (F34.1), Generalized anxiety disorder (F41.1), and/or Persistent mood disorder, unspecified (F34.9). Given Ms. H's reports of withdrawing into her room when feeling overwhelmed, you might also consider Agoraphobia (F40.01). You also wonder whether her sleep difficulties and memory problems warrant separate diagnoses (e.g., Sleep disorder not due to a substance or known physiological condition, unspecified [F51.9] and Other amnesia [R41.3], respectively), or whether they are manifestations of a primary diagnosis.

The patient's symptoms clearly point to a disorder of mood, in some manner. The major question is its apparent cause. In Ms. H's case, her history and the medical record indicate that the onset of her mood disturbance followed her car accident, and the course of her depressive and anxious symptoms tends to covary with her pain. In addition, the psychological testing data suggest that her mood disturbances, although clinically significant and interfering with her life, are directly related to her chronic pain. Thus, on the basis of these interview and testing data, we can rule out Dysthymic disorder (F34.1) and Persistent mood disorder, unspecified (F34.9) because the onset and chronicity of her difficulties are best accounted for by her medical condition. Although Ms. H also has a history of anxiety (F41.1), her testing revealed positive coping strategies, and per her presentation, the anxiety only became an issue during situations in which she felt overwhelmed, so anxiety does not appear to be primary. You can likely rule out Agoraphobia (F40.0) because you observe that her reports of "withdrawing" and social isolation seem more reflective of her coping style rather than an irrational fear of being trapped or panic about public places.

As a result, the primary diagnoses from the ICD–10–CM that best fit her presentation are Mood Disorder due to known medical condition with mixed features (F06.34) and Adjustment disorder with both depressive and anxious symptoms (F43.23). It seems that sleep and memory problems are secondary issues that result from her pain and contribute to her mood disorder (e.g., difficulty getting to sleep because of pain), although you could list them as secondary diagnoses. You may consider additional consults with neurology or a sleep expert to elucidate the extent to which sleep or memory problems contribute to her depressive and anxious symptoms.

Ethical Considerations—Protecting Your Patient

Because integrated care psychology often requires collaboration with other professionals, issues of confidentiality with respect to professional roles, recordkeeping, and report dissemination are important to consider (American Psychological Association [APA; 2017] *Ethical Principles of Psychologists and Code of Conduct* [APA Ethics Code], Standards 4.01, Maintaining Confidentiality; 6.01, Documentation of Professional and Scientific Work and Maintenance of Records; and 6.02, Maintenance, Dissemination, and Disposal of Confidential Records of Professional and Scientific Work, respectively). The field of psychology is not unified regarding how to structure psychological reports and what to include. In a setting where multiple other professionals have access to psychological data through the EMR, it is important that you include only information specifically relevant to the referral questions and not personal information that would not have a direct impact on the patient's treatment. The concern for patient privacy needs to be balanced, however, with other professionals' needs for information, which may help them understand the patient's medical treatment needs because those needs are likely related to the patient's emotional stability, available coping strategies, behavioral and dispositional traits, potential for substance abuse, and psychosocial history. These factors can influence the patient's health and likelihood of responding to medical treatment. In turn, the medical staff can provide useful information for the psychologist, such as pharmacological data, integrity of brain functioning, and history of adherence to medical recommendations. Although developing firewalls between health and mental health notes may be respectful of the patient's privacy (APA Ethics Code, Standard 4.05, Disclosures), providers who work together with patients to disclose psychological data relevant to their physical health tend to have improved treatment outcomes (APA, 2008). This presents an ethical predicament involving a balance between operating in the best interests of the patient and protecting patient privacy (Richards, 2009; see also Chapter 6, this volume). To that end, the importance of informed consent is especially crucial in medical settings (APA Ethics Code, Standard 3.10, Informed Consent) and should include a thorough discussion with the patient of the information that will be gathered, the way that information will be shared with other providers, and the possible consequences of that sharing, both positive and negative.

Complex patients call for the psychologist to do a comprehensive, sometimes lengthy, evaluation, which can be expensive. Such a circumstance can create an ethical dilemma involving a clash between protecting the patient and revenue generation. For a more in-depth discussion of this issue, see C. B. Fisher (2008) and Pope (1990). Ultimately, when working within the managed care system, psychologists must continually balance their fee practices (APA Ethics Code, Standard 6.04, Fees and Financial Arrangements) and accuracy in reporting (APA Ethics Code, Standard 6.06, Accuracy in Reports to Payors and Funding Sources) against the best interests of their patient.

Integrated care psychologists must also ensure that they have specialized competence related to their role within the integrated care setting (APA, 2007a), above and beyond having the necessary competence to provide the psychological services rendered (APA Ethics Code, Standard 2.01, Boundaries of Competence). Because psychological testing is a common component of integrated care psychology, familiarity with the tests administered and competency in test interpretation is particularly important. Many of the ethical concerns regarding testing are discussed in Schaffer and Rodolfa (2016), including selecting valid and reliable tests, using tests that are appropriate for the patient's language preference and competence, and obtaining informed consent (APA Ethics Code, Standard 9.02, Use of Assessments, and 9.03, Informed Consent in Assessments).

Although there is some support for continuing to use older instruments that have proven reliability and validity (APA Ethics Code, Standard 9.08, Obsolete Tests and Outdated Test Results), updated and current psychological tests with appropriate validity and reliability should be the assessment instruments of choice whenever possible. Tests administered should always be chosen on the basis of presenting problems, clinical questions, and validation for use with similar populations.

Psychologists often provide feedback to patients regarding their assessment results (see APA Ethics Code, Standard 9.10, Explaining Assessment Results), which is a good way to build rapport with the patient and open up dialogue about issues that may not have emerged during the clinical interview. Information regarding test results should be provided in a way the patient understands, which can be done by using language similar to that used by the patient (Fischer, 2000; Levak, Siegel, Nichols, & Stolberg, 2011).

Overlapping of professional roles holds the potential for role confusion in integrated care teams (APA Ethics Code, Standard 3.06, Conflict of Interest). Psychologists must clarify the distinctiveness of their roles in relation to other health care professionals at the onset of treatment. Ultimately, your role in the professional system must be clear to you, your patient, and other providers.

Risk Management—Protecting Your Patient, Protecting Yourself

> **ACTIVITY 1.4:**
>
> What distinct risk management issues does such a medical case raise? Do you view your role in this integrated care context any differently than you did when you formed your first impressions of Ms. H? Why or why not?

Working in an integrated health care setting poses a unique set of risks for a provider. Patients in this setting present with complex medical problems that often require additional time for psychological assessment. The provider attempts to sort out where the psychological distress is located, how it relates to the relevant medical conditions, and how it can best be managed. Becoming familiar with relevant medical conditions and the expected psychological distress (as documented in the literature) is a good strategy for helping to sort out these variables. Working collaboratively with other medical providers and making appropriate referrals are integral to this setting and are good risk management strategies. For instance, a patient with chronic pain should always have a medical evaluation by an expert in pain management, if one is available. These types of decisions are ethically and empirically based, and consultation with medical providers is an important component of protecting yourself from malpractice (Bland, Lambert, Raney, & the American Psychiatric Association, 2014; Guglielmo, 2013).

In particular, when working with a chronic pain population, where opioids are a standard form of treatment and substance abuse is a high risk, the psychologist will often be asked to help in making a decision about the patient's current functioning and whether narcotics can be considered an option for future treatment. This is an important risk management issue for two reasons. First, your professional judgment regarding something that lies outside the range of a psychologist's usual training could have implications for whether the patient will receive pharmacological treatment. Second, it is important that you practice only within your area of professional competence so that you are not accused of practicing medicine without a license (APA Ethics Code, Standard 2.01). Thus, there needs to be a balance between attempting to meet the needs of the patient and not overstepping your areas of competence.

A second and related issue is the appropriate role for a psychologist in providing input in understanding the impact multiple medications could have on the patient's physical and mental health, an issue particularly relevant to patients with chronic pain. Ms. H is prescribed several antidepressant medications, in addition to opioids for her pain and extra medications for her other medical conditions. The side effects of her opioids, such as drowsiness or fogginess, could be contributing to her cognitive complaints and depressive symptoms. What is your role, as the psychologist, in handling these complications? Your awareness of mood and behavioral symptoms and the psychological data you obtained may provide a useful perspective. A related consideration, especially given the number and complexity of her medical treatment regimen and her memory difficulties, is whether she is taking her medications regularly and appropriately. Consultation with the prescribing physician is indicated when there are concerns such as substance abuse, debilitating side effects, or clear contraindications (Eccleston, 2001).

Disposition

ACTIVITY 1.5:

What are the specific goals in working with a chronic pain patient with multiple psychological and medical problems? How might you achieve these goals with Ms. H?

When working in a medical setting, treatment intervention is directed at psychological distress with the aim of reducing the overall health burden and maximizing functionality. For Ms. H, conceptualizing treatment strategies requires an in-depth consideration of the various psychosocial, cognitive, and environmental factors that contribute to her mood disorder and the resulting increases in her chronic pain. Treatment will focus directly on pain management and coping, as well as on the corollary depression resulting from chronic pain. Ms. H also has several psychosocial stressors and symptoms that need to be addressed to treat her pain effectively (e.g., medication management, need for support, memory problems, substance abuse history, suicidality, sleep problems, self-esteem, anxiety symptoms).

There are different approaches to prioritizing the problems a patient like Ms. H presents. In this case, the patient specifically wants to reduce her pain, have better sleep, and develop a better home life with more supportive relationships. In most cases, you will need to determine whether your patient is suicidal, whether she has truly given up abuse of substances, and whether she would benefit from integrated pain management care.

A thorough assessment of suicidality will be an important first step in treatment. Next, you will likely make appropriate referrals, including medication review, neuropsychological testing, and migraine assessment. In keeping with your professional boundaries, it is critical for you to understand when referral is necessary to gather more information before beginning treatment. Given this patient's history, developing rapport, building a connection, and ensuring she feels safe are all integral nonspecific interventions to maintain.

Next, you might consider proximal treatment approaches for reducing Ms. H's pain. These will likely include the use of relaxation and pain management strategies, such as progressive muscle relaxation, guided imagery, exercise, and mindfulness-based coping (Chang, Fillingim, Hurley, & Schmidt, 2015). Beyond direct pain management, you will also need to work on managing Ms. H's emotional distress, particularly her depressive and anxious symptoms. Cognitive behavior therapy (CBT) and acceptance and commitment therapy (ACT) have both been shown to be effective in such situations (Ehde, Dillworth, & Turner, 2014; McCracken & Vowles, 2014). CBT for chronic pain focuses on helping patients evaluate the impact of pain on their lives, gain insight into the relationship between their pain appraisals and negative emotions, and develop more adaptive responses to pain. Motivational interviewing can also be incorporated to facilitate behavioral change and maintain commitment to treatment (Tse, Vong, & Tang, 2013). ACT emphasizes psychological flexibility and values-guided behavior by encouraging patients to acknowledge (rather than avoid) their suffering, engage in the present moment, and behave in ways that are consistent with their internally held goals and values (Hayes, Luoma, Bond, Masuda, & Lillis, 2006).

A final component of Ms. H's treatment will be learning to manage psychosocial stress, because it is a key contributor to her pain. To do this, you might focus on building her existing coping skills and developing a self-care program for herself. Social skills training (Rakos, 1991) may help empower Ms. H to ask for more support from her family. Additionally, psychoeducational interventions regarding sleep habits, scheduling, and related behavior patterns may help improve her sleep hygiene (e.g., Berry et al., 2015). These are brief interventions that can enable Ms. H to better manage daily life stressors and thereby help reduce her pain.

References

American Psychological Association. (2007a). *Guidelines for psychological practice in health care delivery systems.* Retrieved from http://www.apa.org/practice/guidelines/delivery-systems.aspx

American Psychological Association. (2007b). Record keeping guidelines. *American Psychologist, 62,* 993–1004. http://dx.doi.org/10.1037/0003-066X.62.9.993

American Psychological Association. (2008). *Blueprint for change: Achieving integrated health care for an aging population.* Washington, DC: Author.

American Psychological Association. (2017). *Ethical principles of psychologists and code of conduct* (2002, Amended June 1, 2010 and January 1, 2017). Retrieved from http://www.apa.org/ethics/code/index.aspx

Beck, A. T., Steer, R. A., & Brown, G. K. (2000). *BDI–FS FastScreen for Medical Patients: Manual.* San Antonio, TX: Psychological Corporation.

Berry, R., Verrier, M. J., Rashiq, S., Simmonds, M. K., Baloukov, A., Thottungal, J., . . . Dick, B. D. (2015). A brief cognitive–behavioral intervention for sleep in individuals with chronic noncancer pain: A randomized controlled trial. *Rehabilitation Psychology, 60,* 193–200. http://dx.doi.org/10.1037/rep0000035

Bland, D. A., Lambert, K., Raney, L., & the American Psychiatric Association. (2014). Resource document on risk management and liability issues in integrated care models. *The American Journal of Psychiatry, 171*(Data Suppl.), 1–7. http://dx.doi.org/10.1176/appi.ajp.2014.1710501

Brannon, L., Feist, J., & Updegraff, J. A. (2013). *Health psychology: An introduction to behavior and health.* Belmont, CA: Cengage Learning.

Butcher, J. N., Dahlstrom, W. G., Graham, J. R., Tellegen, A., & Kaemmer, B. (1989). *The Minnesota Multiphasic Personality Inventory—2 (MMPI–2): Manual for administration and scoring.* Minneapolis: University of Minnesota Press.

Chang, K. L., Fillingim, R., Hurley, R. W., & Schmidt, S. (2015). Chronic pain management: Nonpharmacological therapies for chronic pain. *FP Essentials, 432,* 21–26.

Cleeland, C. S., & Ryan, K. M. (1994). Pain assessment: Global use of the Brief Pain Inventory. *Annals of the Academy of Medicine, Singapore, 23,* 129–138.

Denollet, J. (2005). DS14: Standard assessment of negative affectivity, social inhibition, and Type D personality. *Psychosomatic Medicine, 67,* 89–97. http://dx.doi.org/10.1097/01.psy.0000149256.81953.49

Eccleston, C. (2001). Role of psychology in pain management. *British Journal of Anaesthesia, 87*(1), 144–152. http://dx.doi.org/10.1093/bja/87.1.144

Egede, L. E. (2007). Major depression in individuals with chronic medical disorders: Prevalence, correlates and association with health resource utilization, lost productivity and functional disability. *General Hospital Psychiatry, 29,* 409–416. http://dx.doi.org/10.1016/j.genhosppsych.2007.06.002

Ehde, D. M., Dillworth, T. M., & Turner, J. A. (2014). Cognitive-behavioral therapy for individuals with chronic pain: Efficacy, innovations, and directions for research. *American Psychologist, 69,* 153–166. http://dx.doi.org/10.1037/a0035747

Feuerstein, M., Labbé, M. F., & Kuczmierczyk, A. R. (2013). *Health psychology: A psychobiological perspective*. New York, NY: Springer Science + Business Media.

Fischer, C. T. (2000). Collaborative, individualized assessment. *Journal of Personality Assessment, 74*, 2–14. http://dx.doi.org/10.1207/S15327752JPA740102

Fisher, C. B. (2008). *Decoding the ethics code: A practical guide for psychologists*. Thousand Oaks, CA: Sage.

Fisher, L., & Dickinson, W. P. (2014). Psychology and primary care: New collaborations for providing effective care for adults with chronic health conditions. *American Psychologist, 69*, 355–363. http://dx.doi.org/10.1037/a0036101

Guglielmo, W. J. (2013, December 23). New malpractice risks under the ACA. *Medscape Business of Medicine: Legal and Malpractice Corner*. Retrieved from http://www.medscape.com/viewarticle/815368

Hathaway, S. R., McKinley, J. C., & the MMPI Restandardization Committee. (1989). *MMPI–2: Minnesota Multiphasic Personality Inventory—2: Manual for administration and scoring*. Minneapolis: University of Minnesota Press.

Hayes, S. C., Luoma, J. B., Bond, F. W., Masuda, A., & Lillis, J. (2006). Acceptance and commitment therapy: Model, processes and outcomes. *Behaviour Research and Therapy, 44*, 1–25. http://dx.doi.org/10.1016/j.brat.2005.06.006

Helgeson, V. S., & Zajdel, M. (2017). Adjusting to chronic health conditions. *Annual Review of Psychology, 68*, 545–571. http://dx.doi.org/10.1146/annurev-psych-010416-044014

Kaptein, A. A. (2014). Ethics in health psychology: Some remarks from an outsider. *The European Health Psychologist, 16*, 90–94.

Kazak, A. E., & Noll, R. B. (2015). The integration of psychology in pediatric oncology research and practice: Collaboration to improve care and outcomes for children and families. *American Psychologist, 70*, 146–158. http://dx.doi.org/10.1037/a0035695

Koran, L. M., Sox, H. C., Jr., Marton, K. I., Moltzen, S., Sox, C. H., Kraemer, H. C., . . . Chandra, S. (1989). Medical evaluation of psychiatric patients. I. Results in a state mental health system. *Archives of General Psychiatry, 46*, 733–740. http://dx.doi.org/10.1001/archpsyc.1989.01810080063007

Levak, R. W., Siegel, L., Nichols, D. S., & Stolberg, R. (2011). *Therapeutic feedback with the MMPI–2: A positive psychology approach*. New York, NY: Taylor & Francis.

McCracken, L. M., & Vowles, K. E. (2014). Acceptance and commitment therapy and mindfulness for chronic pain: Model, process, and progress. *American Psychologist, 69*, 178–187. http://dx.doi.org/10.1037/a0035623

National Institute of Mental Health. (2002). Breaking ground, breaking through: The strategic plan for mood disorders research of the National Institute of Mental Health. *Biological Psychiatry, 52*, 547–588.

National Institute of Neurological Disorders, National Institutes of Health. (2009). Pain: Hope through research. *Journal of Pain and Palliative Care Pharmacotherapy, 23*, 307–322. http://dx.doi.org/10.1080/15360280903099141

Ouwens, M., Wollersheim, H., Hermens, R., Hulscher, M., & Grol, R. (2005). Integrated care programmes for chronically ill patients: A review of systematic reviews. *International Journal for Quality in Health Care, 17*, 141–146. http://dx.doi.org/10.1093/intqhc/mzi016

Patten, S. B., & Barbui, C. (2004). Drug-induced depression: A systematic review to inform clinical practice. *Psychotherapy and Psychosomatics, 73,* 207–215. http://dx.doi.org/10.1159/000077739

Pope, K. S. (1990). Ethical and malpractice issues in hospital practice. *American Psychologist, 45,* 1066–1070. http://dx.doi.org/10.1037/0003-066X.45.9.1066

Rakos, R. F. (1991). *Assertive behavior: Theory, research, and training.* New York, NY: Taylor & Frances/Routledge.

Randolph, C. (1998). *RBANS manual: Repeatable battery for the assessment of neuropsychological status.* San Antonio, TX: The Psychological Corporation.

Richards, M. M. (2009). Electronic medical records: Confidentiality issues in the time of HIPAA. *Professional Psychology: Research and Practice, 40,* 550–556. http://dx.doi.org/10.1037/a0016853

Rosenstiel, A. K., & Keefe, F. J. (1983). The use of coping strategies in chronic low back pain patients: Relationship to patient characteristics and current adjustment. *Pain, 17,* 33–44. http://dx.doi.org/10.1016/0304-3959(83)90125-2

Schaffer, J., & Rodolfa, E. (2016). *A student's guide to assessment and diagnosis using the ICD–10–CM: Psychological and behavioral conditions.* Washington, DC: American Psychological Association.

Tauber, A. I. (2005). *Patient autonomy and the ethics of responsibility.* Boston, MA: MIT Press.

Tse, M. M., Vong, S. K., & Tang, S. K. (2013). Motivational interviewing and exercise programme for community-dwelling older persons with chronic pain: A randomised controlled study. *Journal of Clinical Nursing, 22,* 1843–1856. http://dx.doi.org/10.1111/j.1365-2702.2012.04317.x

World Health Organization. (1993). *The ICD–10 classification of mental and behavioural disorders: Clinical descriptions and diagnostic guidelines.* Retrieved from http://www.who.int/classifications/icd/en/bluebook.pdf

Staci Leon Morris, Ken C. Winters, and Eric F. Wagner

F10.2 Alcohol Dependence

2

lcohol dependence involves a compulsive desire to use alcohol, combined with the inability to control its use. The use of alcohol can increasingly take over a person's life, replacing other life pleasures, while involving a physiological addiction with multiple negative physical, psychological, and social consequences. The use and abuse of alcohol (as well as marijuana) are major behavioral disorders of our time (Tyburski, Sokolowski, Samochowiec, & Samochowiec, 2014), despite being associated with negative consequences (Haberstick et al., 2014), particularly among adolescents (Haberstick et al., 2014; Johnston, O'Malley, Miech, Bachman, & Schulenberg, 2017). The prevalence rate of alcohol use in the United States is estimated to be approximately 48% for those aged 12 years and older, with almost 8% of those aged 12 to 20 engaging in binge drinking (National Institute on Alcohol Abuse and Alcoholism [NIAAA], 2017; Center for Behavioral Health Statistics and Quality, 2016). *Binge drinking* is defined as five or more drinks on one occasion for males and four or more for females (although this definition is somewhat arbitrary, as intoxication is dependent on many other factors than amount consumed, such as gender, body mass and fat content, rate of alcohol use, stomach contents, sleep, tolerance, context, and mood). The annual societal cost in the United States attributed to the misuse of alcohol is more than $249.0 billion (NIAAA, 2017).

http://dx.doi.org/10.1037/0000069-003
An ICD–10–CM Casebook and Workbook for Students: Psychological and Behavioral Conditions, J. B. Schaffer and E. Rodolfa (Editors)

Alcohol use has declined among adolescents in the United States since its peak in 1979, but alcohol remains the most used substance among adolescents in the United States, with more than 61% reporting drinking any alcohol by high school and 23% by eighth grade with almost 10% of eighth graders reporting being drunk at least once (Johnston et al., 2017). Heavy, or binge, drinking continues to be a major public health concern (Johnston, O'Malley, Miech, Bachman, & Schulenberg, 2014).

Although underage drinking cuts across racial/ethnic lines, there are indications that young Hispanics, who comprise a rapidly increasing population demographic, report greater alcohol involvement (i.e., more frequent drinking, binge drinking, and drunkenness) than do their Black and non-Hispanic White counterparts (Johnston, O'Malley, Bachman, & Schulenberg, 2011).

The Case

Joaquin, a 16-year-old Hispanic male, was arrested for public intoxication and referred to the community mental health center (CMHC) where you work for diagnosis and possible treatment. Because this was his first offence, this court-mandated service option was offered to him in place of being sentenced to serve time in a juvenile detention facility. Joaquin was administered a comprehensive psychosocial intake assessment (for an outline of the topics covered in such an interview, see Schaffer & Rodolfa, 2016) and, based on the assessment results and your clinical judgment, he was referred to a brief treatment program for adolescent alcohol and other drug users at the CMHC.

CLINICAL INTERVIEW

Joaquin arrives for the intake with his mother, but he is interviewed alone while she completes some paperwork. During his intake, Joaquin is oriented, personable, sober, cooperative, open, and engaged. He completes the interview with ease. He describes himself as Hispanic White. Born in the United States, Joaquin lives with his mother and father, who were both born in Peru. Joaquin reports that he prefers to speak English most of the time, although he speaks Spanish and English equally with his family. Joaquin names his mother, a stay-at-home mom, as his primary caregiver. According to Joaquin, both of his parents graduated from high school, and he earns grades of "mostly C's" in school. He describes his family as "very religious" and reports that they attend Catholic mass weekly.

Joaquin denies any symptoms of depression, anxiety, learning problems, or behavioral issues, including suicidality. He has never participated in any counseling. When asked about substance use, he denies any recent alcohol use that day, and thus his blood alcohol content is not measured. He reports that he started drinking "around age 13" and currently drinks 2 or 3 nights per week, which he says is "normal." Furthermore, when he does drink, he usually has "a couple of beers" and "so many shots (hard liquor) I can't even count." You comment that this is considered heavy drinking, which is dismissed by Joaquin. He says he often prefers to drink over other activities, such as sketching, playing baseball, practicing his drums, and playing video games, all activities he used to enjoy often but now rarely engages in. Joaquin denies experiencing either withdrawal symptoms when he isn't drinking or tolerance, stating "I drink because I like it, not because I need more." Although he later reports a history of marijuana use, he denies any other illegal substance use in the 6 months before intake. The negative urinalysis obtained during this visit confirms no recent use of amphetamines, cocaine, THC, or morphine. Although urinalysis is not diagnostic, it can serve to either corroborate a patient's denial of recent substance use or to reveal substance use that a patient is trying to hide or can't recall (American Society of Addiction Medicine, 2013).

Joaquin states that he lives with both parents and his 19-year-old brother, whom he describes as a heavy drinker and regular marijuana user. He describes his father as a moderate drinker and his mother as a nondrinker; neither parent uses other illicit substances. Joaquin reports that he, his father, and his brother often drink together, and this causes family arguments with his mother. Joaquin reports having several good friends and being generally satisfied with his peer relationships. However, he also states that his friends are all moderate to heavy drinkers and some are regular users of marijuana.

CLINICAL IMPRESSIONS

You carefully consider not only Joaquin's presenting problem—namely, his alcohol use and being mandated to treatment—but also his crucial developmental period. Adolescence is a period marked by key developmental transformations in multiple domains, including biological (e.g., pubertal status, hormonal changes, physical changes, maturation of prefrontal cortex/limbic system), psychological (e.g., individuation, identity formation, self-regulation, executive functioning, autonomy), social (e.g., intimate relationships; peer and sibling influences; shifts in parental control; and social skills development, including social networking), and roles (e.g., school transitions, driving, working; Wagner, 2008). As reported by Winters and Lee (2008), any drug or alcohol use during this time of rapid brain maturation may make an adolescent like Joaquin more vulnerable to the development of an alcohol use disorder. Issues to consider include the pace at which Joaquin is maturing compared with his peers and whether his brain maturation (i.e., decision-making abilities) is on par with his physical maturation. The timing of these multiple transitions not only varies across individuals but may not be constant, and may even overlap. Each of these transformations, and their interactions, may uniquely influence the role that alcohol plays in Joaquin's life. Furthermore, due to the experience of these transformations, an adolescent not only makes choices and decisions in a different way from a mature adult but cannot necessarily be expected to respond to treatment in the same way as an adult (Morris & Wagner, 2007).

Adolescents may generally be expected to be at the earlier stages of readiness to change (Prochaska & DiClemente, 1986), given their short-lived history of use and the fact that the negative consequences are often fewer in number and less pervasive than they are for adults. However, although adolescents usually do not identify themselves as having problems with substance use (Monti, Barnett, O'Leary, & Colby, 2001), certain circumstances, such as Joaquin's contact with the justice system, may function as a "window of opportunity" situation in which negative consequences are salient, thereby enhancing motivation to make changes.

Assessment Using the ICD–10–CM

ACTIVITY 2.1:

While alcohol abuse is the reason for the referral, Joaquin is an adolescent who has been arrested. Do you begin your diagnostic considerations with block F10–F19 (Behavioral and emotional disorders with onset usually occurring in childhood and adolescence) and focus on the arrest, or on the substance use surrounding the arrest, even though substance use disorders are typically associated more with adults than adolescents?

As part of his intake, Joaquin was given several assessment measures. Alcohol consumption was measured using the Timeline FollowBack Interview (TLFB; Sobell & Sobell, 1996). The TLFB is a widely used research and clinical assessment tool with good reliability and validity for various groups of individuals with alcohol use problems. Data from the TLFB are summarized to yield the following variables: total number of alcohol use days, total number of drug use days, number of days abstinent from alcohol, and number of days abstinent from drugs, as well as average number of drinks per drinking day.

Hispanic/Latino adolescents may be especially vulnerable to alcohol problems due to acculturation and perceived discrimination (Acosta, Hospital, Graziano, Morris, & Wagner, 2015). However, a practitioner must do a thorough cultural assessment as Hispanic/Latinos are a diverse group who require specific attention to be paid not only to risk factors but also to protective factors, such as parental involvement and religiosity (Salas-Wright, Hernandez, Maynard, Saltzman, & Vaughn, 2014).

Diagnosis Using the ICD–10–CM

Joaquin denied symptoms of depression and suicidality. He also did not appear to have any other emotional, behavioral, or learning problems. All information was similarly reported by his mother. Corroboration, especially in the case of substance use, can be quite informative.

Because Joaquin is an adolescent who has been arrested, it is certainly worth considering whether he meets criteria for an ICD–10 diagnosis of Conduct disorder

(F91.x)[1] or Oppositional defiant disorder (F91.3), given some reported family conflict around his use of alcohol. To meet criteria for a diagnosis of conduct disorder, Joaquin would have to present a consistent pattern of repeated *dissocial, aggressive, or defiant conduct*. This diagnosis is a quick rule-out because this is Joaquin's first offense, and he does not have a history of the oppositional or antisocial behaviors typically associated with a conduct disorder (see World Health Organization [WHO], 1993).

Using the ICD–10–CM, and given Joaquin's presenting history, the remaining diagnostic possibilities are all classified under Category F10: Alcohol related disorders. Although alcohol users may also be polysubstance users, Joaquin reported no current illicit drug use and stated that he had not smoked marijuana in the past 6 months. He is not currently under the influence of alcohol, and thus Alcohol abuse with intoxication (F10.12x) and Alcohol dependence with intoxication (F10.22x) can be ruled out.

Alcohol abuse (F10.1xx) may seem like an appropriate diagnosis for Joaquin, but this diagnosis requires specific negative consequences from alcohol use, such as medical issues or depression (WHO, 1993), which Joaquin denied, so this diagnosis would not fit. Furthermore, if he had reported depressive symptomatology, the depressive symptoms would have to be the result of his alcohol use for Alcohol abuse to be the correct diagnosis.

ACTIVITY 2.2:

As you proceed to narrow down your diagnostic hypotheses and rule-outs, consider how an alcohol use disorder manifests in an adolescent. How might an adolescent who is dependent on alcohol report different symptoms, patterns of use, and consequences than an adult who probably has a longer drinking history, easier access to alcohol, and can consume it legally?

Although alcohol dependence is often characterized by withdrawal and tolerance, Joaquin denied experiencing either of these conditions. This is not uncharacteristic for underage drinkers because they typically do not have long enough histories of use for these conditions to develop fully. This also applies to medical conditions caused by extensive alcohol use (e.g., cognitive dysfunction, liver damage) for the same reasons. However, an ICD–10–CM diagnosis of Alcohol dependence uncomplicated (F10.20) requires further consideration. The symptoms of Alcohol dependence have in common the overwhelming desire for and need for the substance, in this case alcohol, so that one often chooses the use of that substance over participation in other activities.

---

[1]The designation *x* in an ICD–10–CM code is a placeholder to designate that a number of subtypes of the diagnosis are possible but not yet determined.

To meet ICD–10–CM criteria for Alcohol dependence, Joaquin would have to meet at least three of the following criteria together over the previous year (Hasin, Hatzenbuehler, Keyes, & Ogburn, 2006; see WHO, 2017):

(a) a strong desire to use the substance, (b) difficulties in controlling substance-taking behavior, (c) a physiological withdrawal state, (d) evidence of tolerance, (e) progressive neglect of alternative pleasures, and (f) persisting with substance use despite clear evidence of overtly harmful consequences. (WHO, 2017, p. 5)

Upon careful review of the criteria, it is clear that although Joaquin is not experiencing tolerance or withdrawal symptoms, he does, in fact, meet three of the required criteria: a strong desire for alcohol, he has difficulty saying no to alcohol and managing his use to the point that he often cannot report an accurate measure of his alcohol intake, and he has stopped participating in previously enjoyable activities.

Therefore, Joaquin does merit a diagnosis of Alcohol dependence (F10.2x) because he meets the minimum threshold of three criteria. Joaquin is not abstinent, which rules out the in-remission code (F10.21). Similarly, because he is not experiencing withdrawal or delirium due to withdrawal, the F10.23x codes are also ruled out. He is, however, a recent alcohol user. Therefore, his most appropriate ICD–10–CM diagnosis is Alcohol dependence, uncomplicated (F10.20).

Ethical Considerations—Protecting Your Patient

ACTIVITY 2.3:

What unique ethical issues do you need to consider when working with Joaquin, a Hispanic, adolescent alcohol user, court-mandated to attend treatment? What are the ethical and legal implications of his being a minor regarding maintenance of confidentiality?

As an ethical practitioner, you practice according to the five principles outlined in the American Psychological Association's (APA's; 2017) *Ethical Principles of Psychologists and Code of Conduct* (APA Ethics Code), as follows.

PRINCIPLE A: BENEFICENCE AND NONMALEFICENCE

Your work with Joaquin is guided not only by doing him no harm but, more importantly, selecting a program and interventions that will benefit him after careful consideration of his presenting problems, needs, and unique cultural and developmental issues. With court-referred clients like Joaquin, the clinician needs to balance carefully professional responsibilities to Joaquin (e.g., right to privacy) versus professional responsibilities to the court (and thereby society). This is a complex issue and beyond the scope of the current chapter (see APA, 2013; Greenberg & Shuman, 1997, 2007).

PRINCIPLE B: FIDELITY AND RESPONSIBILITY

You develop and maintain appropriate professional relationships with the judge presiding over Joaquin's case, always protecting Joaquin as your client. If any potential conflicts arise, you consult with colleagues or the CMHC attorney. Moreover, you carefully balance professional responsibilities to Joaquin versus professional responsibilities to the court (see Greenberg & Shuman, 1997, 2007; Strasberger, Gutheil, & Brodsky, 1997).

INTEGRITY

You demonstrate professional integrity by consistently communicating in a truthful and honest manner. You are clear about your commitment to Joaquin, being on time for scheduled sessions and returning phone calls and responding to requests within a reasonable and previously agreed-on amount of time. Most important for Joaquin, you send reports to the judge on time. Considering his age and the widespread use of technology, you communicate a clear policy with regard to social media contact with patients (no social media relationships, friending, or following) and the use of texting only as a means of appointment reminders.

JUSTICE

Before agreeing to treat Joaquin, and throughout the course of treatment, you consider your feelings about adolescents, alcohol users, juvenile offenders, and Hispanics to ensure that you have no bias toward Joaquin that could negatively affect his treatment. Moreover, you consider the broader implications of treatment for Joaquin, especially in regard to his having been arrested and his relations with family, to ensure that he is treated justly. If any of these issues arise during the course of treatment, you seek consultation with colleagues and CMHC administrators.

RESPECT FOR PEOPLE'S RIGHTS AND DIGNITY

You consistently demonstrate respect for Joaquin and his rights to privacy, confidentiality, and involvement in decision making regarding his treatment. This may be especially salient for Joaquin, who may be vulnerable due to his age, minority status, and legal involvement.

The issue of client–therapist confidentiality (see APA Ethics Code, Section 4: Privacy and Confidentiality) when a client is a minor is complicated. Whereas clinical practice and ethics are relevant, state laws need to be considered. States vary as to what age defines a minor and what type of information is or is not considered confidential. Most state laws give the parent access to the child's treatment until the child is 18 years of age, but exceptions exist (e.g., some states allow those age 16 or older to seek treatment without parent consent). Nonetheless, these limits must consistently be explained to

Joaquin. You not only explain the limits of confidentiality that apply to all of your patients (harm to self, neglect, or abuse) but also stress the content of communication required by the judge, as well as what may happen if his records get subpoenaed.

Because he is a minor, Joaquin's mother, as his legal guardian, signs the consent form, and Joaquin signs the assent form, further demonstrating respect for him as the patient (see Grady et al., 2014). The consent form is the legal consent to treatment provided by the legal guardian on behalf of the minor. The assent form, although it may be considered more of a formality, conveys to the minor a respect for his or her involvement in the treatment process. Both are provided with copies of the signed documents that detail their rights and responsibilities, including confidentiality, fees, right to withdraw, and voluntary consent.

They also sign an Authorization to Release Confidential Information form as attendance and treatment updates are to be sent to the judge that mandated Joaquin to treatment as a condition of his arrest and subsequent referral. The information that you are authorized to release is specific and time limited and includes periodic urinalysis test results. It is important to check with your state regulations regarding authorization to release information. In many (but not all) jurisdictions, the parent has a legal right to access all information regarding their teenager's treatment, including reports on how the treatment is progressing. This may present a challenge for respecting and protecting the privacy of your client, Joaquin, and needs careful consideration.

Risk Management—Protecting Your Patient; Protecting Yourself

ACTIVITY 2.4:

How would you describe the way in which you protect yourself in your professional role? What unique risk management issues do you need to consider when working with Joaquin and communicating with the judge ruling on his case?

Although you take great care to protect Joaquin as your patient, you must simultaneously be aware of any risks involved so that you may protect yourself as a psychologist, as well as the CMHC in which you work. According to Schaffer and Rodolfa (2016), the way in which you protect yourself is to (a) maintain a professional relationship, (b) practice in an ethical manner, (c) demonstrate competence, and (d) consider professional threats.

Thus, you maintain your professional license and keep up with current advancements in evidence-based practices. Before accepting Joaquin as a patient, you consider whether you have the expertise to treat (a) an adolescent (b) with an alcohol-related diagnosis (c) who identifies as Hispanic. You also take the time to explain to Joaquin how your training and experience make you qualified to treat him.

Joaquin is Hispanic, so you ask him about his language preference and assess his fluency. You also ask him during treatment about his family and how culture influences their relationships and beliefs about alcohol use. You ask Joaquin's mother about her fluency in and comfort with the English language to ensure that she is aware of her rights and responsibilities, understands the limits to confidentiality (especially regarding reports to the court), and gives informed consent.

As previously stated, you not only consult with the attorney for the CMHC, but you are fully versed in laws and rules regulating your profession, as well as participate in continuing education to keep up with changes in the laws and rules. The importance of this is only highlighted by Joaquin's legal involvement.

Finally, you comply with the rules of the federal Health Insurance Portability and Accountability Act (HIPAA), which includes among its stipulations the right to have a copy of the case record and to be able to provide corrections to it, and requires that Joaquin's personal health information (PHI) be protected when it is electronically sent or detailed in records. Joaquin and his mother should be provided with a copy of the HIPAA rules as required by law.

Disposition

Now that your intake interview and assessment are complete and you have been able to make an accurate diagnosis, it is time to use that information and make a decision on how to proceed with Joaquin's treatment, which should consider his age and developmental period, presenting problem, and legal involvement, as well as the programs available and the potential benefits and length and intensity of those treatments. The fact that he is not interested in reducing his drinking is an important consideration.

ACTIVITY 2.5:

Currently, Joaquin is only motivated to attend treatment to avoid juvenile detention and does not see a need to reduce his drinking. What do you think an ideal treatment program would be for Joaquin? What components would be appealing to him? How can you motivate him to make changes?

You determine that Joaquin is an appropriate candidate for a brief treatment program for adolescent alcohol and other drug users at your CMHC. Additionally, you believe this program will allow Joaquin to move from being externally motivated by the court mandate to being internally motivated for his own personal reasons to reduce his alcohol use.

Employing a Guided Self Change format (Sobell & Sobell, 1998), the five-session program synthesizes motivational and cognitive behavioral interventions (Miller &

Rollnick, 2013) for treating substance abuse. This approach is especially well-suited to meet the developmental needs of adolescents. Motivational components of the program, such as exploring ambivalence about substance use and setting personal goals for substance use reduction or abstinence, are developmentally compatible with an adolescent's need for increasing self-direction when making choices about his or her behavior. Furthermore, in general, it has been recognized that one strategy for strengthening motivation for making changes in substance use is to allow choices in setting goals for treatment (Sobell & Sobell, 1995). Motivational interventions appear to be especially effective in treating individuals at the earlier stages of readiness to change (i.e., those who have not yet identified themselves as having a substance use problem; Heather, Rollnick, Bell, & Richmond, 1996; Waldron, Miller, & Tonigan, 2001).

Initial sessions focus on exploring motives for substance use, reasons to reduce or stop use, and heightening awareness of the situational, cognitive, and emotional factors relating to use. Additional sessions focus on stress management (how to cope with stress without alcohol), developing communication skills (how to tell his friends when he chooses not to drink or limit drinking), and identifying and preparing for risky situations. Helping the patient build coping skills is essential for promoting and maintaining change, with learning to formulate detailed plans regarding how to handle high-risk trigger situations (e.g., with friends who may promote drinking) and replacing current methods with alternative, non–alcohol-related behaviors being particularly helpful.

Identifying weekly goals for reduction or abstinence is also initiated in the first session and continued throughout the program. The identification of longer term goals for alcohol use reduction, as well as for other areas of life, is important. Highlighting the relationship between substance use and life goals can further enhance motivation as the patient explores how continued patterns of use may interfere with accomplishments in other areas of life. This likely will be the first time that the individual has articulated life goals, which in and of itself may foster motivation to make changes.

You recognize that Joaquin's family plays an important role in his drinking: He often drinks with his brother and father, and their drinking has caused conflict with his mother. Therefore, you decide that involvement of the family—and in particular, the father—in psychoeducation regarding use of drugs and alcohol will be important.

Adhering to the motivational foundation of the program, you work with Joaquin in a collaborative manner. Open-ended questions examine reasons for change (or lack thereof), ways to promote further change, and how to maintain those changes that have been made. Relapse prevention (Marlatt & George, 1984) will also be addressed via education about specific thoughts, feelings, and behaviors that might develop if he does have a "slip" back to previous patterns of use after making changes. Identifying those who could offer support in helping him to make and sustain changes is also an important element of relapse prevention. Finally, it will be important to have a plan for how you will evaluate any changes made in the context of the goals set.

References

Acosta, S. L., Hospital, M. M., Graziano, J. N., Morris, S., & Wagner, E. F. (2015). Pathways to drinking among Hispanic/Latino adolescents: Perceived discrimination, ethnic identity, and peer affiliations. *Journal of Ethnicity in Substance Abuse, 14,* 270–286. http://dx.doi.org/10.1080/15332640.2014.993787

American Psychological Association. (2013). *Specialty guidelines for forensic psychology.* Retrieved from http://www.apa.org/practice/guidelines/forensic-psychology.aspx

American Psychological Association. (2017). *Ethical principles of psychologists and code of conduct* (2002, Amended June 1, 2010 and January 1, 2017). Retrieved from http://www.apa.org/ethics/code/index.aspx

American Society of Addiction Medicine. (2013, October 26). *Drug testing: A white paper of the American Society of Addiction Medicine.* Chevy Chase, MD: Author.

Center for Behavioral Health Statistics and Quality. (2016). *Key substance use and mental health indicators in the United States: Results from the 2015 National Survey on Drug Use and Health* (HHS Publication No. SMA 16-4984, NSDUH Series H-51). Retrieved from https://www.samhsa.gov/data/sites/default/files/NSDUH-FFR1-2015/NSDUH-FFR1-2015/NSDUH-FFR1-2015.pdf

Grady, C., Wiener, L., Abdoler, E., Trauernicht, E., Zadeh, S., Diekema, D. S., . . . Wendler, D. (2014). Assent in research: The voices of adolescents. *Journal of Adolescent Health, 54,* 515–520. http://dx.doi.org/10.1016/j.jadohealth.2014.02.005

Greenberg, S. A., & Shuman, D. W. (1997). Irreconcilable conflict between therapeutic and forensic roles. *Professional Psychology: Research and Practice, 28,* 50–57. http://dx.doi.org/10.1037/0735-7028.28.1.50

Greenberg, S. A., & Shuman, D. W. (2007). When worlds collide: Therapeutic and forensic roles. *Professional Psychology, Research and Practice, 38,* 129–132. http://dx.doi.org/10.1037/0735-7028.38.2.129

Haberstick, B. C., Young, S. E., Zeiger, J. S., Lessem, J. M., Hewitt, J. K., & Hopfer, C. J. (2014). Prevalence and correlates of alcohol and cannabis use disorders in the United States: Results from the national longitudinal study of adolescent health. *Drug and Alcohol Dependence, 136,* 158–161.

Hasin, D., Hatzenbuehler, M. L., Keyes, K., & Ogburn, E. (2006). Substance use disorders: *Diagnostic and Statistical Manual of Mental Disorders, fourth edition* (DSM–IV) and *International Classification of Diseases, tenth edition* (ICD–10). *Addiction, 101,* 59–75. http://dx.doi.org/10.1111/j.1360-0443.2006.01584.x

Heather, N., Rollnick, S., Bell, A., & Richmond, R. (1996). Effects of brief counselling among male heavy drinkers identified on general hospital wards. *Drug and Alcohol Review, 15,* 29–38. http://dx.doi.org/10.1080/09595239600185641

Johnston, L. D., O'Malley, P. M., Bachman, J. G., & Schulenberg, J. E. (2011). *Monitoring the future national survey results on drug use, 1975–2010: Vol. I. Secondary school students.* Ann Arbor: Institute for Social Research, University of Michigan.

Johnston, L. D., O'Malley, P. M., Miech, R. A., Bachman, J. G., & Schulenberg, J. E. (2014). *Monitoring the future national survey results on drug use: 1975–2013: Overview, key findings on adolescent drug use.* Ann Arbor: Institute for Social Research, University of Michigan.

Johnston, L. D., O'Malley, P. M., Miech, R. A., Bachman, J. G., & Schulenberg, J. E. (2017). *Monitoring the future national survey results on drug use: 1975–2016: Overview, key findings on adolescent drug use.* Ann Arbor: Institute for Social Research, University of Michigan.

Marlatt, G. A., & George, W. H. (1984). Relapse prevention: Introduction and overview of the model. *British Journal of Addiction, 79,* 261–273. http://dx.doi.org/10.1111/j.1360-0443.1984.tb03867.x

Miller, W. R., & Rollnick, S. (Eds.). (2013). *Motivational interviewing: Helping people change* (3rd ed.). New York, NY: Guilford Press.

Monti, P. M., Barnett, N. P., O'Leary, T. A., & Colby, S. M. (2001). Motivational enhancement for alcohol-involved adolescents. *Adolescents, alcohol, and substance abuse: Reaching teens through brief interventions* (pp. 145–182). New York, NY: Guilford Press.

Morris, S. L., & Wagner, E. F. (2007). *Adolescent substance use: Developmental considerations, Florida Certification Board/Southern coast* (ATTC Monograph Series 1). Retrieved from http://www.academia.edu/22044953/Adolescent_Substance_Use_Developmental_Considerations

National Institute on Alcohol Abuse and Alcoholism. (2017, January). *Alcohol facts and statistics.* Retrieved from https://pubs.niaaa.nih.gov/publications/AlcoholFacts&Stats/AlcoholFacts&Stats.pdf

Prochaska, J. O., & DiClemente, C. C. (1986). Toward a comprehensive model of change. In W. R. Miller & N. Heather (Eds.), *Treating addictive behaviors: Processes of change* (Vol. 13, pp. 3–27). http://dx.doi.org/10.1007/978-1-4613-2191-0_1

Salas-Wright, C. P., Hernandez, L., Maynard, B. R., Saltzman, L. Y., & Vaughn, M. G. (2014). Alcohol use among Hispanic early adolescents in the United States: An examination of behavioral risk and protective profiles. *Substance Use & Misuse, 49,* 864–877. http://dx.doi.org/10.3109/10826084.2014.880725

Schaffer, J., & Rodolfa, E. (2016). *A student's guide to assessment and diagnosis using the ICD–10–CM: Psychological and behavioral conditions.* http://dx.doi.org/10.1037/14778-000

Sobell, L. C., & Sobell, M. B. (1995). *Alcohol Timeline FollowBack* [computer software]. Toronto, Ontario, Canada: Addiction Research Foundation.

Sobell, L. C., & Sobell, M. B. (1996). *Timeline FollowBack users' manual for alcohol use.* Toronto, Ontario, Canada: Addiction Research Foundation.

Sobell, M. B., & Sobell, L. C. (1998). Guided self-change treatment. In W. R. Miller & N. Heather (Eds.), *Treating addictive behaviors: Process of change* (2nd ed., pp. 189–202). New York, NY: Plenum.

Strasberger, L., Gutheil, T., & Brodsky, A. (1997). On wearing two hats: Role conflict in serving as both psychotherapist and expert witness. *American Journal of Psychiatry, 154,* 448–456.

Tyburski, E. M., Sokolowski, A., Samochowiec, J., & Samochowiec, A. (2014). New diagnostic criteria for alcohol use disorders and novel treatment approaches—2014 update. *Archives of Medical Science, 10,* 1191–1197. http://dx.doi.org/10.5114/aoms.2014.47829

Wagner, E. F. (2008). Developmentally informed research on the effectiveness of clinical trials: A primer for assessing how developmental issues may influence treatment responses among adolescents with alcohol use problems. *Pediatrics, 121*(Suppl. 4), S337–S347. http://dx.doi.org/10.1542/peds.2007-2243F

Waldron, H. B., Miller, W. R., & Tonigan, J. S. (2001). Client anger as a predictor of differential response to treatment. *Project MATCH Hypotheses: Results and Causal Chain Analyses, 8,* 134–148.

Winters, K. C., & Lee, C.-Y. S. (2008). Likelihood of developing an alcohol and cannabis use disorder during youth: Association with recent use and age. *Drug and Alcohol Dependence, 92,* 239–247. http://dx.doi.org/10.1016/j.drugalcdep.2007.08.005

World Health Organization. (1993). *The ICD–10 classification of mental and behavioural disorders: Clinical descriptions and diagnostic guidelines.* Retrieved from http://www.who.int/classifications/icd/en/bluebook.pdf

World Health Organization. (2017). *Management of substance abuse: Harmful use.* Retrieved from http://www.who.int/substance_abuse/terminology/definition2/en

Katherine Elliott and Nicola Wright

F20.0 Paranoid Schizophrenia

3

Schizophrenia is a family of diagnoses that is generally considered to be characterized by some set of positive symptoms (the presence of distinctive behaviors, such as delusional thinking, hallucinations, perceptual disturbances, and/or bizarre behaviors) and negative symptoms (the absence of normal behavior, such as social withdrawal, poverty of speech [alogia], flat affect, lack of motivation and initiative, and/or anhedonia). Schizophrenia is a complex mental disorder that affects people globally at a prevalence rate of approximately 0.5%; however, such epidemiological data are often controversial due to different approaches to assessment (e.g., differing duration criteria in different diagnostic approaches over time), as well as differing assessment methods used in many studies. There is still no truly valid definition of schizophrenia (Castle & Morgan, 2008). Given that the diagnosis of "schizophrenia" actually has little predictive value in treatment outcome (e.g., Mortimer, 2007), it is likely that the way in which lived experience of psychosis is viewed by mental health professionals will continue to evolve. Psychologists increasingly play an important and meaningful role in the assessment and treatment of those with lived experience of psychosis (cf. American Psychiatric Association, 2004; National Institute for Clinical Excellence, 2014).

http://dx.doi.org/10.1037/0000069-004
An ICD–10–CM Casebook and Workbook for Students: Psychological and Behavioral Conditions, J. B. Schaffer and E. Rodolfa (Editors)

The Case

You are a psychologist who works in the schizophrenia program at your local hospital. You are contacted with the following case: A 23-year-old biracial young woman named Kaya has attended 2 years of university majoring in biology but gradually became more withdrawn and avoidant of social contact. A family physician's report briefly refers to some form of assault of her that occurred before the beginning of her social withdrawal. The physician report also indicates that Kaya began "using drugs" with a small network of friends around the same time. Reportedly, there was a steady decline in Kaya's grades until she eventually dropped out of the university, moved home, and began living in her parents' basement. According to her family physician, Kaya has continued to withdraw, even from her family. Her parents have initiated this assessment because they are very concerned about their daughter's well-being.

You met with Kaya on several occasions, and she did not initially want to speak with you. However, with time, empathy, and a clear interest in trying to understand, she was gradually willing to share more details about her experiences. Kaya's speech was organized, but her thoughts and beliefs were imbued with a suspicious and paranoid flavor. Throughout the meetings, she would either look down or at the wall. At times, she appeared distracted, so you needed to repeat yourself and attempt to reengage her. On one occasion, Kaya insisted you change rooms because she was convinced the room in which you were meeting was bugged. She was in visible distress during some of the meetings, indicating that she did not trust you and was concerned about how the information she provided would be used. You noted that Kaya appeared very tired, and she said she had a difficult time getting out of bed. One issue to consider here is whether some, or even all, of what Kaya is telling you includes elements of truth. For example, there may be cameras in your room for training purposes. You should not automatically think that everything a person says is "delusional." Look for corroboration whenever possible and listen carefully to what the person believes and on what basis.

When gathering some history about her during the interview, you learned that Kaya is one of two children (she has a younger sister, age 16) of a couple who has been married for 25 years. Both parents are professionals; her father, a Black African by upbringing, is a high school teacher in biology, and her mother, who is Caucasian and Canadian born, works for the government. Kaya's sister is in high school. Kaya frequently commented that her parents think she is "crazy" and are "making" her speak with "doctors." Kaya has repeatedly indicated that she feels her parents just don't understand or believe what she tells them. When you asked her about why she wears sunglasses during the interviews, Kaya reported that when other people look into her eyes, she gets a tightening in her chest, which is a signal that others are trying to hurt her. By wearing the sunglasses, she feels protected. Kaya did not appear to see her behaviors or beliefs as indicative of a problem.

You asked Kaya for consent to speak with her parents; however, it was not until you indicated that she could withdraw her consent at any time and any information shared by her family would be disclosed to her that Kaya reluctantly gave consent.

Given her hesitation, you asked if she would like to be a part of the meeting with her parents. Kaya visibly appeared less guarded when this option was offered.

Kaya's mother reported taking time off work because she was afraid to leave Kaya home alone. Her mother reported that she and other members of the family would frequently try to convince Kaya that her beliefs were not true; however, this seemed to be making things worse. Her mother indicated that on several occasions Kaya has accused her parents of being "in on it" and has threatened to move out. Her mother reported that her concern had increased since Kaya covered all the windows in the basement with towels and kept her room locked to ensure "no one would get in." Kaya's mother reported being very concerned about her daughter and not knowing what to do.

Kaya's father appeared more stoic and indicated that, although he had concerns about his daughter, he believed his wife might be overreacting in her concerns regarding Kaya. He said that if they could just push Kaya to go back to school or at least get a job, then she would not be so isolated. He also appeared to be skeptical about Western ways of viewing psychological problems. He reported concern about any potential consequences for his daughter in being assessed and diagnosed with a mental illness. These differences in perspective were clearly leading to tensions between him and his wife.

You feel considerable pressure from the family to determine what is happening, but you are also concerned, given the different perspectives of Kaya and each of her parents, how each family member will respond to a diagnosis. You are especially concerned about how Kaya may respond, given her insistence that her beliefs are accurate.

Assessment Using the ICD–10–CM

ACTIVITY 3.1:

What are the specific challenges in diagnosing Kaya? What role, if any, do you think the family plays in her presentation?

This patient is indicating reluctance about coming in to speak with "doctors" and insisting that she is not being heard or believed. The family is experiencing fear and frustration around what is happening and what to do, which is resulting in tension and arguments. What would an effective assessment look like in such a situation?

You would need to take time to gain a detailed history, ideally from Kaya herself, as one would do with any psychological assessment (see Schaffer & Rodolfa, 2016), as well as detailed accounts of behavioral observations (e.g., disorganized speech, hallucinations). In particular, given her family physician's reference to an assault, you will want to explore for any history of experiences with bullying or other kinds of trauma because such experiences are highly associated with psychosis (e.g., Bentall et al., 2014). A trauma-informed approach to assessment and treatment are critical in working with individuals with psychosis.

You also know that Kaya has been using drugs. Getting further information about the types of drugs used, frequency and amount of use, reasons for use, current use, and timeline of drug use related to the onset of symptoms would be important because use of cannabis, cocaine, amphetamines, and hallucinogens, in particular, can trigger psychosis in people with a vulnerability for psychosis (Gururajan, Manning, Klug, & van den Buuse, 2012).

Conducting a clinical interview is highly recommended for assessing psychosis (Rudnick & Roe, 2008) because it provides the most flexibility in exploring symptoms, as well as opportunities for observation of the patient.

Approaching Kaya with warmth, empathy, genuineness, and an open, curious style will help facilitate your engagement with her and your ability to conduct her assessment. Having been challenged or discounted by others, a patient may ask whether you believe her or him. A response of genuine caring and interest in the experience of the patient and his or her understanding of the situation and experiences can enhance engagement. Yet you may be fearful of "colluding" with the patient if you do not refute his or her inaccurate beliefs. In our experience, exploration of the content and themes underlying delusions and hallucinations often links to the patient's past experiences and provides valuable information on underlying emotions. Given that delusions and hallucinations are culturally defined, just as in any comprehensive assessment, it will be essential to use a culturally informed approach to assessment and assess the content of delusions and hallucinations in relation to the patient's belief system, as well as religious and cultural background and influences.

ICD–10–CM Diagnosis

Any diagnosis involving psychotic symptoms can be challenging because the presence of psychosis does not necessarily denote schizophrenia. For example, psychosis can be a feature of a mood disorder, the result of a medical condition, or use of certain drugs (e.g., cannabis, cocaine, amphetamines; cf. Gururajan et al., 2012). Other possible diagnoses should be ruled out before considering the diagnosis of schizophrenia. For example, one can experience a Manic episode, severe with psychotic symptoms (F30.2); Bipolar affective disorder, current episode manic with psychotic symptoms (F31.2); Bipolar affective disorder, current episode severe depression with psychotic symptoms (F31.5); a Major depressive disorder, single episode, severe with psychotic features (F32.3); or Major depressive disorder, recurrent, severe with psychotic symptoms (F33.3). The key issue to keep in mind is that it is not the severity of either the psychotic or affective symptoms that defines the diagnosis, it is the timing of the symptoms (Rudnick & Roe, 2008). If the psychotic symptoms only occur while the person is experiencing mania or depression (and are absent in the absence of a mood or affective disorder), the person is diagnosed with the specific affective disorder with psychotic features.

Schizoaffective disorder is a little more complicated. To qualify for a diagnosis of Schizoaffective disorder (either the bipolar type, F25.0, or depressive type, F25.1), the person must experience the associated mood symptoms, as well as at least one or more symptoms of schizophrenia in the same episode of illness. What distinguishes this disorder from a mood or affective disorder with psychotic features is that there is a period of time when the symptoms of an affective disorder are absent (i.e., the person recovers from the associated depression or mania), but the symptoms of schizophrenia remain. Unfortunately, the only way to differentiate Schizoaffective disorder from a mood disorder with psychotic features is through time and observation of the presence and absence of symptoms.

In the ICD–10–CM, there is an Exclusion1 (i.e., the excluded disorder cannot co-occur with the listed disorder) of Involutional paranoid state (F22.8) and Paranoia (F22.0), which are considered Delusional disorders (F22). As with mood and schizoaffective disorders, the differential here can be quite tricky and a thorough clinical interview is necessary. According to the *Blue Book* (World Health Organization, 1993), a delusional disorder occurs when a person has one or more delusions (i.e., belief systems) that are often persecutory, hypochondriacal, or grandiose. To make things really complicated, depressive symptoms can occasionally occur (i.e., a depressive episode is not an exclusion for a delusional disorder). The key separation from paranoid schizophrenia is that other key symptoms of schizophrenia (e.g., clear and persistent auditory hallucinations, delusions of control, thought broadcasting) are absent. Additionally, the delusions must be present for at least 3 months (vs. 1 month for schizophrenia).

ACTIVITY 3.2:

What information do we have that we need to consider in the differential diagnosis? What additional information do we need? How might you phrase questions to Kaya and each member of her family to obtain this information?

You will recall that you needed to take several sessions in interviewing Kaya; sometimes this was because she was in visible distress and other times because she was extremely fatigued. In addition, Kaya believed the interview room was bugged on one occasion, which can affect the quality of the assessment information. We would want more specifics on the behavioral observations. For example, why did you think Kaya was "visibly distressed"? Does this mean agitation (a potential symptom of a mood disorder) or fear (which would be consistent with the flavor of paranoia that was mentioned and therefore a possible symptom of paranoid schizophrenia)? We would also want more information from Kaya. For example, was her reason for being tired and having a difficult time due to fatigue related to a low mood, or was it because she was having difficulty sleeping given her fears that people might attack her (or perhaps a completely different reason that we have not thought of)? It is important never to assume that you understand another person's experience; always ask. Asking Kaya more in-depth questions about why she was tired and why she was covering up windows and locking the doors of her room would be an excellent way to investigate these observations. Do not just assume it is a symptom of paranoid schizophrenia. Kaya's responses will also likely provide valuable diagnostic information. For example, her belief that the interview room was bugged and her insistence on changing locations provide information that is suggestive of a delusion of persecution (which is a symptom of Paranoid schizophrenia [F20.0]).

You would additionally want more information on why Kaya occasionally appeared distracted (i.e., when she was looking around the room or not hearing your questions). One key symptom of Paranoid schizophrenia is the experience of auditory hallucinations (i.e., hearing voices). Patients who are hearing voices are distracted and may be reluctant to tell you (possibly because they fear your reaction and possibly because the voices may be telling them something about you). It will take a strong alliance, with sensitivity and gentleness, to have a conversation about this.

Another important issue you would want more information about is Kaya's drug use. It is not clear from the information you have gathered whether the drug use preceded symptoms or is an attempt to cope with difficult emotions, to manage symptoms, or another reason. Is Kaya still using drugs? Which ones? In what quantity? How often? We would want to rule out the effects of current drug use before pronouncing a diagnosis of Paranoid schizophrenia (F20.0).

Finally, is this Kaya's first episode of symptoms? Have the symptoms been consistently present for at least 1 month (the minimum time requirement for a diagnosis of Paranoid schizophrenia [F20.0] in the ICD–10–CM)? If this is her first episode of psychosis, it could be difficult to do a differential diagnosis. You may need to rule out a schizoaffective disorder or mood disorder with psychotic features if it is not yet clear how the affective and psychotic symptoms relate to each other. This is also where additional information from family (and any prior experiences noted by other health professionals) can be invaluable to help construct a more accurate timeline of symptoms, as well as the presence and absence of symptoms that a person may have difficulties identifying (e.g., if Kaya were experiencing an episode of mania, it is more likely that those around her would notice this shift in her mood than she would).

Finally, it can be useful to assess for a possible personality disorder. Someone experiencing Schizotypal disorder (F21) can have paranoid or suspicious ideas, obsessive ruminations, unusual perceptual experiences and occasional transient quasi-psychotic episodes with intense illusions, auditory or other hallucinations and delusion-like ideas, although usually occurs external provocation. Kaya appears to have experienced one or more possible initiating events (i.e., assault, drug use) prior to the onset of symptoms, which you would want to clarify.

In the ICD–10–CM, Schizotypal disorder is an "Excludes2" disorder, meaning that it could exist at the same time as a diagnosis of Schizophrenia. Typically, Schizotypal disorder is considered a personality disorder in which symptoms do not meet threshold (i.e., either there are not enough symptoms, or the frequency/duration of the symptoms do not meet full criteria to pronounce a diagnosis) for a psychotic disorder. This disorder can evolve into Schizophrenia, and patients experiencing residual symptoms of Schizophrenia may resemble Schizotypal disorder. If an episode of Schizophrenia occurs first, however, one would not typically give a diagnosis of Schizotypal disorder (Kleiger & Khadivi, 2015). The question is whether the personality disorder was premorbid (i.e., existing before) the onset of Schizophrenia. The same can apply to Paranoid personality disorder (F60.0) and Schizoid personality disorder (F60.1). If there is evidence of a premorbid personality disorder, then both the personality disorder and schizophrenia can co-occur (as reflected in the Excludes2 coding in the ICD–10–CM for each of these disorders). However, one must not confuse residual symptoms of an episode of schizophrenia as a personality disorder, nor confuse a premorbid personality disorder with schizophrenia. A detailed history and timeline can help sort through these complex differential diagnoses. In the case of Kaya, her symptoms have continued to worsen for at least 2 years (possibly more), she is experiencing clear persecutory delusions and paranoia (based on your observation and corroborated by family members), a withdrawal and decline in functioning (which may be negative symptoms of schizophrenia), and a possibility of auditory or visual hallucinations (you would want to query this when Kaya appeared distracted during the clinical interview). Thus, your working diagnosis is Paranoid schizophrenia (F20.0).

Ethical Considerations—Protecting Your Patient

The referral question requested some clarification of potential differential diagnoses. What ethical issues would you need to take into consideration in responding to this question? Whether you are competent is an important first step (Canadian Psychological Association [CPA; 2017] Code of Ethics, Standards II.6, 9; American Psychological Association [APA; 2017] *Ethical Principles of Psychologists and Code of Conduct* [APA Ethics Code], Standard 2.01, Boundaries of Competence). Although there is currently no requirement, from a registration or licensure standpoint, to have specific training in psychosis to treat someone with schizophrenia (apart from competency in mental health, as well as the age range you intend to work with), do you think it would be ethical to treat someone with this disorder without any previous training or supervision? Do you see the potential to do harm without extensive supervision? (See also Chapters 5 and 8, this volume.) Obtaining and documenting Kaya's informed consent to the assessment is an important second step (CPA Code of Ethics, Standards I.16–I.26; APA Ethics Code, Standards 3.10, Informed Consent, and 9.03, Informed Consent in Assessments). If Kaya is experiencing a lot of fear about others being "out to get her," she will likely have a number of concerns regarding what will be happening in her interactions with various mental health professionals. It will be important that you are well prepared and able to explain in a clear and understandable way what the purpose of the assessment is, how information will be used and stored, and who will have access to this information and for what purpose (these are important aspects of informed consent with any patient).

Kaya may have concerns about her parents' involvement (possibly as a result of her paranoid thinking and possibly for reasons of which we are not aware). It is important not to assume everything a person says or does while experiencing psychosis is inherently untrue or merely a result of symptoms. This situation can put you in an uncomfortable position, particularly in cases like Kaya's, where it appears that her family is concerned and wanting to help. Ideally, Kaya would want to involve her family because family can play an important role in treatment adherence and outcomes in people experiencing schizophrenia (e.g., Glick, Stekoll, & Hays, 2011; see also Chapter 5, this volume).

ACTIVITY 3.3:

What would you do if a family member called to ask about Kaya's symptoms or treatment progress? What impact do you think talking to Kaya's parents without her consent would have on conducting this or future assessments or providing treatment? What would you do if she reported command hallucinations to hurt a family member or someone else?

First, let's look at this from the perspective of the codes of ethics for psychologists. Kaya is 23 years old and has not been declared incompetent in a court of law; therefore, she is a legally competent adult assumed to be capable of providing informed consent. As discussed in the CPA Code of Ethics, Standard I.45, and the APA Ethics Code, Standard 4.05, Disclosures, you are only to share confidential information with the informed consent of the patient (in this case, Kaya), except as justified by law or due to concerns about possible serious harm or death. Thus far, Kaya has not indicated that she has any intent to harm herself or anyone else, and there are no legal reasons why you would be justified in sharing her information without her informed consent (e.g., no subpoena for her medical records for any legal reason). Therefore, although her family may have good intentions in wanting more information (and you may agree this would be helpful), unless Kaya provides informed consent that you may share information from the assessment, you may not do so. In fact, if a family member were to call simply asking if you were her psychologist, you would be obliged to say that you are unable to provide even that information.

Let's consider for a moment the scenario of Kaya being at risk of harming herself or someone else, whether because of a command hallucination or some other reason. What is your ethical and legal responsibility? As Schaffer and Rodolfa (2016) discussed, the California Supreme Court in the *Tarasoff* case in 1976 ruled that mental health professionals have a duty to warn a potential victim, although a 2015 State Supreme Court decision in Minnesota stipulates that providing information—in this case, testimony in court—beyond such warning is not supported by the law (*State of Minnesota vs. Jerry Expose, Jr.*, 2015). Thus, you are required to inform the potential victim of any legitimate threats, but you should not share additional information with anyone, including the family.

Third, let's look at this from the perspective of therapeutic alliance. If you were to decide that you could ethically justify informing Kaya's parents about the assessment without Kaya's full informed consent, how would this affect your relationship with Kaya? If you were in her shoes, what would your trust level be if you found out that information you had shared under the assumption that it would be maintained in strict confidentiality were shared with someone else, even a family member? Doing so could essentially prevent any future professional relationship.

Risk Management—Protecting Your Patient, Protecting Yourself

ACTIVITY 3.4:

What specific risks can you identify in a case where there is considerable mistrust of traditional mental health approaches? How would you manage these risks?

Most of the examples described in the previous section (i.e., protecting the patient) apply to this section (i.e., protecting yourself) as well. The most important thing to remember in a case such as this (or any case, for that matter) is to document, document, document. People who are experiencing paranoia may have concerns about writing things down; therefore, in addition to oral consent, you may want written consent to assessment/treatment (CPA Code of Ethics, Standard I.22; APA Ethics Code, Standard 3.10), as well as what you explained and what Kaya's understanding was of what you explained.

Another important issue, as emphasized earlier, is the importance of being genuine and transparent throughout the process (CPA Code of Ethics, Standard III.14; APA Principle C: Integrity). Do not assume what Kaya tells you is inherently untrue or simply a result of symptoms, and be forthright with her as to who will have access to her information and what it will be used for. You may be afraid that if you say too much about risks to her, someone like Kaya (due to her fears) may decide not to see you. That is her choice, and we need to respect that (CPA Code of Ethics, Standard I.30; APA Ethics Code, Standard 10.01, Informed Consent to Therapy). Not being forthright with a patient or not being fully transparent (even with the best of intentions or due to discomfort) can cause significant problems in the future.

Finally, respect the limits of your knowledge and competency (CPA Code of Ethics, Standards II.6, II.8; APA [2017] Ethics Code, Standard 2.01). As a supervisor once told one of the authors of this chapter, the biggest mistake psychology students and young psychologists can make is to act first and consult afterward to make sure what they did was correct. Although the intention is generally good, the result could put you at risk. Ethical consultation means consulting before acting and then, of course, remembering to document, document, document.

Disposition

ACTIVITY 3.5:

Do you think there is anything you as a psychologist can do in so complex a case with such serious psychological problems? What can you do to motivate Kaya to stay engaged in treatment? How would you get her family involved, if at all?

Although you may think there is not much you can do when it comes to patients experiencing psychosis, we want to emphasize hope about how much you *can* do in helping a patient like Kaya (Kingdon & Turkington, 2008; Wright et al., 2014). First, as we have been commenting throughout this chapter, building a positive therapeutic relationship with the patient throughout this process is one of the most important things you can do. In addition to showing her respect, it will allow you to complete a more accurate assessment (because Kaya is more likely to be open and honest about her experiences with someone she trusts). This will also pave the way for providing psychotherapy (if this is the direction taken) or providing Kaya with a positive experience with a mental health provider that may pave the way for mental health treatment in the future. In this way, even a diagnostic assessment can be therapeutic for a patient. In addition, the National Institute for Clinical Excellence (2014) guidelines in the United Kingdom (a set of guidelines that promote evidence-based practice) recommend that cognitive behavior therapy for psychosis be offered to people experiencing psychosis (Sections 1.3.7, 1.3.4.1). The American Psychiatric Association (2004) has similar recommendations.

A second important issue is that although a diagnosis is important for directing one to the most evidence-based practice and for billing purposes, it is not vital to Kaya's recovery that she accept the diagnosis of "paranoid schizophrenia." Although there are some patients who may not have difficulties with this label, there are many who will due to stigma (see also Chapter 8, this volume). Although we do not condone hiding a diagnosis from a patient, if he or she is clearly having difficulties in accepting the diagnosis, this does not need to be a hindrance in providing psychotherapy that will help promote the process of recovery (i.e., living a satisfying, hopeful, and contributing life in the presence of mental health problems; Mental Health Commission of Canada, 2016).

Additionally, given the multicultural component in this case, we would encourage you to consult with Kaya on cultural issues. Given that Kaya's father immigrated from Africa and seems skeptical about purely Western approaches, to provide culturally informed care, you should discuss cultural norms and values, including beliefs and practices related to mental health with Kaya (see APA, 2002; Comas-Díaz, 2012; Hays, 2016). Given her biracial heritage, one should not make any assumptions about whether Kaya identifies with one or both cultures and how her cultural self-identity may affect her involvement in assessment and treatment. Educating oneself around the specific cultural issues in this case, including appropriate consultation, would be essential for the culturally informed and competent psychologist.

Finally, finding a way to bring the family together (either in family therapy or just to involve them as supports for Kaya) would be helpful (if Kaya provides her consent). This could involve psychoeducation or family therapy, depending on the results of ongoing assessment. Additionally, providing the family with information on where they can seek support would also be beneficial to help them cope with caregiver stress and to remind them of the importance of self-care. We saw in this example that there is a 16-year-old sibling who is likely feeling invisible in the family and a mother who is missing work to stay at home. Although Kaya is the patient, the family (who is expected to be the main provider of care) is often forgotten. Any support that can be provided to help the family improve its functioning and enhance its self-care will only further promote recovery in Kaya (Glick et al., 2011; National Institute for Clinical Excellence, 2014).

References

American Psychiatric Association. (2004). *Schizophrenia practice guideline*. Retrieved from http://psychiatryonline.org/pb/assets/raw/sitewide/practice_guidelines/guidelines/schizophrenia.pdf

American Psychological Association. (2002). *Guidelines on multicultural education, training, research, practice and organizational change for psychologists*. Retrieved from http://www.apa.org/pi/oema/resources/policy/multicultural-guidelines.aspx

American Psychological Association. (2017). *Ethical principles of psychologists and code of conduct* (2002, Amended June 1, 2010 and January 1, 2017). Retrieved from http://www.apa.org/ethics/code/index.aspx

Bentall, R. P., de Sousa, P., Varese, F., Wickham, S., Sitko, K., Haarmans, M., & Read, J. (2014). From adversity to psychosis: Pathways and mechanisms from specific adversities to specific symptoms. *Social Psychiatry and Psychiatric Epidemiology, 49*, 1011–1022. http://dx.doi.org/10.1007/s00127-014-0914-0

Canadian Psychological Association. (2017). *Canadian code of ethics for psychologists* (4th ed.). Retrieved from http://www.cpa.ca/docs/File/Ethics/CPA_Code_2017_4thEd.pdf

Castle, D. J., & Morgan, V. (2008). Epidemiology. In K. T. Mueser & D. V. Jeste (Eds.), *Clinical handbook of schizophrenia* (pp. 117–124). New York, NY: Guilford Press.

Comas-Díaz, L. (2012). *Multicultural care: A clinician's guide to cultural competence*. http://dx.doi.org/10.1037/13491-000

Glick, I. D., Stekoll, A. H., & Hays, S. (2011). The role of the family and improvement in treatment maintenance, adherence, and outcome for schizophrenia. *Journal of Clinical Psychopharmacology, 31*, 82–85. http://dx.doi.org/10.1097/JCP.0b013e31820597fa

Gururajan, A., Manning, E. E., Klug, M., & van den Buuse, M. (2012). Drugs of abuse and increased risk of psychosis development. *Australian and New Zealand Journal of Psychiatry, 46*, 1120–1135. http://dx.doi.org/10.1177/0004867412455232

Hays, P. A. (2016). *Addressing cultural complexities in practice: Assessment, diagnosis, and therapy* (3rd ed.). http://dx.doi.org/10.1037/14801-000

Kingdon, D. G., & Turkington, D. (2008). *Cognitive therapy of schizophrenia*. New York, NY: Guilford Press.

Kleiger, J. H., & Khadivi, A. (2015). *Assessing psychosis: A clinician's guide*. New York, NY: Routledge.

Mental Health Commission of Canada. (2016). *Guidelines for recovery-oriented practice*. Retrieved from https://www.mentalhealthcommission.ca/sites/default/files/2016-07/MHCC_Recovery_Guidelines_2016_ENG.PDF

Mortimer, A. M. (2007). Symptom rating scales and outcome in schizophrenia. *The British Journal of Psychiatry, 191*, s7–s14. http://dx.doi.org/10.1192/bjp.191.50.s7

National Institute for Clinical Excellence. (2014). *Psychosis and schizophrenia in adults: Treatment and management.* Retrieved from http://www.nice.org.uk/guidance/cg178/chapter/1-recommendations

Rudnick, A., & Roe, D. (2008). Diagnostic interviewing. In K. T. Mueser & D. V. Jeste (Eds.), *Clinical handbook of schizophrenia* (pp. 117–124). New York, NY: Guilford Press.

Schaffer, J., & Rodolfa, E. (2016). *A student's guide to assessment and diagnosis using the ICD–10–CM: Psychological and behavioral conditions.* http://dx.doi.org/10.1037/14778-000

State of Minnesota vs. Jerry Expose, Jr., A13-1285 (Minn., 2015). Retrieved from https://mn.gov/law-library-stat/archive/supct/2015/OPA131285-120915.pdf

World Health Organization. (1993). *The ICD–10 classification of mental and behavioural disorders: Clinical descriptions and diagnostic guidelines.* Retrieved from http://www.who.int/classifications/icd/en/bluebook.pdf

Wright, N., Turkington, D., Kelly, O., Davies, D., Jacobs, A., & Hopton, J. (2014). *Treating psychosis: A clinician's guide to integrating acceptance and commitment therapy, compassion-focused therapy and mindfulness approaches within the cognitive behavioral therapy tradition.* Oakland, CA: New Harbinger.

Genny Lou-Barton and John Preston

F31 Bipolar Disorder

4

ipolar affective disorders are characterized by disturbances in emotion, energy, and activity typically involving alternating episodes of elevated, irritable, or depressive moods. They have a lifetime prevalence rate ranging from 1.5% to 5% (variability due to differences in diagnostic criteria). Bipolar affective disorder presents unique challenges for assessment and diagnosis. Only 20% of cases are accurately diagnosed during the first year of symptoms, and up to 35% are not correctly diagnosed or not appropriately treated for more than 10 years after the first episode (Hirschfeld, Lewis, & Vornik, 2003; Suppes et al., 2001). This disorder can become progressively more severe and more difficult to treat if not appropriately treated early, so accurate diagnosis is particularly crucial (Goodwin & Jamison, 2007). To complicate matters, an estimated 40% of those diagnosed as unipolar major depressive disorder (F32.xx or F33.xx) actually turn out to be suffering from bipolar affective disorders (F31.xx; Angst, 2013). When the first episode of bipolar disorder is one of severe depression and no manic or hypomanic symptoms have yet emerged, the differential diagnosis—unipolar depression versus bipolar depression—can be especially challenging (Berk et al., 2007). An inaccurate diagnosis can lead to treatments that are either harmful or ineffective, thus making this important distinction much more than

http://dx.doi.org/10.1037/0000069-005
An ICD–10–CM Casebook and Workbook for Students: Psychological and Behavioral Conditions, J. B. Schaffer and E. Rodolfa (Editors)

academic; inaccurate diagnosis can contribute significantly to a worsening of the condition and may adversely affect the longer-term trajectory of the disorder.

Bipolar disorders have the highest rates of completed suicide among all psychiatric disorders (15%–18.9%; Goodwin et al., 2003; Sharma & Markar, 1994). Inadequately treated bipolar disorders also result in significant health problems—most notably, high rates of cardiovascular disease, obesity, stroke, and Type 2 diabetes (see Depression and Bipolar Support Alliance for specific articles on a host of medical conditions associated with bipolar disorder: http://www.dbsalliance.org). The World Health Organization predicts that by 2030, severe mood disorders will be the number one cause of burden of disease (lost years of healthy life) and the number two cause of decreased life expectancy worldwide (Mather & Loncar, 2005).

Bipolar disorders affect people from all socioeconomic classes, with an average age of onset of 18 (American Psychiatric Association, 2013). Unless this disorder is successfully treated, patients will invariably experience recurring episodes of increased frequency, severity, and duration and, potentially, mortality (Goodwin & Jamison, 2007).

The Case

Because bipolar disorders present with discrete episodes that are clinically very different from each other, this case includes a description of two phases of the illness.

FIRST ENCOUNTER

Craig is a 25-year-old single White man. He has a college education and works as a city planner. Three months ago, he began to develop symptoms that included depressed mood, significant fatigue, and hypersomnia (excessive sleeping: 10 or more hours a night). Before the onset of depressive symptoms, he normally slept 7 or 8 hours a night and did not experience noticeable daytime fatigue. He also experienced slight weight gain. Increasingly, he has become more socially withdrawn and has reduced some of his normal activities (e.g., attending church, hiking, going out with friends). He states that he has felt tired, depressed, apathetic, and disinterested. Additionally, many activities that normally have been enjoyable hold little interest for him (e.g., going out to eat, watching movies, and playing his guitar; he also notes a greatly diminished sex drive). Craig's thinking has become progressively more negative and pessimistic. Often he feels irritable and has begun to lose confidence in himself.

Craig sought out counseling at a local mental health clinic. You, the psychologist, inquire about possible precipitating events that may have triggered his mood changes. Craig is unable to identify clearly any specific adverse life events, except for some work-related stress. However, he doubts these problems were significant enough to warrant his severe symptoms.

Further inquiry reveals the following: no prior depressive episodes, no suicidal ideation, no obvious psychotic symptoms, no severe manic symptoms, and no apparent past episodes of hypomania or mania. Craig denies a significant history or current pattern of substance abuse (however, because minimization or denial of drug and alcohol abuse is common, this cannot be completely ruled out). Craig states that his physical health is good, although sometimes there are underlying medical disorders with few if any noticeable physical symptoms that can cause psychiatric symptoms. It is always important to evaluate and rule out underlying medical disorders that may present with depressive symptoms.

On the basis of the information gathered so far—in particular, his mood, fatigue, excessive sleeping, anhedonia, and their short duration—you give Craig the diagnosis of Major depressive episode, single episode, moderate (F32.1). As a result, individual therapy is recommended. Craig continues to meet with you for six additional sessions but then decides it is not helping him, and he drops out of treatment. Craig's depression lasts about 5 months, and then it gradually disappears.

ACTIVITY 4.1:

What are the clinical signs that could suggest that your initial diagnosis might have been incorrect and which alternative diagnoses should be considered?

There are a number of clues in this case that should lead you to think more broadly than unipolar depression. First, Craig reported "atypical symptoms" of unipolar depression that include hypersomnia, extreme fatigue, and weight gain. These symptoms may be seen in people with unipolar depression but also in those suffering from Seasonal affective disorder (F33.x). Second, the lack of clear-cut precipitating events ushering in the depressive episode raises speculation about possible bipolar disorder. Although stressful life events may trigger bipolar episodes (especially depressive episodes), spontaneous/endogenous episodes are often seen. Third, despite the report of Craig having no medical conditions, some underlying subtle medical disorders (that frequently go undetected in a routine medical examination) may play a role in causing or aggravating mood episodes. Thus, a number of medical diagnoses should be considered in addition to a mental health diagnosis. Fourth, the overuse of caffeine (F15.xxx or T43.615) and alcohol (F10.xxx) can also significantly impair the quality of sleep and need to be evaluated. Sleep deprivation is a critical factor underlying the onset of mood disorders and in general plays a role in interfering with long-term mood stabilization. Fifth, in diagnosing affective disorders one must always screen for psychotic symptoms and rule out Schizophrenia (F20.x) and drug-induced psychoses (F10–F19). Psychotic symptoms can occur in severely ill patients with unipolar depression but are more often seen in bipolar affective disorders.

SECOND ENCOUNTER

Two years later Craig experienced his second mood episode. Now 27, Craig began staying at work long after his normal work hours. He became enthusiastic about his novel rezoning project associated with his city planning job. Over a period of 3 days, fellow employees reported that he appeared increasingly energetic, excited, and animated. He told a coworker that he had only been sleeping about 3 or 4 hours a night and feeling no daytime fatigue. He became more and more hyperactive and at times somewhat agitated and irritable, behaviors that were uncharacteristic for Craig. He mentioned to coworkers that with his revolutionary rezoning plan, homeless people could be flown in from around the country and put in housing that he planned to outline in his new project. He was drinking enormous amounts of coffee, and his personal hygiene deteriorated. At one point, he began speaking so fast that no one could follow what he was saying.

Assessment Using the ICD–10–CM

This clinical picture brings up a number of important diagnostic issues that were not adequately addressed during the initial assessment. In particular, you did not take a family history. In the diagnosis of mood disorders, it often is important to determine whether there is a strong history of mood problems in blood relatives, although that is complicated by the fact that many people do not know the details of psychiatric problems in their relatives either because mental disorders are not discussed or they do not know the terminology (manic-depressive illness was the name used for bipolar disorders before 1980). However, the following behaviors and symptoms can alert the clinician to possible affective disorders in relatives: completed suicides; psychiatric hospitalizations; severe substance abuse and, in the case of bipolar disorder, abnormal behavior such as starting and stopping multiple businesses, multiple marriages, or significant problems with the law, as well as excessive gambling, spending sprees, and poor judgment. The vulnerability for bipolar disorder is one among the few mental illnesses that clearly appear to be genetically transmitted (Craddock & Sklar, 2009), and thus family histories, if they can be obtained, are important data. If Craig and other family members do not know of mental illness in their family, your direct interviewing of family members or close friends, if acceptable to the client, could also provide useful information about Craig's history and any noticeable changes in behavior. Such collateral data have long been considered to be a high-yield strategy in diagnosing mood disorders.

ICD–10–CM Diagnosis

ACTIVITY 4.2:

What are the indicators in your second encounter with Craig that would lead you to consider differential diagnostic categories other than a unipolar depression?

Let us consider the possible differential diagnoses in turn, taking into account all of the data you have available (i.e., from both the first and the second encounters). Of course, any good assessment considers all of the information available. The most important condition that may signal seasonal affective disorder is regularity in the onset of depressive episodes (occurring each year in the late fall or winter months and remitting in spring). It is also important to note that other situations resulting in decreased bright light exposure can trigger this kind of depression (e.g., beginning to work the night shift). Craig did not show this pattern. A primary medical diagnosis that can present as a mood disorder is subclinical hypothyroidism (E02 or E03.9), which results from only slight elevations of thyroid-stimulating hormone (TSH). For most people, such mild TSH elevations (in the high end of the normal range, e.g., 2.0–3.0) are not a reason for concern, but they may be problematic in those with mood disorders. Up to 10% of people with unipolar depression and two thirds of bipolar patients have signs of underlying thyroid disease (Goodwin & Jamison, 2007; Phelps, 2016).

The other two conditions that often exacerbate mood symptoms and are often not suspected or identified in routine medical exams are Sleep apnea (G47.3x) and Restless leg syndrome (G25.81). In this case, you might have asked Craig about his sleep and whether his medical checkup included a review of his thyroid. However, because subtle (subclinical) thyroid disease has few if any physical symptoms and symptoms of apnea and restless legs occur during sleep, they may or may not be noticed by the patient. If Craig has a bed partner, interviewing that person may be helpful. Obstructive sleep apnea is generally hard to miss when it is observed by a bed partner, given up to 200 to 400 spells of gasping for breath during the night. But many bed partners assume it is just snoring and habituate to the noises (i.e., tune it out). Restless legs are also quite noticeable to bed partners or even to those without a bed partner because covers are commonly knocked off the bed each night. Significant daytime fatigue can be an important clue for either condition (always seen with sleep apnea). A referral to the primary care doctor, and likely a sleep specialist, would be indicated for further evaluation.

Clients often underreport alcohol use or abuse and generally fail to consider caffeine to be a major factor influencing the quality of sleep, so such conditions warrant further investigation.

In schizophrenia or drug-induced psychoses, the psychotic symptoms usually involve more disorganized thinking and bizarre behavior than Craig exhibits, compared with psychotic symptoms due to a mood disorder.

Although you could not have known this at the time Craig was initially seen, he later experienced a spontaneous remission after 5 months. Episodes of unipolar depression, if untreated, usually last 9 to 12 months (followed by spontaneous remission), whereas depressions in bipolar disorder generally are of shorter duration (e.g., 6 months), suggesting this might be something other than a unipolar depressive disorder (Goodwin & Jamison, 2007; Sobel, 2012). Severe depressive episodes with short duration are a red flag for possible bipolar disorder. Additionally, in at least half of adults and teenagers who have bipolar disorder, the first episode is depression, with no manic or hypomanic episodes (Goodwin & Jamison, 2007). In other words, the manic "pole" of the disorder has not yet emerged. The first manic or hypomanic episode (on average) follows 18 months later (although there is a good deal of individual variability). Thus, this represents a major challenge in making a diagnosis (i.e., bipolar depression vs. unipolar), if it is a first episode. What is important is that the possibility of a bipolar depression should be kept in mind.

Bipolar disorders are associated with certain comorbidities (i.e., co-occurring disorders), such as substance use disorders (SUDs; F10–F19), anxiety disorders (F41–F43), Attention-deficit hyperactivity disorder (F90.x), and Eating disorders (F50.x; Krishnan, 2005). In the current case, you could have assessed for signs of these disorders as well. Of all the comorbidities, SUDs appear to be most common. It is estimated that 60% of individuals with bipolar disorder have an SUD (Ostacher, 2011). Although in this case, you asked Craig about his substance use, SUDs can easily be overlooked without a detailed line of questioning that includes asking about specific amounts and frequencies, due to the frequency of denial or minimization of use of drugs and alcohol (Frances, 2013). Identifying the existence of an SUD in cases of bipolar disorder is crucial. Not only can substance use underlie the causes of some symptoms, but, along with the other comorbidities mentioned, it can significantly interfere with treatment and lead to poorer outcomes (Ostacher, 2011). It cannot be overemphasized that failure to diagnose and treat these psychiatric comorbidities or underlying medical conditions is a common reason for patients' inability to maintain long-term mood stability, which is an important goal in treating this highly recurrent disorder.

One of the largest challenges in making a correct diagnosis of bipolar disorder, as discussed earlier, is that the diagnosis typically is based on the presence or history of both a major depressive and a manic or hypomanic episode. Craig may not note a few days of an "upbeat mood" if it caused no distress or impairment. He may assume that those are periods of normal "good feelings" that have nothing to do with his current psychological problems. When assessing for hypomania, it may be helpful for the psychologist to be detailed when describing characteristics of a hypomanic episode (distinguishing symptoms outlined subsequently). Most important, however, is the value in having a third party's perspective. Here is where information from a close relative, friend, or spouse can be informative. Very mild hypomania is not pathological; however, when significant others notice striking behavioral changes in the patient (e.g., very rapid speech), this should alert the clinician to a bona fide hypomanic episode.

There is some disagreement among mood disorder experts regarding the duration of symptoms required to diagnose a hypomanic episode. Many have pointed out that hypomanic episodes that last 2 to 3 days are actually the norm, whereas other experts have argued that an episode requires a minimum of 4 days. Higher rates of bipolar disorder in the general population are seen when 2 to 3 days of hypomanic symptoms are considered to be bona fide hypomanic episodes (Goodwin & Jamison, 2007).

For many years in the United States, two versions of bipolar disorder have been recognized: bipolar I (severe depressive and manic episodes) and bipolar II (severe depressions and hypomanic episodes). This nosology and subtyping have been seen throughout the research and professional literature. ICD–10–CM approaches this issue from a slightly different perspective. The terms bipolar I and II are not used, although the ICD–10–CM diagnoses do describe similar conditions (see Exhibit 4.1).

On the basis of Craig's history and clinical picture and ruling out interepisode psychotic symptoms or substance-induced mania, the most likely ICD–10–CM diagnoses

EXHIBIT 4.1

ICD–10–CM: Bipolar Affective Disorder Diagnoses

1. Bipolar disorder, current episode hypomania (ICD–10–CM Code: F31.0)
2. Bipolar disorder, current episode manic[a] (ICD–10–CM Code: F31.1x or F31.2)
3. Bipolar disorder, current episode depressed, mild or moderate depression[a] (ICD–10–CM Code: F31.3x)
4. Bipolar disorder, current episode depressed[a] (ICD–10–CM Code: F31.4 or F31.5)
5. Bipolar affective disorder, current episode mixed[a] (ICD–10–CM Code: F31.6x)

[a]May include specifiers: With or without psychotic symptoms; with or without somatic symptoms (melancholic symptoms), mild, moderate, severe.

would be first episode: Bipolar disorder, current episode depressed, severe, without psychotic features (F31.4). Second episode: Bipolar disorder, current episode manic with psychotic features (F31.2). It would be important to question Craig carefully about his apparently grandiose plan, for example, to fly in homeless people, to determine whether these beliefs are truly grossly unrealistic and thus delusional. Finally, in a case of bipolar affective disorder, the diagnosis is not static: The clinical picture will be quite different whether the patient is in a manic or depressive episode.

Ethical Considerations—Protecting Your Patient

ACTIVITY 4.3:

Given the diagnostic complications in this case, what are the particular ethical issues you need to keep in mind? Why would or wouldn't it be ethical to involve Craig's family in his treatment? What ethical issues might arise if they do become involved?

Involving the family is often important, although it also raises ethical questions involving confidentiality (American Psychological Association [APA; 2017] *Ethical Principles of Psychologists and Code of Conduct* [APA Ethics Code], Standard 4.01, Maintaining Confidentiality; Roberts & Jain, 2011; Srivastava, 2011). Diagnosing and treating bipolar disorders can be particularly challenging. Often the history of the current and prior episodes gleaned from the patient may not be fully accurate. People in the throes of a major mood episode rarely can provide an accurate history. This is where the involvement of a significant other or the family can be invaluable in providing useful information about the patient's history and support for the patient, encouraging his or her regular use of medications and continued engagement in psychotherapy, acting as a coach to help the patient exercise or make other helpful lifestyle changes, and being on the alert for early signs of another episode. This necessitates a discussion with the patient about involving family members and requires that he or she sign an appropriate release of information form. There are times when the informed consent process is difficult, especially if the patient is psychotic. Additionally, many manic patients, whether or not psychosis is present, exhibit severely impaired judgment. They may drive their families into bankruptcy or act in ways that can be dangerous to themselves or others. For example, poor impulse control, extremely poor judgment, and agitation can lead to potentially dangerous behaviors, such as reckless driving, driving while intoxicated, excessive restlessness and hyperactivity, and grandiose delusions, such as the belief that one can fly, and then jumping off a bridge. If you assess the person as at imminent physical danger to self or others, this creates a special circumstance in which violating patient privacy may even be legally mandated (see the discussion of the *Tarasoff* case in Chapter 3, this volume). In the absence of dangerousness, however, there arises a complex ethical dilemma if the patient does not agree to allow the psychologist to speak with family members. Optimal care may be impossible without family involvement, yet the patient's right to privacy remains primary (Schaffer & Rodolfa, 2016; see also Chapter 3, this volume). In this circumstance, working carefully with the patient to develop sufficient trust that involvement of family is acceptable is a principal goal.

If there are sufficient dysfunctional emotions and behavior present, another potential means of response is involuntary hospitalization, a relatively rare circumstance in which the ethical principle of avoiding harm (APA Principle A: Beneficence and Nonmaleficence; APA, 2017) trumps privacy (APA Principle E: Respect for People's Rights and Dignity; APA, 2017). Most times when people are in a manic episode, they have no insight that they are ill and may refuse treatment. You should be familiar with specific protocols for dealing with involuntary hospitalizations in your community. Initiating involuntary treatment presents a significant ethical dilemma because it involves depriving a person of a constitutional right to self-determination. Here protection of the patient's privacy and autonomy may be superseded by the need to provide safety when the patient is gravely disabled or incompetent to make these important decisions (see APA Ethics Code, Principle A: Beneficence and Nonmaleficence and Principle E: Respect for People's Rights and Dignity [APA, 2017]; see also Pope & Vasquez, 2016).

Risk Management—Protecting Your Patient, Protecting Yourself

ACTIVITY 4.4:

What specific risks would you face working with Craig, especially if you decide to involve his family or hospitalize him?

A number of risks are involved in working with a person like Craig. Given the earlier discussion regarding hospitalization and violating privacy, the psychologist can be "damned if you do and damned if you don't." The strategy of maintaining privacy and doing the best one can leaves the psychologist open to an accusation of inadequate treatment. Violating privacy leaves one open to the accusation of doing so without adequate foundation. In such a circumstance, careful documentation regarding not only the actions taken but also the data you collected and the rationale you used to make decisions is especially important.

Second, it is essential to refer bipolar clients for medication treatment. This is one psychiatric disorder for which psychopharmacology is imperative, and failure to make a referral leaves you open to an accusation of incompetent practice because lack of adequate medical treatment carries significant risks (e.g., progressive worsening of the disorder, suicide). Between episodes, when there are not severe symptoms and judgment is intact, discussing the need for medication treatment is particularly important. This includes carefully explaining how medications work and the risks and benefits of medical treatment. If, during these times, the patient refuses medications, it will be important to carefully document in your records what you have done to address these issues with her or him. During severe manic episodes, when the patient may not recognize or admit to the presence of problems, involvement of the family may be beneficial (Roberts & Jain, 2011; Srivastava, 2011).

Disposition

ACTIVITY 4.5:

What specific intervention strategies would be most appropriate in this case? What role could Craig's family or other health care professionals play in his treatment, and what would your role as a psychologist be in this integrated care context?

The overall goals of therapy should include successful resolution of the current episode, longer term relapse prevention and mood stabilization, and treatments aimed at helping Craig deal with what is a chronic mental illness. Additionally, an especially important goal is to reduce the risk of suicide in this group of patients with high suicide rates. If suicidal ideation is present, specific steps should be taken to develop a safety plan; for instance, determining whom to call if a crisis occurs during the evening or weekend or having the family remove weapons from the house. Specific plans for possible hospitalization, including involuntary hospitalization, need to be designed. Once again, these intervention strategies are more effective when family members are involved (if the patient or a court-appointed guardian consents).

The treatment of bipolar disorder is complex and requires integrative approaches, including psychotherapy, lifestyle management, and use of psychiatric medication.

The forms of psychotherapy that have empirical support in treating bipolar disorder include family-focused psychoeducational treatment (Miklowitz et al., 2000), cognitive behavior therapy (Newman, Leahy, Beck, Reilly-Harrington, & Gyulai, 2002), and interpersonal and social rhythm therapy (Frank, Swartz, & Kupfer, 2000). Additionally, the American Psychiatric Association (2002) *Practice Guidelines for the*

Treatment of Bipolar Disorder and the website of the APA Society of Clinical Psychology (Division 12; APA, 2015) provide reviews of research on these approaches to psychotherapy with bipolar patients. All three empirically supported treatments focus on active problem-solving, reduction of extreme stressful interactions in the family, and adherence to medication treatments. In addition, supportive therapy for both patient and family can contribute significantly to positive treatment outcomes. Family members may need treatment to deal with their significant stress, especially in the case of long-term mood stabilization (Frank et al., 2000).

Lifestyle management is also crucial (this approach is highlighted in interpersonal and social rhythm therapy; Frank et al., 2000). Most important are the following: maintain regular sleeping schedules (especially important is awakening at the same time each day, a strategy referred to as *dawn simulation*); avoid sleep deprivation, if possible; avoid disruption of the circadian rhythm (e.g., a significant problem for shift workers and also seen with jet lag); engage in regular exercise; reduce or eliminate caffeine, especially in the afternoon or evening; avoid intense physical activities or emotionally charged situations in the late evening; and, very important, avoid recreational substances such as alcohol (provide treatment for substance abuse when necessary).

Most people diagnosed with bipolar disorder in the United States only receive medication treatment. Thus, you play a crucial role in identifying cases of bipolar disorders, carrying out comprehensive evaluations, and recommending and providing integrative treatments. Medication treatment for bipolar disorder is beyond the scope of this book, but standard medications used include mood stabilizers (e.g., lithium, Depakote, Tegretol, Lamictal) and antipsychotics (e.g., Seroquel, Zyprexa, Abilify, Latuda, and others). Note that antidepressants carry significant risks and should either be avoided or used cautiously (Preston, 2015). Psychologists can play a vital role on the collaborative treatment team by tracking medication adherence and following closely any side effects that may arise, necessitating a referral back to the prescribing physician. For instance, Shea (2006) provided numerous suggestions to help practitioners use their clinical alliance to explore their patients' difficulty with medication adherence. In addition, in following closely any side effects that may arise, a psychologist may find it necessary to refer the patient back to the prescribing physician. For reasons such as negative stigma, side effects, denial, and lack of positive treatment effects, medication nonadherence rates are high among those being treated for bipolar disorder, and nonadherence is the major cause for recurring episodes. Psychologists are often front-line professionals in managing this concern by encouraging open discussion concerning negative thoughts regarding medications that can occur either in the patients themselves or in significant others.

Because of the highly recurrent nature of bipolar disorder, the therapist can also work with the patient and family members to become alert to the first signs of an impending episode (providing treatment early may avoid a full-blown episode; Phelps, 2016). Patients and family members can be coached to be especially alert to behavioral changes in the following areas: physical symptoms; change in daily activities; sleep patterns; work, school, and social activities; sexual behavior; eating; substance use or abuse; and spending. Instruction to monitor these behaviors carefully is key to relapse prevention. In addition to psychotherapy, it is helpful for all people suffering from bipolar disorder to become knowledgeable about the disorder and long-term illness management.

Finally, it is often helpful to provide referrals to support groups for people with bipolar disorder (e.g., National Alliance for Mental Illness: http://www.nami.org) and Depression and Bipolar Support Alliance (http://www.dbsalliance.org).

In conclusion, assessing and diagnosing a client such as Craig is not a quick process. Bipolar disorders involve a pattern that occurs over a lifetime, so more than a snapshot of the current episode—that is, a cross-sectional perspective—is needed for an accurate diagnosis. In addition, time and care are needed for an accurate diagnosis, particularly when there is no obvious indication of previous episodes.

References

American Psychiatric Association. (2002). *Practice guideline for the treatment of patients with bipolar disorder* (2nd ed.). Retrieved from http://psychiatryonline.org/pb/assets/raw/sitewide/practice_guidelines/guidelines/bipolar.pdf

American Psychiatric Association. (2013). *Diagnostic and statistical manual of mental disorders* (5th ed.). Washington, DC: Author.

American Psychological Association. (2011). Practice guidelines regarding psychologists' involvement in pharmacological issues. *American Psychologist, 66,* 835–849. http://dx.doi.org/10.1037/a0025890

American Psychological Association. (2017). *Ethical principles of psychologists and code of conduct* (2002, Amended June 1, 2010 and January 1, 2017). Retrieved from http://www.apa.org/ethics/code/index.aspx

American Psychological Association, Society of Clinical Psychology. (2015). *Description.* Retrieved from https://www.div12.org/psychological-treatments/disorders/bipolar-disorder

Angst, J. (2013). Bipolar disorders in *DSM–5*: Strengths, problems and perspectives. *International Journal of Bipolar Disorders, 1,* 12. http://dx.doi.org/10.1186/2194-7511-1-12

Berk, M., Dodd, S., Callaly, P., Berk, L., Fitzgerald, P., de Castella, A. R., . . . Kulkami, J. (2007). History of illness prior to a diagnosis of bipolar disorder or schizoaffective disorder. *Journal of Affective Disorders, 103,* 181–186. http://dx.doi.org/10.1016/j.jad.2007.01.027

Craddock, N., & Sklar, P. (2009). Genetics of bipolar disorder: Successful start to a long journey. *Trends in Genetics, 25,* 99–105. http://dx.doi.org/10.1016/j.tig.2008.12.002

Frances, A. (2013). *Essentials of psychiatric diagnosis: Responding to the challenge of DSM–5.* New York, NY: Guilford Press.

Frank, E., Swartz, H. A., & Kupfer, D. J. (2000). Interpersonal and social rhythm therapy: Managing the chaos of bipolar disorder. *Biological Psychiatry, 48,* 593–604. http://dx.doi.org/10.1016/S0006-3223(00)00969-0

Goodwin, F. K., Fireman, B., Simon, G. E., Hunkeler, E. M., Lee, J., & Revicki, D. (2003). Suicide risk in bipolar disorder during treatment with lithium and divalproex. *JAMA, 290,* 1467–1473. http://dx.doi.org/10.1001/jama.290.11.1467

Goodwin, F. K., & Jamison, K. R. (2007). *Manic-depressive illness*. Oxford, England: Oxford University Press.

Hirschfeld, R., Lewis, L., & Vornik, L. (2003). Perceptions and impact of bipolar disorder: How far have we really come? Results of the National Depressive and Manic-Depressive Association 2000 survey of individuals with bipolar disorder. *Journal of Clinical Psychiatry, 64*, 161–174. http://dx.doi.org/10.4088/JCP.v64n0209

Krishnan, K. R. (2005). Psychiatric and medical comorbidities of bipolar disorder. *Psychosomatic Medicine, 67*(1), 1–8. http://dx.doi.org/10.1097/01.psy.0000151489.36347.18

Mather, C., & Loncar, D. (2005). *Updated projections of global mortality and burden of disease, 2002–2030: Data sources, methods and results*. Retrieved from the World Health Organization website: http://www.who.int/healthinfo/statistics/bodprojectionspaper.pdf

Miklowitz, D. J., Simoneau, T. L., George, E. L., Richards, J. A., Kalbag, A., Sachs-Ericsson, N., & Suddath, R. (2000). Family-focused treatment of bipolar disorder: 1-year effects of a psychoeducational program in conjunction with pharmacotherapy. *Biological Psychiatry, 48*, 582–592. http://dx.doi.org/10.1016/S0006-3223(00)00931-8

Newman, C., Leahy, R., Beck, A., Reilly-Harrington, N., & Gyulai, L. (2002). *Bipolar disorder: A cognitive therapy approach*. http://dx.doi.org/10.1037/10442-000

Ostacher, M. (2011). Bipolar and substance use disorder comorbidity. *Journal of Lifelong Learning in Psychiatry, 9*, 428–434. http://dx.doi.org/10.1176/foc.9.4.foc428

Phelps, J. (2016). *A spectrum approach to mood disorders*. New York, NY: Norton.

Pope, K., & Vasquez, M. (2016). *Ethics in psychotherapy and counseling: A practical guide* (5th ed.). San Francisco, CA: Jossey-Bass.

Preston, J. (2015). *Bipolar disorder medications: A concise guide to the medical treatment of bipolar disorder in adolescents and adults* [Amazon Digital Services e-book]. Retrieved from https://www.amazon.com/Bipolar-Medications-Medication-Treatments-Adolescents-ebook/dp/B005GWFQGK and http://www.psyd-fx.com

Roberts, L. W., & Jain, S. (2011, May 6). Ethical issues in psychopharmacology. *The Psychiatric Times*. Retrieved from http://www.psychiatrictimes.com/articles/ethical-issues-psychopharmacology

Schaffer, J., & Rodolfa, E. (2016). *A student's guide to assessment and diagnosis using the ICD–10–CM: Psychological and behavioral conditions*. http://dx.doi.org/10.1037/14778-000

Sharma, R., & Markar, H. R. (1994). Mortality in affective disorder. *Journal of Affective Disorders, 31*, 91–96. http://dx.doi.org/10.1016/0165-0327(94)90112-0

Shea, S. (2006). *Improving medication adherence: How to talk with patients about their medications*. Philadelphia, PA: Lippincott, Williams and Wilkins.

Sobel, S. (2012, August 2). Effective personalized strategies for treating bipolar disorder. *Psychiatric Times*. Retrieved from http://www.psychiatrictimes.com/bipolar-disorder/effective-personalized-strategies-treating-bipolar-disorder

Srivastava, S. (2011). Ethical considerations in the treatment of bipolar disorder. *The Journal of Life-long Learning in Psychiatry, 9*, 461–464. http://dx.doi.org/10.1176/foc.9.4.foc461

Suppes, T., Leverich, G. S., Keck, P. E., Jr., Nolen, W. A., Denicoff, K. D., Altshuler, L. L., . . . Post, R. M. (2001). The Stanley Foundation Bipolar Treatment Outcome Network: II. Demographics and illness characteristics of the first 261 patients. *Journal of Affective Disorders, 67*, 45–59. http://dx.doi.org/10.1016/S0165-0327(01)00432-3

Mark S. Barajas and Claytie Davis III

F32 Major Depressive Disorder, Single Episode

5

Major depressive disorder consists of a set of symptoms that include depressed mood, loss of interest and enjoyment, and reduced energy resulting in increased fatigability and diminished activity. Other possible symptoms include difficulties with concentration, sleep, and appetite, lowered self-esteem, pessimism, and suicidality. Depression is one of the most common psychological disorders, occurring in an estimated 7% of the general population (Center for Behavioral Health Statistics and Quality, 2016). It is a common problem in university settings, which is the focus of this chapter.

Rates of students seeking therapy at university and college counseling centers are increasing, as are reports of acuity. In 2009, 93% of university counseling center directors reported an increase in the number of clients presenting with severe psychological problems on their campus (Gallagher, 2009). More recently, the Association of University College Counseling Center Directors survey (Center for Collegiate Mental Health, 2017) revealed that depression was the second most common presenting concern (49%) at college counseling centers; anxiety (61%) was the most commonly reported issue leading students to seek therapy. Researchers have found financial concerns, difficult relationships with faculty, irregular patterns of sleeping and eating, and competitiveness among students to be predictors of depression, especially

http://dx.doi.org/10.1037/0000069-006

An ICD–10–CM Casebook and Workbook for Students: Psychological and Behavioral Conditions, J. B. Schaffer and E. Rodolfa (Editors)

among students from historically marginalized populations (Ibrahim, Kelly, Adams, & Glazebrook, 2013; Posselt & Lipson, 2016).

The Case

Linda, a 19-year-old, first-generation Taiwanese American college student in her second year at the university, arrives at the university counseling center, accompanied by her roommate, Traci. Linda is reluctant to complete the initial paperwork and complies only after being informed that it will help the therapist better understand her needs. She identifies as a single female and declines to report her sexual orientation. Her top three concerns are academic concerns, depression issues, and family concerns. Linda is considering withdrawing from school and reports no previous counseling or psychiatry history. She denies using alcohol or drugs and does not respond to any of the items related to risk to self or others (i.e., suicidal and homicidal ideation). She further denies any past physical or sexual traumas. She reports receiving little to no support from her mother, father, or brother. She asks if Traci can join her in the session, adding, "it will make me feel more comfortable."

While staring at the floor with her legs crossed and both hands covering her face, Linda shares that she stopped attending class 6 weeks ago because she is "not sure of the point of going to school anymore." She learned last month she has not been admitted to the College of Business and therefore needs to choose another major, which has increased her anxiety. Since she stopped attending class, Linda feels increasingly sad and has difficulty concentrating, finding herself preoccupied with thoughts of "what went wrong" and trying to imagine what her future might look like. She states that the only reason she came to the university was to "major in business, get a high-paying job in consulting, and take care of my parents." She reports having a twin brother, who also attends the university and is doing well as a computer science major. Traci interjects that Linda's parents have tended to "play favorites," and Linda often feels like the "other child." She states that Linda has difficulty sleeping at night and feels tired most of the time. Traci goes on to indicate that she became concerned after Linda failed to leave her room for 3 days in a row, and she says Linda looks like she has lost 10 pounds over the course of the past 2 months. Moreover, it is apparent that Linda has not bathed in some time, and her appearance is disheveled.

Traci is concerned about Linda's suicidality and reports that Linda has enough pain pills to kill herself. Linda states she is currently at a 7 on a 1-to-10 scale on suicide likelihood because "if I let my family down, there is nothing left to live for, and God will understand as I would no longer be a burden to my family." She denies engaging in other self-harm behaviors (e.g., cutting) or contemplating harming anyone else. Regarding strengths, Linda is a good athlete and is considerate of others. She states that she is open to therapy but is not confident it will help her "unless it can get me into my major." She adds that she attended three sessions of family therapy during her sophomore year of high school when her mother was struggling with alcoholism, and she did not recall therapy helping her or her mother.

Linda's parents own a restaurant where she and her brother worked while in high school. Her parents immigrated to the United States to provide greater educational opportunities for their children. Her parents repeatedly tell her of the sacrifices they made for her when she is not meeting their expectations of academic success. She is scolded if she fails to answer their calls and if she is not in her room by 10 p.m. Linda is worried that if she cannot find a way to get into her preferred major, her family will once again disapprove of her and blame her for not trying hard enough.

Assessment Using the ICD–10–CM

ACTIVITY 5.1:

In what ways might Linda's family background and past experiences with family therapy be relevant in assessing her? What concerns does Traci's presence during your initial session with Linda raise for you?

A focused, concise intake interview will facilitate efficient information gathering and the development of diagnostic hypotheses. In Linda's case, the intake process is complicated by the fact that she is accompanied by her friend, Traci. In such a situation, you need to remain mindful of validating Traci's concern for Linda while maintaining focus on Linda's experience and needs and ensuring that you gather as much information as possible directly from Linda.

In addition to a focused clinical interview, you may wish to consider the use of brief assessments to aid in the assessment process. Brief assessment tools can be useful in gathering domain-specific information and may facilitate initial diagnosis in a time-efficient manner, especially with clients who may be unaccustomed to, or uncomfortable with, sharing personal information verbally with a stranger. The Beck Depression Inventory—II (BDI–II; A. T. Beck, Steer, & Brown, 1996) provides brief screening for a variety of concerns endorsed by college students. Given her endorsement of suicidal ideation, Linda's risk level could be further explored with an instrument such as the Suicidal Ideation Questionnaire (SIQ; Reynolds, 1988).

Consultation with colleagues is an important practice that can help you think through complicated cases and uncover areas you may wish to explore in greater depth. After a complex clinical interview such as Linda's, we suggest consultation with a supervisor or discussion of the case in agency-wide case conference. Returning to your case, after discussing her in case conference, a staff social worker asks you about previous treatment. This leads you to reconsider the importance of exploring her reference to having been in family therapy and motivates you to ask Linda if she would be open to signing a release of information (ROI) allowing you to talk with her former family therapist.

ICD–10–CM Diagnosis

Once Linda's presenting concerns have been summarized and relevant information compiled, you are ready to formulate a set of differential diagnoses. At this point, we recommend clinicians have several materials at hand for reference. The ICD–10–CM, because of its federal status as the billing and coding standard for the United States, is necessary. For more thorough descriptions of diagnostic criteria, discussion of depression in specific populations, and an overview of the epidemiology of depression, we suggest you consult one of two handbooks of depression (Friedman & Anderson, 2014; Gotlib & Hammen, 2014).

ACTIVITY 5.2:

How would you organize the information gained during Linda's intake? Also list any additional information you would want. How will cultural considerations influence your approach to diagnosis?

Although there are many potential methods for conceptualizing Linda's concerns, we prefer grouping the information gathered as follows: cognitive, affective, and behavioral symptoms; suicidal/homicidal ideation and self-harming behavior; alcohol and other drug concerns; and direct behavioral observations. We encourage you also to note Linda's strengths, level of insight, and presence of help-seeking behaviors. While organizing information in the aforementioned manner, it is important to remain mindful of cultural factors affecting both the clinician's interpretation and the client's presentation of relevant information. One heuristic that may help is Hays's (2016) ADDRESSING framework: Age, Developmental and acquired Disabilities, Religion, Ethnicity, Social Class, Sexual Orientation, Indigenous Background, National Origin, and Gender. It is critical to address the client's identities, as these explorations often lead to important clinical information (Comas-Díaz, 2012).

Following the suggested organizing method, you are able to conceptualize Linda's case as follows. Regarding cognitive symptoms, she reported difficulty concentrating, racing thoughts, diminished self-esteem, and self-doubt. Affective symptoms consist of depressed mood and increased anxiety. Her behavioral symptoms include lethargy, chronic fatigue, disturbed sleep, social withdrawal, and difficulty getting out of bed. Furthermore, Traci speculated that Linda's eating has become irregular and that she has lost approximately 10 pounds. Suicidal ideation is present, manifesting as passive and vague (i.e., "there is nothing left to live for"), and she strongly denied engaging in self-harm behavior or having an active plan or intent to harm herself or anyone else. Reassuringly, she also denied any use of alcohol or other drugs, including caffeine and nicotine. Behavioral observations gleaned from the intake interview include her withdrawn posture (i.e., hands and hair covering her face) and her disheveled appearance. In considering a holistic conceptualization of Linda, it is important to note her reported strengths, her moderate level of insight into the present concerns, her future-orientated thinking, and her help-seeking behaviors. Using the ADDRESSING framework, we see that she is a traditionally aged college student, able-bodied, Taiwanese American from a middle or working-class family, nonnative, first-generation U.S.-born, cisgender-female (i.e., gender assigned at birth matches gender identity); at this point, you do not have information regarding her sexual orientation or religious affiliation.

To assist in determining a diagnosis for Linda, we recommend you consult a general psychopathology text (e.g., Blaney, Krueger, & Millon, 2015) in addition to the previously mentioned handbooks (Friedman & Anderson, 2014; Gotlib & Hammen, 2014). Let us first consider Reaction to severe stress (F43.x), as well as adjustment disorder, as possible diagnoses. Although Linda tells you she feels stressed and is having difficulty concentrating, both symptoms of Acute stress reaction (F43.0), her depressed mood and self-doubt are not accounted for by this diagnosis and thus allow you to rule it out. You might consider Posttraumatic stress disorder (PTSD; F43.1) because depression symptoms are common with PTSD. However, she did not report experiencing a discrete, exceptionally threatening event. Moreover, her symptoms have not included periods of numbness nor has she reported flashbacks, also allowing a rule-out. Finally, Linda does endorse many symptoms present in Adjustment disorder (F43.2); however, her physical symptoms (e.g., lethargy, irregular appetite) and suicidal ideation are not characteristic of this disorder, again facilitating a rule-out.

Linda's symptoms might also be understood as manifestations of anxiety, perhaps diagnosed as Generalized anxiety disorder (F41.1) or Mixed anxiety and depressive disorder (F41.2). Although she discloses feeling anxious, her physical symptoms do not include muscle tension, lightheadedness, or heart palpitations, typically present in Generalized anxiety disorder (F41.1). Furthermore, her endorsement of suicidal ideation, depressed mood, and feelings of self-doubt allows you to rule out Generalized anxiety disorder (F41.1). The diagnosis of Mixed anxiety and depressive disorder (F41.2) is also not appropriate for Linda because she endorses relatively few anxiety symptoms compared with the amount of depressive symptoms present.

Might she be suffering from a personality disorder? Although depressive personality disorder does not exist in the ICD–10–CM, her feelings of doubt are characteristic of Obsessive-compulsive personality disorder (F60.5). However, you have no reason to suspect Linda is stubborn, perfectionistic, or preoccupied with details. Moreover, Obsessive-compulsive personality disorder (F60.5) can be ruled out because Linda recognizes her current state of being as a departure from her regular personality rather than a long-standing pattern of symptoms.

Given the diagnoses ruled out so far and her cluster of symptoms, the most appropriate diagnosis appears to be either Depressive episode (F32.x) or Recurrent depressive disorder (F33.x). Because all information suggests this is the first time she has experienced this constellation of symptoms, we can rule out Recurrent depressive disorder (F33), leaving us with F32.x. Next, you need to categorize her episode as mild, moderate, or severe. According to the *Handbook of Depression* (Friedman & Anderson, 2014), the presence of four symptoms signifies a mild episode (F32.0), whereas the presence of five or six symptoms and considerable difficulty continuing with usual activities indicates a moderate episode (F32.1). For the depressive episode to be considered severe, at least seven symptoms must be present, and the individual is very unlikely to be able to continue with usual activities. Additionally, in Severe depressive episode (F32.3), somatic symptoms and suicidal ideation or suicidal actions are common.

Because more than seven symptoms are present, she has stopped attending classes, and rates her risk of suicidal as 7 out of 10, Linda's depressive episode is considered severe. We must now differentiate between F32.2 Severe depressive episode without psychotic features and F32.3 Severe depressive episode with psychotic features—the key difference being the presence of hallucinations, delusions, psychomotor retardation, or severe stupor rendering ordinary activities impossible (Friedman & Anderson, 2014). She has not reported hallucinations, she does not appear delusional or psychotic, and although fatigued and socially withdrawn, she has been able to carry out ordinary activities. Given this configuration of symptoms, it appears that the best ICD–10–CM diagnosis for her is F32.2 Severe depressive disorder, without psychotic features.

Whereas Linda presented with several discrete symptoms, students presenting at university counseling centers do not always exhibit such clearly identifiable symptoms. In such cases, ICD–10–CM Z codes might help you categorize the reasons the student is seeking help. ICD–10–CM Z codes identify circumstances other than diseases or injuries influencing health status and contact with health services. Although several Z codes could be used to categorize her visit, we present a sample of codes representative of common student concerns. For example, students may experience difficulty transitioning into a 4-year university, whether from high school or community college, and their counseling sessions might be coded as Educational maladjustment and discord with teachers and classmates (Z55.4). More generally, students might seek counseling services to help adjust to living independently for the first time, living far away from home, or other developmental transitions; in these cases, Problems of adjustment to life-cycle transitions (Z60.0) might best represent their concerns. Students of color attending predominately White universities, international students, and members of other underserved student groups may seek counseling to help them navigate campus culture, accounted for by Acculturation difficulty (Z60.3). Finally, students may seek counseling services to help them understand family of origin concerns. Imagine that you were granted permission to talk to her former family therapist and you learned that her mother had abused alcohol while Linda was an adolescent and has since been sober for 5 years. Her visit to the counseling center could be coded under Alcoholism and drug addiction in family (Z63.72), which accounts for children affected by the alcoholism of a parent. We have presented a few Z codes to consider; however, given their versatile and broad topic coverage, we encourage clinicians to familiarize themselves with ICD–10–CM's Chapter 21, "Factors Influencing Health Status and Contact With Health Services."

Ethical Considerations—Protecting Your Patient

ACTIVITY 5.3:

What are the ethical and practical issues involved in Linda's request to have Traci sit in on that first session and the high level of parental involvement in Linda's life?

Several ethical considerations need to be addressed to ensure quality care. First, is there any reason you are not qualified to provide Linda's care? And what does it mean to be qualified or competent to work with a particular client or clinical presentation? (See also Chapters 3 and 8, this volume.) At first glance, the case seems straightforward and typical of a college student presenting at a university counseling center. However, the case becomes more complex as cultural considerations are introduced. For example, how much knowledge do you need to have regarding a client's cultural background? The American Psychological Association (APA; 2017) *Ethical Principles of Psychologists and Code of Conduct* (APA Ethics Code; Standard 2.01, Boundaries of Competence) states "(a) Psychologists provide services, teach and conduct research with populations and in areas only within the boundaries of their competence, based on their education, training, supervised experience, consultation, study or professional experience," which might lead some to say, no, this therapist is not qualified to work with Linda. However, on further reading you will see that section (c) of 2.01 states, "Psychologists planning to provide services, teach or conduct research involving populations, areas, techniques or technologies new to them undertake relevant education, training, supervised experience, consultation or study." Thus, with a modicum of previous training or experience, it is permissible to work with new clinical presentations and populations, as long as you receive supervision from someone with the requisite competence.

The decision to have Traci in the session, for that first encounter, is a clinical one. It seems that Linda is likely to be more forthcoming with her friend present. That said, Linda needs to be reminded that her friend will be privy to all she shares in the session, and there may be questions you need to ask whose answers Linda might prefer her friend to not hear. If you allow Traci to stay, you can remind Linda that she can ask Traci to leave at any point during the session; similarly, you might inform Linda that you may request that Traci leave the session should it be therapeutically indicated. You would want to explain these issues to Linda before inviting Traci into the office. It is at that time that you will also review confidentiality and the limits of confidentiality, then confirm that Linda still wants Traci to be present in the session.

Linda's family is actively involved in her life and, by Western standards, might be categorized as "overly involved" or, even, "enmeshed" (Minuchin, 1974). What would you do if her mother called reporting that she found your business card in Linda's backpack and wants to know "what's wrong with Linda?" A request for information from parents is an increasingly frequent phenomenon on college campuses. Even the most novice psychologist-in-training knows to respond with something akin to "I cannot confirm or deny . . . without a release of information." Responding to an anxious or tearful parent is a challenging situation, especially when you know that what they know is in fact accurate (i.e., you are seeing their child). Imagine the ramifications of Linda's learning that you talked about her care to any of her family members. Assuming you do not have an ROI, if her mother called you, it is important to gather whatever information she wants to share to ensure there is no reason to believe Linda is at risk; after that, it behooves you to remind her mother of confidentiality and encourage her to reach out to her daughter directly. At your next session with Linda, unless it is not clinically indicated, sharing with her that her mother called and what you communicated (and did not) might strengthen the therapeutic relationship by serving as a reminder to Linda that what she shares with you will not be disclosed to her family, or anyone else, without her permission.

Risk Management—Protecting Your Patient, Protecting Yourself

ACTIVITY 5.4:

What risks can you envision working in a college counseling center? What risks might Traci's involvement pose? How would you address these risks?

Several potential scenarios could arise on a college campus related to risk management. For example, what would you do if you got a call from the dean of students at your school claiming that he needs to know if Linda is, or was, being treated in the counseling center and, more importantly, whether she is a threat to the campus? The dean adds that she has received calls from a professor and a residential (housing) director stating that Linda has been acting odd and her peers are concerned about her. Before you are able to remind the dean about confidentiality, she informs you, "It is OK for you share any necessary information because the request is related to campus safety." There are, in fact, situations in which sharing information without the client's consent is "permissible" (e.g., coordinating care with another provider, addressing crisis situations in which there is a clear risk of imminent harm). It is not clear from the dean's description that this is one of them, unless you have also assessed Linda as being a risk to others (see Koocher & Keith-Spiegel, 2008). In such a circumstance, it is always good practice to discuss the request with your client and, if the decision is to allow you to release information, to obtain written consent using an ROI form. This form outlines the dates of treatment being discussed, what information is to be shared and with whom, and an expiration date for when you are no longer able to communicate with others about the client. Finally, the client needs to be informed that this consent to have information shared may be withdrawn at any time. It is also important that the discussion leading up to obtaining written consent also includes what the individual does not want to be shared with anyone. If you do not have an ROI, we strongly encourage clinicians always to consult with colleagues before considering sharing clinical information. Similarly, you are encouraged to discuss with your supervisor(s) and legal counsel, if available, how best to respond to requests such as court orders.

Documentation is one of the best ways to avoid risk to yourself and your agency. Documenting what you do and what your thinking process is as you decide what to do and what not to do is of critical importance. Thus, you want to document why you let Traci join the session and how you evaluated Linda's suicidality, particularly because there is some discrepancy in the screening data and the information you obtained during the clinical interview. Your supervision should also be documented, particularly if Traci's diagnosis and treatment plan stretches your scope of competence.

If you believe that Linda is at significant risk for self-harm, then it may be necessary to consider the initiation of an involuntary hold (see also Chapter 4, this volume). Once again, consulting and following the processes and procedures of your agency are critical.

Disposition

ACTIVITY 5.5:

Provide a treatment plan for Linda. What are the critical elements necessary for therapeutic success? How would the severity of Linda's depression influence your approach in the early stages of therapy? Would you focus more on immediate symptom relief or on creating long-term change, and how would that focus influence what you do?

There are many possible paths for treatment with someone like Linda (Cuijpers, 2017). Given the trend toward brief therapy approaches prevalent in college counseling centers, you might consider the following goals for a client presenting with symptoms similar to Linda's: (a) provide a culturally congruent environment that facilitates sharing her concerns (see Comas-Díaz, 2012; Hays, 2016), (b) include the client in the construction of goals for therapy, (c) decrease suicidal ideation, (d) increase awareness of adaptive coping skills and resources already in place, (e) normalize and validate feelings, and (f) build on strengths.

The beginning phase of therapy would focus primarily on information gathering and rapport building. If there is any ambivalence about counseling, establishing a solid therapeutic relationship is imperative (Norcross, Krebs, & Prochaska, 2011). In working with a client with a diagnosis of Major depressive episode (F32.x), it is critical to ensure client safety. This might include asking the client about suicidal ideation or having her complete an assessment (e.g., BDI, SIQ) at each session; if there is significant concern, obtaining an ROI to talk with roommates, loved ones, and friends as additional sources of information might be helpful. After establishing a therapeutic relationship, a depressed client might respond well to an empirically supported treatment like cognitive behavior therapy (CBT; J. S. Beck, 2011). If your client is new to therapy or not informed about how CBT can lead to change, take time to provide psychoeducation about what is involved, what to expect, and what you will ask of her (e.g., homework, challenging thoughts).

It is important, early on, to provide the client with strategies that might provide some immediate relief. This might include having the client begin some form of exercise, practicing mindfulness, or journaling—all of which have been found to have a significant positive impact on mood (Hayes, Follette, & Linehan, 2004). Next you can begin to teach the individual how to manage negative self-talk by identifying alternative thoughts, such as the impact on her life of not being able to meet parental expectations. The primary objective during this phase of therapy is to have the client make the connection between mood and thoughts; for many, intense feelings (e.g., anxiety, sadness) will trigger negative self-talk. An example the second author likes to use to help clients understand the thought–mood connection is to share the following story: Today I saw two students from the same class. Student A received a B+ on his exam and was upset, and Student B received a C− and was elated. Thus, it is not the grade (event) that leads to certain feelings, it is the interpretation of what that grade means. Often our interpretations lead us to negative emotions that can spiral out of control (e.g., "I won't get into law school now that I have B on my transcript; I should have gone to a different school; I am such a failure!" Or in Linda's case, "My parents will be disappointed and as a result my life is over because I didn't get into business school"). Asking clients to provide data for their thoughts leading to intense emotions provides a glimpse into their worldview and allows you to address more directly their particular thought–mood interaction. It is important that you work in a culturally congruent manner and pay attention to any verbal or nonverbal feedback the client provides. Thus, we like to check in often with our clients (e.g., "How was today for you?" "What would you want more of? less of?"). As you continue helping the client learn new strategies to alleviate depression, it is also important to remind her of coping skills she is already using or has used in the past (e.g., talking with a friend, keeping up with exercise).

The middle phase of therapy is also the time when you might consider medication evaluation if symptoms do not appear to be improving despite your client being actively involved (i.e., doing the work of therapy). This is especially important if your client is struggling with getting adequate sleep, because lack of sleep can increase depressive symptoms. Given many clients' reservations to take medication, we like to remind them that meeting with a psychiatrist does not mean they will have to take medication should it be recommended. A medication evaluation can also be thought of as an opportunity for a second opinion.

The last phase of therapy includes summarizing the skills developed, providing your thoughts for next steps for your client, and referrals (e.g., continued individual therapy, group therapy if needed). If assessments were completed during therapy, you might consider sharing the data with the client as a visual representation of progress. Finally, it is important to remind clients of any crisis counseling support services that are available should the need arise.

References

American Psychological Association. (2017). *Ethical principles of psychologists and code of conduct* (2002, Amended June 1, 2010 and January 1, 2017). Retrieved from http://www.apa.org/ethics/code/index.aspx

Beck, A. T., Steer, R. A., & Brown, G. K. (1996). *Manual for the Beck Depression Inventory—II*. San Antonio, TX: Psychological Corporation.

Beck, J. S. (2011). *Cognitive behavior therapy: Basics and beyond*. New York, NY: Guilford Press.

Blaney, P. H., Krueger, R. F., & Millon, T. (Eds.). (2015). *Oxford textbook of psychopathology* (3rd ed.). New York, NY: Oxford University Press.

Center for Behavioral Health Statistics and Quality. (2016). *Key substance use and mental health indicators in the United States: Results from the 2015 National Survey on Drug Use and Health* (HHS Publication No. SMA 16-4984, NSDUH Series H-51). Retrieved from https://www.samhsa.gov/data/sites/default/files/NSDUH-FFR1-2015/NSDUH-FFR1-2015/NSDUH-FFR1-2015.htm

Center for Collegiate Mental Health. (2017). *2016 annual report of the Center for Collegiate Mental Health*. Retrieved from https://sites.psu.edu/ccmh/files/2017/01/2016-Annual-Report-FINAL_2016_01_09-1gc2hj6.pdf

Comas-Díaz, L. (2012). *Multicultural care: A clinician's guide to cultural competence*. Washington, DC: American Psychological Association.

Cuijpers, P. (2017). Four decades of outcome research on psychotherapies for adult depression: An overview of a series of meta-analyses. *Canadian Psychology, 58,* 7–19. http://dx.doi.org/10.1037/cap0000096

Friedman, E. S., & Anderson, I. M. (2014). *Handbook of depression* (2nd ed.). London, England: Springer Healthcare.

Gallagher, R. P. (2009). *National Survey of Counseling Center Directors*. Retrieved from http://d-scholarship.pitt.edu/28170/1/survey_2009.pdf

Gotlib, I. H., & Hammen, C. L. (Eds.). (2014). *Handbook of depression* (3rd ed.). New York, NY: Guilford Press.

Hayes, S. C., Follette, V. M., & Linehan, M. M. (Eds.). (2004). *Mindfulness and acceptance: Expanding the cognitive-behavioral tradition*. New York, NY: Guilford Press.

Hays, P. A. (2016). *Addressing cultural complexities in practice: Assessment, diagnosis, and therapy* (3rd ed.). Washington, DC: American Psychological Association.

Ibrahim, A. K., Kelly, S. J., Adams, C. E., & Glazebrook, C. (2013). A systematic review of studies of depression prevalence in university students. *Journal of Psychiatric Research, 47,* 391–400. http://dx.doi.org/10.1016/j.jpsychires.2012.11.015

Koocher, G. P., & Keith-Spiegel, P. (2008). *Ethics in psychology and the mental health professions: Standards and cases*. New York, NY: Oxford University Press.

Minuchin, S. (1974). *Families and family therapy*. Boston, MA: Harvard.

Norcross, J. C., Krebs, P. M., & Prochaska, J. O. (2011). Stages of change. In J. C. Norcross (Ed.), *Psychotherapy relationships that work* (2nd ed.). http://dx.doi.org/10.1002/jclp.20758

Posselt, J. R., & Lipson, S. K. (2016). Competition, anxiety, and depression in the college classroom: Variations by student identity and field of study. *Journal of College Student Development, 57,* 973–989. http://dx.doi.org/10.1353/csd.2016.0094

Reynolds, W. M. (1988). *Suicidal ideation questionnaire: Professional manual.* Odessa, FL: Psychological Assessment Resources.

Rainey Sealey Temkin and Larry E. Beutler

F33 Major Depressive Disorder, Recurrent

6

Depression is a symptom of many different disorders, both medical and functional, and both within and outside of the depressive spectrum. In fact, depression may be likened to a fever in medical practice: Its presence indicates that a problem is present, but the depression may not be the central problem but a symptom of some other primary problem. When a disorder within the spectrum of depression-related conditions is identified, one can be assured of its seriousness and must consider the possibility that there are comorbid conditions as well.

The prevalence rates for major depressive disorder are among the highest of any psychological disorder, with a lifetime prevalence rate of more than 15% of men and 25% of women (Kessler et al., 1994). Half of those who experience one episode of depression have one or more additional episodes in their lifetime (Kupfer, Frank, & Wamhoff, 1996), typically within 5 years (Lewinsohn, Clarke, Seeley, & Rohde, 1994) and have, on average, five (Kessler & Walters, 1998) to nine (Kessler, Zhao, Blazer, & Swartz, 1997) depressive episodes throughout their lives.

A common issue encountered when diagnosing depressive episodes concerns what constitutes the beginning and end of an episode—what is the cause and what is the effect. The boundaries between episodes can be blurry and hard to delineate because certain symptoms are transitory and others

http://dx.doi.org/10.1037/0000069-007
An ICD–10–CM Casebook and Workbook for Students: Psychological and Behavioral Conditions, J. B. Schaffer and E. Rodolfa (Editors)

are quite stable. These complex issues involved in diagnosis should lead the clinician to carefully rule out diagnoses or other common mood disorders and to be aware of how depression interacts with other symptoms, as both a cause and an effect. Risk factors and cultural components are important factors to consider when managing this multifaceted diagnosis.

The Case

Darius is a 34-year-old, heterosexual African American man who is seeking treatment because of increasing suicidal ideation and a desire to "get back on track" before things are totally hopeless. He feels like a failure at everything he tries and sees little reason to go on. You are a staff psychologist in the community mental health center and have taken this patient on a regular rotation referral from the intake clinician. In addition to a history of depressive symptomatology, suicidal ideation, and thoughts of dying, he also has a variety of general somatic complaints for which he has not sought treatment. He was previously diagnosed with Attention-deficit hyperactivity disorder, predominantly inattentive type (ADHD; F90.0) and has been inconsistently taking Adderall, a stimulant commonly prescribed to treat ADHD.

Darius severely burned his face in an accident while working as an assistant mechanic a little more than a year ago, due to a malfunction in one of the power tools. This traumatic event forced him to quit his job and precipitated a weight gain of more than 80 pounds. Darius had always struggled with his weight, but just before the accident had successfully lost more than 100 pounds, moving him below the obesity range on the body mass index (BMI; a measure of body fat based on height and weight; Darius used to have a BMI of 35, considered severely obese). He reports frequent binge-eating episodes, which are sometimes so bad that he has chest pains and dizziness. He believes that if he could "lose the weight," all of his problems would be solved.

Over the next few sessions, you learn that Darius lives at home with his mother and sometimes with his father, who shows up periodically for a few months and then leaves again. The family has significant financial concerns. Darius has few friends and a pattern of failed relationships, some of which start on Internet dating sites. Until recently, he was very involved in his church, which gave him a strict moral foundation but also caused distress over his behavior and thoughts involving premarital sex, pornography, and feelings of moral inadequacy.

Darius reports feeling the lowest when his father comes home because this brings up intense feelings of fear that he will turn into his father, toward whom he expresses intense hatred and anger. Although he has verbally expressed motivation to change during the sessions themselves, you notice he engages in little follow-through between sessions and seems ambivalent toward initiating the behavior changes that will lead to his immediate goal of successful weight loss.

Throughout his childhood, Darius was teased about his weight. His ADHD (F90.0) was diagnosed in adulthood, so as a child, he was told he was stupid and slow—not only by his peers but by his siblings, mother, and father. He always lacked assertiveness and deferred to his parents and others to guide him. His chronic feeling of failure leaves him believing "there is no point anymore" and anxious about much of his life.

Darius dropped out of high school in his senior year to work as a mechanic with his father. He made numerous attempts to study for his GED but never followed through. Prior traumatic experiences recounted were the burn Darius sustained to his face, intense public humiliation by his father in work-related situations, and an embarrassing first sexual experience with a girl. He reports being greatly traumatized by these experiences, and, compounded with his weight gain, they have inhibited his ability to meet and become intimate again with a woman.

Darius has the capacity to report in depth on the thoughts and feelings he is experiencing while actively avoiding the painful and uncomfortable feelings underneath. His coping style is one of internalization and self-blame. He frequently perceives others as being critical of him and as having a negative impression not just of his looks but of his character as well. In turn, he withdraws and becomes self-critical.

You notice numerous strengths that will positively inform Darius's response to therapy. He has a highly developed ability to self-reflect. Although quick to self-blame and to predict negative outcomes on the basis of past failures, Darius presents with thoughtful and insight-oriented reflections on his behaviors and interactions with others, although his acting-out behaviors prevent him from processing his underlying feelings, emotions, and motivation.

Assessment Using the ICD–10–CM

ACTIVITY 6.1:

What are your primary concerns as you consider the information provided by Darius in the initial sessions? How will these concerns affect your assessment of Darius?

At the earliest stage, you will want to outline primary concerns and thoughts about potential diagnoses based on the information you have. Most pressing will be your concerns about suicide risk, and these should be addressed immediately. Another task will be to determine Darius's readiness for change because he expresses passivity and negativity, both of which may impede his ability to work in therapy and to develop relationships. You will want to assess carefully current and past symptomatology to help with differential diagnosis.

Psychologists often use testing to help gather information, for accuracy of diagnosis and to fill in gaps in information obtained. You will want the assessment materials that you select to shed light on the questions and issues that have been raised in your initial assessment. For example, you may want to clarify the level for risk of suicide and the severity of his depression and anxiety, gain a general sense of his quality of life, and establish a basis for treatment recommendations. The tests discussed in this section can also be used as measures to monitor therapeutic outcomes.

You decide to give Darius the 21-item Depression, Anxiety, and Stress Scale (Lovibond & Lovibond, 1995), which measures the severity of a range of symptoms common to both depression and anxiety over the past week, and the Outcome Questionnaire 45.2 (OQ–45.2; Lambert et al., 1996). The OQ–45.2 can also be given weekly; it evaluates a patient's progress over the course of treatment and provides a snapshot of current functioning across a variety of factors, as well as risk assessment items for suicide potential and substance abuse. You also use the Systematic Treatment Selection (STS) Innerlife (http://www.innerlife.com; Beutler, Williams, & Norcross, 2008), which generates a report that provides a basis for treatment recommendations and will help you understand more fully the relative severity of the most usual symptoms (most importantly the risk of suicide) and clarify any secondary symptoms, such as reported disordered eating, attention and concentration problems, and family distress.

The STS Innerlife program suggests clinically elevated depression, anxiety and distress, and thoughts of self-harm. Darius's secondary symptoms of concern are attention and concentration difficulties, family conflict, and problems with anger (ICD–10–CM diagnostic possibilities include Parent perpetrator of maltreatment and neglect [Y07.1]; Problem related to primary support group, unspecified [Z63.9]; and Irritability and anger [R45.4]). The STS coping style trait scale (i.e., the usual way one behaves when faced with challenge) confirms your impression of both high levels of internalization (e.g., self-depreciation, worry, social withdrawal, introversion) and externalization (e.g., acting out, drinking, blaming).

ICD–10–CM Diagnosis

ACTIVITY 6.2:

Rank order the ICD–10–CM diagnoses that you believe may be most applicable to Darius at this time and the symptoms that support these diagnoses. Given the number of severe symptoms, how do you ensure that you adequately consider all of the diagnostic possibilities?

A refined differential diagnosis can be identified only after a detailed clinical interview with full psychosocial history is conducted, in addition to examining all relevant assessment results. Many times, what initially looks like one diagnosis may change on the basis of further clinical information or an evolving constellation of symptoms.

When reviewing the history, it is essential that you consider whether Darius may have experienced an Acute stress reaction (F43.0) after burning part of his face. Darius met initial criteria in that his response was to an exceptional physical stressor, but his symptoms did not resolve rapidly or diminish within 3 days, as suggested by the *ICD–10 Classification of Mental and Behavioural Disorders: Clinical Descriptions and Diagnostic Guidelines* (the *Blue Book*; World Health Organization, 1993) criteria.

Another possible diagnosis worthy of consideration, given Darius's history, is Post-traumatic stress disorder (PTSD; F43.1). When a patient has experienced an intense trauma, clinicians must look carefully at the possibility that presenting symptoms, including depressive symptoms, may be a component of a PTSD diagnosis. Again, although Darius met criteria in his exposure to a stressful event or situation of exceptionally threatening or catastrophic nature, on initial diagnostic interview, it was clear that Darius was not experiencing persistent remembering or "reliving" the stressor, avoidance of the circumstances resembling or associated with the stressor, or inability to recall some of the incident or persistent symptoms of increased arousal—all necessary criteria for diagnosis.

Another important diagnostic consideration after Darius's accident would be any one of the adjustment disorders, including F43.20, Adjustment disorder, unspecified, F43.21, Adjustment disorder with depressed mood, or F43.23, Adjustment disorder with mixed anxiety and depressed mood. The most appropriate diagnostic possibility for Darius appears to be F43.23, but his symptoms were too severe for an adjustment disorder. In addition, Darius's initial constellation of symptoms ended up persisting well beyond the 6-month time frame. Therefore, all adjustment disorders were ruled out.

With a depressive disorder, you must initially and throughout treatment conduct a careful review of potential manic or hypomanic symptoms (in addition to any psychotic features within the context of his mood disorder) to responsibly rule out any of the Bipolar disorders (F31.xx) because treating a person with bipolar disorder with depression medications can be catastrophic (see Chapter 4, this volume). Darius has never met the criteria for either hypomania or mania and denies any psychotic symptoms. After a careful assessment and obtaining a release of information and speaking to Darius's primary care physician, you rule out current and past substance use (Mental and behavioral disorders due to psychoactive substance use, F10–F19) and organic mental disorders (Mental disorders due to known physiological conditions, F01–F09) as possibilities. Because Darius presented with many anxiety-related symptoms, some attention should be given to Generalized anxiety disorder (F41.1). Upon further follow-up, you conclude that Darius more fully meets criteria for a specific depressive disorder because he did not meet the following criteria for an anxiety disorder: apprehension (worries about future misfortunes, feeling on edge), motor tension (restless fidgeting, tension headaches, inability to relax), and autonomic overactivity (sweating, lightheadedness, dry mouth).

The evidence provided in the interview and in test results points in particular to one of the major depressive disorders. Darius's symptoms have been present for more than 2 weeks and include a loss of self-esteem, unreasonable feelings of self-reproach, recurrent thoughts of suicide, difficulties in concentration and indecisiveness, sleep disturbance and difficulty getting out of bed, and, finally, a significant increase in appetite and notable weight gain. Darius does not report any hallucinations, delusions, or depressive stupor. His considerable distress and distinct danger of suicide, with limited ability to continue with social and work-related activities, suggest a severe range of impairment. This constellation of symptoms leads to your diagnosis of Major depressive disorder, single episode, severe without psychotic features (F32.2), with the previously diagnosed ADHD, predominantly inattentive type (F90.0) as a comorbid diagnosis. This is a significant area to address because certain aspects of ADHD, such as difficulty with concentration and low self-esteem, may overlap with criteria for a Major depressive episode and pose additional complications in diagnosing later depressive episodes.

You refer Darius for psychotherapy, but because of your significant concerns about his ongoing well-being, you schedule a follow-up assessment appointment in 6 months. At that session and in reports from his therapist, you gather the following information. Therapy has gone well, he has been increasingly compliant with homework assignments, he has shown motivation to adopt healthier eating and exercise habits, and he has become interested in dating again. He had continued to progress well and no longer met criteria for a severe depressive episode. About a month ago, his father returned to the home, at which point his mood shifted dramatically.

In the current session, Darius appears disheveled and fatigued. You are concerned with elevations in depressive symptoms since his father's return. Risk items on the OQ–45.2 indicate current suicidal thoughts. Within session, Darius endorses changes in appetite with almost daily binge-eating episodes, low mood, difficulty sleeping, problems with concentration despite ADHD medication compliance, and a significant reduction in self-esteem, which is negatively affecting his relationship with his girlfriend.

You diagnose an additional depressive episode and change your overall diagnosis to Major depressive disorder, recurrent, severe without psychotic features (F33.2). The fact that 1 month ago Darius no longer met criteria for a current depressive episode indicates that this is a recurrent depression and not just a continuation of the previous episode. Darius's most recent recurrence of suicidal ideation necessitates a return to a focus on risk management.

On the basis of careful assessment, clinical judgment, and consultation with your supervisor and clinic director, you make the appropriate entries in the chart, remembering that your diagnosis of his attention disorder has not changed. These are as follows:

- Major depressive disorder, recurrent, severe without psychotic features (F33.2)
- Overeating associated with other psychological disturbances (F50.4)

You believe the following issues are relevant and under clinical consideration, but at this stage you do not have sufficient supporting evidence to confirm them. You mention them in your chart because they will help guide therapy and assist future therapists and health care providers to most accurately understand this complex case. The first concern is whether Darius's father has perpetrated maltreatment or neglect (Parent perpetrator of maltreatment and neglect [Y07.1]). Another general concern is the extent of problems related to his primary support group such as family conflict, discord, and stress (Problem related to primary support group, unspecified [Z63.9]). These psychosocial stressors are relevant in that they may perpetuate symptoms and make it difficult for Darius to recover fully.

Ethical Considerations—Protecting Your Patient

ACTIVITY 6.3:

What do you see as the specific ethical issues in this case, and how do you manage them? Would you plan on talking with Darius about the possibility of another depressive episode and its associated risks?

The first ethical component to this case is confidentiality (American Psychological Association [APA], 2017, *Ethical Principles of Psychologists and Code of Conduct* [APA Ethics Code], Standards 4.01–4.07). Given the complexity of the symptoms Darius presents, you want to speak with other professional providers. To do so, you must ensure that Darius understands the issues involved and has signed a release of information. Confidentiality is paramount to effective therapy, and before you enter into a clinical consultation about Darius, his history, and his current symptomatology, the responsibility is in your hands to consider carefully whether Darius understands what will transpire and what the risks and advantages are before you contact any outside sources. Make sure to use a detailed release form so that Darius is clear on whom you will be contacting, at what point in therapy, what information you hope to receive, and how that information will be used. (See also Chapter 1, this volume.)

Although you likely discussed limits to confidentiality in your first encounter with Darius (including risk to self; risk to others; child, elder, and dependent adult abuse; court-mandated release of records; and the possibility of becoming unable to care for himself), it would be in Darius's best interest to review these exceptions in your follow-up encounter. It is the ethical obligation of each provider to discuss confidentiality and not to assume that another professional has already done so. This case carries a strong risk component as a result of Darius's endorsement of suicidal ideation. Therefore, it is imperative that he understands that if you deem him at imminent risk of harming himself, you would need to break confidentiality and, in serious cases, initiate an involuntary hold in a state-approved hospital for evaluation and treatment. In many states, a legally designated person such as a police officer or mobile crisis team must take the individual into custody. As a psychologist, your role would be to initiate this hold after a thorough risk assessment and consultation have taken place. Taking away an individual's freedom should not be taken lightly and is a major consideration for all practicing psychologists.

Understanding what constitutes a thorough suicide risk assessment is imperative to your training and is an essential component of your ethical responsibility to protect Darius (APA [2017] Ethics Code, Standard 4.02, Discussing the Limits of Confidentiality; see also Chapter 15, this volume). In the best-case scenario, you are able to integrate information from a variety of sources and generate an estimate of the probability that Darius is going to attempt suicide. Indirect assessment of this risk includes evaluating demographics and environmental factors that may be associated with high risk. Some of these indicators are a history of suicide attempts, behaviors that suggest a wish to die, recent life stressors, and isolation or lack of social support. Direct assessment of risk requires that you are comfortable asking difficult questions, even if you are just beginning therapy. Stated intent to commit suicide is the best single predictor of risk, and this becomes even greater if there is a plan in place and the individual has the means to carry it out. It is imperative to assess whether the patient has access to lethal means, including guns and medications (Harvard School of Public Health, 2008). Another predictor of risk is a high level of hopelessness, which clinicians should regularly assess. As mentioned in the previous section on assessment, psychological testing can be useful in these higher risk individuals, and speaking to family members or physicians may provide a richer context, but releases of information must be obtained. In your first session, developing a safety plan is critical and may include hotline numbers, individuals Darius could call when he is in crisis, possible safety checks by close relatives or friends, and discussing reasons for living, ways to decrease stress, and possibly increasing sessions to provide additional support.

The next ethical consideration is whether you are competent to provide psychological services to Darius (APA Ethics Code, Standard 2.01, Boundaries of Competence). Consultation and supervision may be useful in answering this question, as may self-reflection and a close evaluation of your experience and knowledge in working with individuals with major depressive disorders. Because risk of death is especially high with severe problems, if you do not feel qualified to handle the case after seeking supervision, a referral is appropriate. For students, your supervisor would ultimately make the final decision. (See also Chapters 3 and 5, this volume.)

There is no indication of a multiple relationship in this case (APA Ethics Code, Standard 3.05, Multiple Relationships), but it is important to maintain your relationship within the boundaries of professional practice. Clear guidelines about your expectations for therapy, as well as understanding Darius's expectations for therapy, can be a useful framework to discuss these ethical considerations. Finally, as a developing psychologist, you should understand the general components of the Health Insurance Portability and Accountability Act of 1996, developed to protect the confidentiality, security, and accuracy of health care information.

Risk Management—Protecting Your Patient, Protecting Yourself

ACTIVITY 6.4:

Are there any specific risks to you as a clinician in this case, and if so, what are they? Do you think the fact that you changed your diagnosis from Major depressive disorder, single episode, severe without psychotic features (F32.2) to Major depressive disorder, recurrent, severe without psychotic features (F33.2) during your assessment of Darius puts you at any risk?

Many psychologists express concern that patients may take legal actions against them for negative outcomes in therapy or interventions that do more harm than good. A complaint could be made to a licensing board, and for this reason, many therapists choose not to work with suicidal patients. Fortunately, there are protective and proactive measures you can use to help minimize this possibility.

First and foremost, thorough and timely documentation, not only on what interventions you use as a therapist but the rationale behind your actions, provides protection, as discussed in more detail in Chapter 1.

Supervision or consultation is an excellent practice and learning tool for both graduate students and licensed professionals and can be useful and reassuring especially with difficult cases that entail risk. Through careful consultation, the therapist can gain a broader perspective and obtain the support he or she may need if questions arise as to the nature of therapy or how decisions were made. Therapy, by nature, can feel and become an isolated practice if we allow it to. Seeking supervision, consultation, and participation in continuing education minimizes this possibility and allows the therapist to stay current, supported, and well advised. These practices minimize risk and ultimately protect you as a therapist.

A final comment about risk is related to your diagnosis of Darius. During the course of your assessment, you changed his diagnosis. This change may lead to the accusation that you don't really understand Darius or his diagnosis. However, your careful, systematic assessment, including review of the documentation of increasing amounts of data, along with a clear description of your thought process, can demonstrate that rather than being incompetent or careless, you are in fact proceeding as any careful, competent psychologist should.

Disposition

ACTIVITY 6.5:

Given the information provided to you at this point, what are the first things you would want to work on in treatment? What would be next in the level of importance? What results or trends would you expect to see during the early stage of treatment in terms of depressive symptomatology and risk items?

When managing any depressive or mood disorder, collaboration with the client on a safety plan is paramount if there is any indication of suicidal ideation or intent. Including community resources and integrating friends or family may help facilitate wellness checks and provide additional social support. Establishing rapport and consistently working on the therapeutic alliance will increase engagement in therapy and other behavioral interventions. You reason that discussing the therapist's and Darius's expectations for therapy may help prevent misunderstandings and establish reachable goals for treatment outcome. Collaboration with clients on treatment planning is essential, and therapists should use best practices and evidence-based therapies, keeping all aspects of culture in mind (Comas-Díaz, 2012; Hays, 2016). In our own practice, and because most research evidence fails to support the outcomes of any one model of treatment over another (Wampold, 2001), we prefer a cross-cutting approach that is tailored to each patient. STS (Beutler, Clarkin, & Bongar, 2000) is particularly well suited to this task. The STS approach focuses on empirically derived principles of how patient, context, and treatment factors interact to optimize change. The STS Innerlife, the instrument that was used in the initial assessment, will provide guidance in developing a principle-based treatment focusing on individualized patient qualities. Thus, Darius's high degree of impairment and chronicity of the condition would lead us to plan for a long-term intervention that concentrates on helping the patient develop a healthy social support system; Darius's level of resistance will lead us to select evocative over directive interventions, and his internalizing coping style will lead us to emphasize the use of procedures that foster insight and understanding as mediators of change (Castonguay & Beutler, 2006).

In your treatment formulation, you conclude that Darius fundamentally wishes for acceptance and love from his father. You conclude that this lack of paternal acceptance has led to a deep and chronic depression that, in turn, becomes the force that gives rise to his other maladaptive and self-destructive symptoms. Reviewing and exploring this focal theme can help Darius gain greater internal control of his behavior and mood.

Major depressive disorders often carry a high component of risk; referrals to psychiatry or other medical providers are also highly recommended. These will further refine and cultivate an integrated approach to treatment and recovery, covering more areas that may be affected by the depression.

Darius refuses the initial suggestion of an antidepressant medications regimen, but he agrees to comply more regularly with his ADHD medications. His resistance to taking medications might be related to shame or stigma associated with psychiatric medication in general, and you recommend that his therapist make a note to periodically address these factors in therapy.

The STS model also focuses on the value of describing the phases (e.g., Howard, Kopta, Krause, & Orlinsky, 1986) that characterize change over time so that the patient will know what to expect. Darius's affective state, associated with hopelessness, low self-esteem, and self-depreciation, will likely change fairly quickly if he works hard at treatment and develops confidence in the therapy and therapist. More complex symptoms, such as disordered eating patterns and depressogenic social relationships, may take several months to change, and the fears and needs that reflect the core of his struggles with his father's rejection and his own self-depreciation will probably require even more time to change (Beutler & Harwood, 2000). Early treatment will focus on trust and building confidence, perhaps even developing new social relationships. Later sessions may focus more on symptom change and then, ultimately, on the conflicts with his father and his own self-depreciation. This will require both self-awareness and learning to take risks that will combat these fears. Focusing on the client's strengths, not just the pathology, symptoms, weaknesses, and deficits, is more likely to lead to growth and recovery.

Finally, ethnic and cultural factors should be considered in selecting the nature and patterns of interventions. For instance, many African American patients indicate considerable cultural shame in seeking mental health services, and the stigma attached to going outside the family to seek assistance can be a barrier to treatment (Sanders Thompson, Bazile, & Akbar, 2004). Culturally sensitive therapy addresses the nature of needed support systems and the patients' beliefs and preferences, all of which emerge in the early assessment and treatment.

References

American Psychological Association. (2017). *Ethical principles of psychologists and code of conduct* (2002, Amended June 1, 2010 and January 1, 2017). Retrieved from http://www.apa.org/ethics/code/index.aspx

Beutler, L. E., Clarkin, J. F., & Bongar, B. (2000). *Guidelines for the systematic treatment of the depressed patient.* New York, NY: Oxford University Press.

Beutler, L. E., & Harwood, T. M. (2000). *Prescriptive psychotherapy: The treatment of co-morbid depression and substance abuse.* http://dx.doi.org/10.1093/med:psych/9780195136692.001.0001

Beutler, L. E., Williams, O. B., & Norcross, J. N. (2008). *Innerlife.com* [Cloud mobile platform].

Castonguay, L., & Beutler, L. (Eds.). (2006). *Principles of therapeutic change that work: Vol. 1. Integrating relationship, treatment, client, and therapist factors.* New York, NY: Oxford University Press.

Comas-Díaz, L. (2012). *Multicultural care: A clinician's guide to cultural competence.* Washington, DC: American Psychological Association.

Harvard School of Public Health. (2008, July). *Means matter: Lethal means counseling.* Retrieved from http://www.hsph.harvard.edu/means-matter/lethal-means-counseling

Hays, P. A. (2016). *Addressing cultural complexities in practice: Assessment, diagnosis, and therapy* (3rd ed.). Washington, DC: American Psychological Association.

Health Insurance Portability and Accountability Act of 1996 (HIPAA), Public Law 104-191.

Howard, K. I., Kopta, S. M., Krause, M. S., & Orlinsky, D. E. (1986). The dose–effect relationship in psychotherapy. *American Psychologist, 41,* 159–164.

Kessler, R. C., McGonagle, K. A., Zhao, S., Nelson, C. B., Hughes, M., Eshleman, S., . . . Kendler, K. S. (1994). Lifetime and 12-month prevalence of *DSM–II–R* psychiatric disorders in the United States: Results from the National Comorbidity Survey. *Archives of General Psychiatry, 51,* 8–19.

Kessler, R. C., & Walters, E. E. (1998). Epidemiology of *DSM-III-R* major depression and minor depression among adolescents and young adults in the National Comorbidity Survey. *Depression and Anxiety, 7,* 3–14.

Kessler, R. C., Zhao, S., Blazer, D. G., & Swartz, M. (1997). Prevalence, correlates, and course of minor depression and major depression in the National Comorbidity Survey. *Journal of Affective Disorders, 45,* 19–30. http://dx.doi.org/10.1016/S0165-0327(97)00056-6

Kupfer, D., Frank, E., & Wamhoff, J. (1996). Mood disorders: Update on prevention of recurrence. In C. Mundt & M. Goldstein (Eds.), *Interpersonal factors in the origin and course of affective disorders* (pp. 289–302). London, England: Gaskell/Royal College of Psychiatrists.

Lambert, M., Hansen, N., Umphress, V., Lunnen, K., Okiishi, J., Burlingame, G., . . . Reisinger, C. (1996). *Administration and scoring manual for the Outcome Questionnaire (OQ–45.2)*. Wilmington, DE: American Professional Credentialing Services.

Lewinsohn, P., Clarke, G., Seeley, J., & Rohde, P. (1994). Major depression in community adolescents: Age at onset, episode duration, and time to recurrence. *Journal of the Academy of Child & Adolescent Psychiatry, 33*, 809–818. http://dx.doi.org/10.1097/00004583-199407000-00006

Lovibond, S., & Lovibond, P. (1995). *Manual for the Depression Anxiety Stress Scales* (2nd ed.). Sydney, Australia: Psychology Foundation.

Sanders Thompson, V., Bazile, A., & Akbar, M. (2004). African Americans' perceptions of psychotherapy and psychotherapists. *Professional Psychology: Research and Practice, 35*, 19–26. http://dx.doi.org/10.1037/0735-7028.35.1.19

Wampold, B. (2001). *The great psychotherapy debate: Models, methods, and findings.* Mahwah, NJ: Erlbaum.

World Health Organization. (1993). *The ICD–10 classification of mental and behavioural disorders: Clinical descriptions and diagnostic guidelines.* Retrieved from http://www.who.int/classifications/icd/en/bluebook.pdf

Maryann E. Owens, Deborah C. Beidel, and Jennifer A. Scheurich

F40.1 Social Phobia

7

S ocial phobia is a significant fear of social interactions, whether individually or in groups. Situations that may induce fear include social conversations, meeting unfamiliar people, being observed while doing something such as eating or drinking in front of others, or engaging in formal performances such as giving a speech or playing an instrument. Approximately 11% of the population will suffer from social phobia at some time in their lives (Kessler, Petukhova, Sampson, Zaslavsky, & Wittchen, 2012). People with social phobia fear that they will do or say something that will be evaluated negatively by others. The extent and severity of fear in people with social phobia vary, but the symptoms significantly impair their social, occupational, and academic functioning. People with social phobia go to great lengths to hide their fears and try to hide the accompanying characteristic physiological symptoms such as a racing heart, sweating, and blushing. Blushing is particularly problematic because it is an anxious response that is clearly visible to others, resulting in an individual's feeling uncomfortable not just because of the social interaction but also because of worry that others will negatively evaluate this visible manifestation of anxiety. Thus, this creates a vicious cycle of distress—social anxiety, the belief that others will perceive one's distress, more anxiety—and this leads to a pattern of social avoidance and functional impairment.

http://dx.doi.org/10.1037/0000069-008
An ICD–10–CM Casebook and Workbook for Students: Psychological and Behavioral Conditions, J. B. Schaffer and E. Rodolfa (Editors)

The Case

Your first appointment today at the university's training clinic is with Elizabeth, a 38-year-old White woman who lives in a small apartment with her two sons (aged 9 and 11 years). Elizabeth moved to the area about 10 years ago, shortly after becoming pregnant with her second son. She presents as intelligent, pleasant, and cooperative, yet very soft-spoken. You often have to ask Elizabeth to speak up because it is difficult to hear her. She appears visibly anxious: Her hands tremble and her voice is shaky. Elizabeth tells you that she was "very anxious" about her appointment and almost did not make it to the session.

Elizabeth is currently separated from her husband of 15 years because of an ongoing history of verbal and emotional abuse. She reports struggling with intense anxiety during social situations throughout her life, but she describes her symptoms as particularly problematic during the separation: "I guess I always just hid behind my husband. Now that I have to deal with my own job, with repairs, or worry about making friends, it's terrifying!" She describes how her husband's abuse caused her self-esteem and self-confidence to diminish (see Foran, Beach, Smith Slep, Heyman, & Warnboldt, 2013; Healy, 2014): "He was always telling me I was either stupid or an idiot and telling me how lucky I was to have him because no one else would want to deal with me, and I believed him."

Elizabeth expresses her desire to develop her sense of individuality and to become independent. She states that she always regretted not attending college and describes how last year she had wanted to get certified as a physical therapy assistant through coursework at the local community college, but she took one class and never returned:

> It had been so long since I was in school. It was too hard to keep up with the teacher. All the other students were young and seemed to understand everything and know each other. I just felt like I was going to make a fool of myself. I found out there was going to be a speech at the end of the semester and the thought of getting up in front of everyone and talking . . . that was it for me, I never went back.

Elizabeth reports desperately needing to find work to support herself and her children but that she is terrified of doing something to embarrass herself and looking stupid in front of job interviewers. She relates a situation in which she was invited to a job interview, but her anxiety was so intense, even thinking about it, that she did not go: "I had gotten myself all dressed up, got in my car, and I just felt so overwhelmed. I just sat there for an hour picturing all these people in suits staring at me." She describes situations requiring her to be the center of attention, interact with authority figures, and be assertive as the most difficult. She also reports extreme anxiety when meeting new people, going to parties, and having conversations where she does not know what to say or do, stating, for example, "I am worried about looking weird if there is an awkward pause or I forget what to say."

Elizabeth reports that these fears have interfered with every aspect of her life. These difficulties have left her feeling sad and down "briefly, most days," and she reports some passive suicidal ideation, saying, "I'd never do anything, but some days I think it would be OK if I just didn't wake up." She expresses concern that her children may pick up her habits and that she wants to be a good role model for her boys.

After you collect this information, you ask Elizabeth about her goals for treatment. She blushes and seems hesitant to respond, but after a few moments and some encouragement, she provides the following treatment goals:

1. to reduce my anxiety in social situations to where I feel confident and not overwhelmed;
2. to be able to go to a job interview and make it all the way through—and, she hopes, even to get a job;
3. to meet new people and make new friends;
4. to be more comfortable being assertive and "standing up for myself so I don't feel like a doormat";
5. to be more confident being the center of attention and doing public speaking; and
6. to not feel so sad and "down on myself all the time—to feel happy most of the time."

Assessment Using the ICD–10–CM

ACTIVITY 7.1:

What can you do during the assessment process to help provide a framework for reaching Elizabeth's goals? What specific additional information do you need as you consider assessment and diagnostic possibilities for her?

Conducting an accurate assessment is the most critical step when approaching case conceptualization. Clinical judgment and knowledge of the empirical literature are essential to synthesize the information, interpret the findings, and provide appropriate recommendations.

Given the seemingly endless options of questionnaires and diagnostic methods available, it is easy to wonder where to begin. It is often helpful to form hypotheses about what diagnosis (or diagnoses) may best account for the patient's symptoms, on the basis of the patient's presenting complaints. Next, spend some time considering what additional information you would need to confirm or disconfirm these hypotheses. Consider what measures you could use and what unique pieces of the diagnostic puzzle they may contribute.

When someone presents with anxiety in social situations, it is important to gather as much information as possible because anxiety in social situations may result from a variety of disorders, such as depression, panic disorder, or adjustment disorder. What additional information might help you with Elizabeth? First, you need to disentangle the various emotions and life events that Elizabeth is experiencing. Some issues to consider are her depression, panic symptoms, and marital separation. People who are depressed often isolate themselves socially because of their low energy and lack of interest. However, depression can also be a result of lifelong anxiety in social situations. Elizabeth noted that she sometimes has panic symptoms. Do her panic symptoms only occur in stressful or social situations? Or do they occur "out of the blue"? Marital separation is stressful. Are all of these emotions the result of her failed marriage and simply the result of an abusive relationship? Or did all of these emotions lead her to select a partner whom she thought would "take care of her"? It is important to understand the relationships among her feelings, behaviors, and experiences because that will allow you to appreciate fully Elizabeth's experiences, which in turn will help you develop your assessment and recommend a treatment plan.

You might continue by considering the administration of self-report measures for her anxiety- and mood-related symptoms and a measure of personality. The Personality Assessment Inventory is a good instrument to assess adult personality. The Social Phobia Scale and the Social Interaction Anxiety Scale have been validated for use with patients with anxiety concerns, experiences and disorders (Brown et al., 1997). If resources allow, a behavioral assessment may help you understand Elizabeth's anxiety during social interactions. You may also provide her with some self-monitoring forms to track her anxiety and mood during the week. By tracking when and where these different emotions occur, you will begin to understand what factors precipitate or are associated with them. Not only do these approaches help you arrive at a diagnosis, they also provide convenient baseline information that you can use for tracking her progress.

ICD–10–CM Diagnosis

A variety of possible diagnoses exist for Elizabeth at this point, among them social phobia, a depressive disorder, panic disorder, adjustment disorder, a personality disorder, or a combination of these. Referring to a manual with diagnostic criteria for mental disorders may aid you in differential diagnosis (see Schaffer & Rodolfa, 2016, Chapter 10, for suggested resources).

According to the *Blue Book* (World Health Organization [WHO], 1993), a diagnosis of Social phobia (F40.1) is appropriate when the person either has a marked fear of being the focus of attention or behaving in an embarrassing or humiliating way, or the person has a marked avoidance of being the focus of attention or situations in which there is fear of behaving in an embarrassing or humiliating way. Elizabeth reported significant anxiety during a wide variety of social situations and specifically expressed a fear of judgment and negative evaluation. It is clear that her symptoms cause significant impairment and marked distress. For example, her anxiety is preventing her from obtaining higher education and a new job, which is necessary for her to continue to support herself and her children.

ACTIVITY 7.2:

Is depression a reasonable primary diagnosis for Elizabeth? What other primary diagnosis would you consider, and why?

You do not have enough information at this point to make an adequate diagnosis of depression (F32.x, F33.x, F34.x, or F.39). However, given the high comorbidity rate for depression and social phobia, it is an important area to explore. Features essential to diagnose depression include onset, course, duration, number and severity of symptoms, and degree of functional impairment (WHO, 1993). Recall that Elizabeth described feeling depressed "briefly, most days." It would be important to clarify what she meant by *briefly*. A few minutes, a few hours, or something more that she is underemphasizing for some reason? An underlying message here is never to assume you know what people mean just because they use common words, such as *briefly*. Explore what words mean to them. Regarding her report of passive suicidal ideation, how often does she have those thoughts, and when do they typically occur? It would also be helpful to understand what she attributes her depression to.

If, upon further evaluation, you find Elizabeth does in fact meet criteria for depression, it is important to determine which diagnosis is primary and which is secondary. Often, socially phobic individuals report feeling down and depressed because of their anxiety. They are socially isolated and sometimes unemployed or underemployed. They often state that if they only felt more confident in social situations and could make some friends, they wouldn't feel so "down." Other times, people who are depressed feel too lethargic and unmotivated to interact with others, and their feelings of social anxiety are related to their feelings of worthlessness. In that case, depression would more likely be the primary diagnosis. A few clues point to social anxiety as Elizabeth's central problem. Recall the observed and self-reported extreme anxiety about the initial appointment, her statement that she has struggled with intense anxiety during social situations her entire life, her multiple examples of anxiety and fear of embarrassment impairing her attempts to improve the quality of her life (dropping out of school and failing to show up for a job interview), and, most important for differential diagnosis, her own admission that her feelings of sadness were due to the difficulties she encountered due to her anxiety.

Elizabeth reported that sometimes her heart felt like it was beating out of her chest. This may be a symptom of a panic attack. It would be a good idea to explore this issue further with her to see if there are other symptoms, such as chest pain, choking sensations, dizziness, or the feeling of unreality. Sometimes a person having a panic attack thinks he or she is dying or going crazy. However, recall Elizabeth's statement that the symptoms come on when she thinks about job interviews. In

Panic disorder (F41.0), the onset of panic symptoms is unpredictable. Thus, we can probably rule out a diagnosis of panic disorder, but it would be prudent to keep an eye on these symptoms and check in with her about them periodically.

Another area to explore is her recent separation from her husband. Although Elizabeth viewed separating from her abusive husband as positive, she reported concerns related to adjusting to single life, caring for her children alone, and needing to increase her independence. At first glance, it seems a diagnosis of an Adjustment disorder (F43.2) may be a good fit. Adjustment disorders are characterized by subjective distress and emotional disturbance in conjunction with an identifiable psychosocial stressor (WHO, 1993). The person responds to the stressful life event with maladaptive depression, anxiety, or behavior. Although this diagnosis appears to account for her symptoms, the symptoms must have only occurred secondary to the stressful life event. In Elizabeth's case, she reported experiencing symptoms of social anxiety long before the separation from her husband. Although her symptoms were exacerbated by the separation and may give the appearance of an adjustment diagnosis, one might consider the separation as a removal of a major avoidance strategy, the "hiding behind [her] husband," which she had used for years. Many people with anxiety disorders find ways to avoid their feared object or situation. Through their avoidance, they are rewarded with decreased anxiety. Thus, they increase their avoidant behavior. Eventually, the avoidant behavior can snowball and become maladaptive. We can see that in Elizabeth's case, she was using her husband as an excuse to avoid the social situations she feared. Given this information, a diagnosis of social phobia continues to describe best Elizabeth's experience.

It could also be suggested that Elizabeth meets criteria for a personality disorder, such as Dependent personality disorder (F60.7). Dependent personality disorder is characterized by pervasive reliance on others to make one's life decisions. It is often associated with fear of abandonment, feeling of helplessness, and passive compliance. At this point, given the lack of additional information, this diagnosis is speculative. More information would be needed before assigning this as an official diagnosis. Regardless of the formal diagnosis, in terms of understanding Elizabeth's behavioral patterns and how she may approach treatment, it will be helpful to be on the lookout for symptoms such as heavy reliance on others, subordination of her own needs to others, and feelings of incompetence.

Elizabeth is fearful of being judged negatively in social situations, and this is impairing her quality of life. This appears to be the central dynamic in this case; hence, it is clear that Elizabeth meets the diagnostic criteria for Social phobia (F40.1x). To assess severity of depression and panic, adjustment, and personality, you would need to gather more information. A good starting point would be to encourage Elizabeth to complete self-monitoring scales to track her mood in the context of her daily experiences. This will provide information and possible insight to both you and Elizabeth about patterns in her behavior, thoughts, and emotions. Even after a primary diagnosis has been assigned, however, it is important to track the patient's other symptoms because they may wax and wane depending on life stressors. It is especially important to track suicidal ideation and behaviors.

Ethical Considerations—Protecting Your Patient

> **ACTIVITY 7.3:**
>
> What are some potential safety and privacy concerns that may be unique to Elizabeth's case? What responsibility, if any, do you have to ensure the well-being of Elizabeth's children?

For every patient, regardless of presenting complaint, it is important to take all measures necessary to ensure privacy and safety. Two potential red flags raised during the assessment were Elizabeth's passive suicidal ideation and her report of living alone with her two young children after escaping an abusive relationship.

With regard to her report of suicidal ideation, it will be important for you to understand thoroughly the nature and severity of her suicidal thoughts (see also Chapters 6 and 15, this volume). The severity of suicidal symptoms might vary depending on the stresses of the day. For example, if Elizabeth has a particularly stressful day, she might experience an increase in suicidal ideation. Given how her daily moods (and not just her diagnoses) may influence her thoughts of suicide, you will need to inquire directly about these thoughts at the beginning of each encounter with her. Although several self-report inventories may be used to quantify suicidal symptoms, this is no substitute for direct questioning by you, her therapist. Knowing that you are comfortable discussing these thoughts will make it easier for her to talk should these thoughts become more frequent or more dangerous, particularly if this happens between scheduled appointments. Elizabeth's thoughts may currently be passive and fleeting, but you will want to ensure that she does not develop a plan or intent. It may be beneficial to develop a written safety plan with Elizabeth to help her identify coping strategies she can use if suicidal thoughts become overwhelming.

Regarding her report of having recently separated from an abusive spouse, the ethical question raised is whether there is any reporting requirement for you. You should follow up with Elizabeth about the nature of the abuse experienced (e.g., physical, emotional, sexual, verbal) and whether the abuse was directed only at her or if her children were also harmed. Just be sure that Elizabeth understands that, if she reveals any physical or sexual abuse toward minors, you are required by law to notify the proper authorities (see also Chapter 3, this volume). State laws designate certain professionals (and in some jurisdictions, all citizens) as mandated reporters. Mandated reporters are legally required to report suspicion of child abuse or neglect (Child Welfare Information Gateway, 2014). Before you begin any assessment or treatment, you will always need to obtain the patient's informed consent, a process in which you provide him or her with information and obtain permission for intervention (see the American Psychological Association [APA; 2017] *Ethical Principles of Psychologists and Code of Conduct* (APA Ethics Code), Standards 3.10, Informed Consent, and Section 4: Privacy and Confidentiality). Part of that information provided should be an explanation of situations in which you would need to break confidentiality, such as when you come to suspect child abuse or neglect.

Concerning privacy, a few standard precautions should be taken. As with any patient, Elizabeth's records should be kept secure. Within the clinic, they should be accessible to others on a need-to-know basis only. Externally, records should only be shared with Elizabeth's prior written consent (see APA Ethics Code, Standard 6). In addition, being aware of the contentious and abusive relationship between Elizabeth and her husband, you should be exceptionally cautious not to reveal even her status as a patient to anyone (i.e., the husband) who may contact the clinic inquiring about Elizabeth's whereabouts or the nature of her care.

Throughout the assessment and treatment process, it will be important for you to be mindful of Elizabeth's reported difficulty asserting herself, particularly with authority figures. A clinician is naturally placed in an authoritative role, so it will be important for you to be mindful that Elizabeth is likely to be hesitant to disagree or express discontent with the services provided. Although most individuals understand that treating anxiety means confronting it, some individuals may initially be frightened to "face their fears." Their expressions of discontent or disagreement may be expressed in the form of missed appointments, not coming prepared for treatment sessions, or even terminating therapy. So be sure to look out for these signs from Elizabeth.

To encourage Elizabeth's active participation, explain that therapy is collaborative and her input is welcomed. Be sure to explain thoroughly the treatment rationale and why she is being asked to engage in certain activities. In some cases, the rationale must be explained several times before the patient feels comfortable. Facilitate a collaborative atmosphere by listening closely and making modifications that remain consistent with the treatment plan. These strategies will help Elizabeth feel more comfortable asserting herself.

Risk Management—Protecting Your Patient, Protecting Yourself

ACTIVITY 7.4:

What are the particular issues involved in protecting yourself when working with Elizabeth, especially considering that therapy for social phobia can occur in public places?

There are many steps you can take to protect yourself as a clinician. First, ensure that you have the training and competency necessary to provide Elizabeth with an appropriate assessment. Once a diagnosis is assigned, you must then decide whether you are the person who is competent to provide effective treatment (see APA Ethics Code, Standard 2). As mentioned earlier and discussed further subsequently, in vivo (real-life) exposure therapy is often a treatment of choice with people with social phobias. Providing this form of treatment involves not only knowledge of the theories and techniques involved, but, preferably, supervised experience providing in vivo treatment. If you are not competent in this kind of treatment and there is no possibility of appropriate supervision, you should make an appropriate referral. Concerning her suicidality, you must perform a detailed suicide risk assessment and continue to follow up on her suicide-related symptoms (as described earlier). Be sure to document carefully all of this information in her case record. In the worst-case scenario that Elizabeth does end up committing suicide or is otherwise harmed, you will need these records to demonstrate that you were not negligent.

If you were the one to provide treatment, in the case that you decide to use therapy techniques in which Elizabeth will be asked to face her fears in a public setting, a common treatment strategy in social phobia, some unique considerations apply, for your protection and the patient's. When therapy occurs outside the therapy room, you should discuss (and role-play) with Elizabeth how to handle any questions such as, "What are you guys doing?" or run-ins with people Elizabeth knows. Let's say a therapy session with Elizabeth requires her to face her social anxiety by going to a shopping mall and asking a store clerk questions. In this case, you will have to consider both how to stay close enough to hear whether she is implementing the instructions correctly and what to do if someone recognizes you or Elizabeth and begins to ask questions. It is possible someone might recognize Elizabeth and interrupt the task. Similarly, an acquaintance of yours might see you and strike up a conversation, making it impossible for you to observe the therapy session. To prepare for these situations, you and Elizabeth should discuss a plan for these possibilities ahead of time. For example, if someone approaches Elizabeth, it may be possible for you to move away and later meet up with her at a predetermined spot. This will decrease the risk that Elizabeth's confidentiality will be violated or that Elizabeth will suddenly feel abandoned, should you need to move away in a public setting to protect her privacy. In general, you will want to be discreet about Elizabeth's identity as a patient performing a treatment exercise.

Disposition

ACTIVITY 7.5:

Now would be a good time to review Elizabeth's treatment goals (described earlier in the chapter). How has your assessment of Elizabeth changed your conceptualization of her goals, if at all? Where on her list would you consider starting?

Before treatment can begin, the therapist needs to know what is being treated and why. It is clear that Elizabeth's primary problem is social phobia. Her depressive symptoms seem to be a response to her inability to interact comfortably with others.

Her avoidance of a job interview far exceeds the typically anxious response to such a high-stakes situation. Her lack of social skills and her inability to be assertive and express her desires and needs create situational distress, which can in turn exacerbate the severity of her symptoms. On the basis of the assessment and Elizabeth's treatment goals, developing a treatment plan that specifically addresses her social phobia is a logical next step. The treatment plan can be adjusted if progress does not occur or if symptoms of depression or another condition become more significant.

Elizabeth communicated a variety of goals. During the assessment, she expressed a dire need to obtain employment to support herself and her children, but severe anxiety prevents her from attending job interviews. Conveniently, the skills needed to be successful in a job interview (e.g., meeting new people, being assertive, having conversations, being the center of attention) are important in many other social interactions as well. Therefore, the second treatment goal on Elizabeth's list about going on job interviews may be a reasonable place to start. If Elizabeth is able to reduce her anxiety to be successful in a high-pressure situation such as a job interview, those gains are likely to carry over to other less stressful interactions.

Currently, cognitive behavior therapy (CBT) has the greatest empirical support for the treatment for social phobia (Hays, 2009; Rodebaugh, Holaway, & Heimberg, 2004). Although CBT is a generic term that encompasses multiple interventions such as cognitive restructuring, applied relaxation, homework assignments, and social skills training (see Henderson, 2014), the most efficacious treatment for anxiety disorders is in vivo exposure therapy (Craske et al., 2008). During exposure therapy, the patient confronts his or her fears in a safe and controlled, but real-life, environment. Through repeated exposure to the stimuli without negative consequences, the patient's physiological and subjective distress decreases, a process known as *habituation*. According to emotional processing theory, habituation occurs because the patient encodes new information that is incompatible with the old belief that the feared stimulus is fear-worthy (Foa, Huppert, & Cahill, 2006). The patient's worst fear is confronted either immediately or gradually, depending on a number of considerations outside the scope of this chapter. (For a more extensive review of when to use intensive or graduated exposure, see Beidel & Turner, 2007.) If you decide to use a graduated approach, your first step will be to construct a hierarchy (Beidel & Turner, 2007). To create a hierarchy, the therapist assists patients in identifying feared situations and ordering the situations according to fear intensity (least to most distressing), using a Likert-type rating scale, sometimes called a Subjective Units of Distress Scale (SUDS) scale. For example, Elizabeth may identify being interviewed by a friendly female interviewer as a 4 (*moderate anxiety*) and doing a group interview with a panel of stern interviewers as an 8 (*extreme anxiety*). Generally, it is a good idea to start exposure with a moderately ranked situation because it will be challenging yet accomplishable. Once the patient habituates to that task, you can move up the hierarchy to a more difficult situation and keep going until you reach the patient's most anxiety-producing task at the top of their hierarchy.

When treating social phobia, a multidimensional approach often works best. Exposure therapy is great for reducing symptoms of anxiety, but it is common for the patient's history of social withdrawal and avoidance to have impeded his or her development of skills needed to be successful in social situations. Therefore, it is often helpful to provide basic training in social skills as part of the treatment plan (Beidel et al., 2014). For Elizabeth, you may recommend that she engage in social effectiveness therapy (Turner, Beidel, Cooley, Woody, & Messer, 1994), a multicomponent intervention consisting of individual exposure sessions and group-based social skills training with relevant homework assignments to promote skill generalization (Turner, Beidel, & Cooley-Quille, 1997). In social effectiveness therapy, Elizabeth can address her anxiety related to job interviews in the individual exposure sessions and develop her interpersonal and presentation skills in the group sessions.

References

American Psychological Association. (2017). *Ethical principles of psychologists and code of conduct* (2002, Amended June 1, 2010 and January 1, 2017). Retrieved from http://www.apa.org/ethics/code/index.aspx

Beidel, D. C., Alfano, C. A., Kofler, M. J., Rao, P. A., Scharfstein, L., & Wong Sarver, N. (2014). The impact of social skills training for social anxiety disorder: A randomized controlled trial. *Journal of Anxiety Disorders, 28,* 908–918. http://dx.doi.org/10.1016/j.janxdis.2014.09.016

Beidel, D. C., & Turner, S. M. (2007). *Shy children, phobic adults: The nature and treatment of social anxiety disorder* (2nd ed.). http://dx.doi.org/10.1037/11533-000

Brown, E. J., Turovsky, J., Heimberg, R. G., Juster, H. R., Brown, T. A., & Barlow, D. H. (1997). Validation of the Social Interaction Anxiety Scale and the Social Phobia Scale across the anxiety disorders. *Psychological Assessment, 9,* 21–27. http://dx.doi.org/10.1037/1040-3590.9.1.21

Child Welfare Information Gateway. (2014). *Mandatory reporters of child abuse and neglect.* Washington, DC: U.S. Department of Health and Human Services, Children's Bureau.

Craske, M. G., Kircanski, K., Zelikowsky, M., Mystkowski, J., Chowdhury, N., & Baker, A. (2008). Optimizing inhibitory learning during exposure therapy. *Behaviour Research and Therapy, 46,* 5–27. http://dx.doi.org/10.1016/j.brat.2007.10.003

Foa, E. B., Huppert, J. D., & Cahill, S. P. (2006). Emotional processing theory: An update. In B. O. Rothbaum (Ed.), *Pathological anxiety: Emotional processing in etiology and treatment* (pp. 3–24). New York, NY: Guilford Press.

Foran, H. M., Beach, S. R. H., Smith Slep, A. M., Heyman, R. E., & Warnboldt, M. Z. (Eds.). (2013). *Family problems and family violence: Reliable assessment and the ICD–11.* New York, NY: Springer.

Hays, K. F. (2009). Performance anxiety. In K. F. Hays (Ed.), *Performance psychology in action: A casebook for working with athletes, performing artists, business leaders, and professionals in high-risk occupations* (pp. 101–120). Washington, DC: American Psychological Association.

Healy, J. (2014). *Issues in society: Domestic and family violence.* Thirroul, Australia: Spinney Press.

Henderson, L. (2014). *Helping your shy and socially anxious client: A social fitness training protocol using CBT*. Oakland, CA: New Harbinger.

Kessler, R. C., Petukhova, M., Sampson, N. A., Zaslavsky, A. M., & Wittchen, H.-U. (2012). Twelve-month and lifetime prevalence and lifetime morbid risk of anxiety and mood disorders in the United States. *International Journal of Methods in Psychiatric Research, 21*, 169–184. http://dx.doi.org/10.1002/mpr.1359

Rodebaugh, T. L., Holaway, R. M., & Heimberg, R. G. (2004). The treatment of social anxiety disorder. *Clinical Psychology Review, 24*, 883–908. http://dx.doi.org/10.1016/j.cpr.2004.07.007

Schaffer, J., & Rodolfa, E. (2016). *A student's guide to assessment and diagnosis using the ICD-10-CM: Psychological and behavioral conditions*. Washington, DC: American Psychological Association.

Turner, S. M., Beidel, D. C., Cooley, M. R., Woody, S. R., & Messer, S. C. (1994). A multicomponent behavioral treatment for social phobia: Social effectiveness therapy. *Behaviour Research and Therapy, 32*, 381–390. http://dx.doi.org/10.1016/0005-7967(94)90001-9

Turner, S. M., Beidel, D. C., & Cooley-Quille, M. R. (1997). *Social effectiveness therapy: A therapist's guide*. North Tonawanda, NY; Toronto, Ontario, Canada: Multi-Health Systems.

World Health Organization. (1993). *The ICD–10 classification of mental and behavioural disorders: Clinical descriptions and diagnostic guidelines*. Retrieved from http://www.who.int/classifications/icd/en/bluebook.pdf

Natacha M. R. Foo Kune and Sinéad Unsworth

F41.1 Generalized Anxiety Disorder

8

eneralized anxiety disorder (GAD; F41.1) is a condition of chronic emotional distress, with anxiety that is generalized and persistent, rather than restricted to any specific environmental circumstance. The symptoms can be quite variable but typically involve apprehension; psychical tension; and autonomic overactivity, such as sweating, dizziness, and epigastric discomfort. According to Kessler et al. (2005), lifetime prevalence for GAD is 5.1% of the adult population, with women being 1.5 to 2 times more likely to suffer from GAD (McLean, Asnaani, Litz, & Hofmann, 2011). Risk factors for this disorder include having a low income; being Caucasian; and being widowed, separated, or divorced (Breslau et al., 2006; Grant et al., 2005). Among college students, anxiety disorders (including GAD) are now the most common diagnoses, surpassing depressive disorders (Center for Collegiate Mental Health, 2015).

GAD is also the most frequent mental health diagnosis for which individuals seek treatment in a primary care medical setting (Wittchen, 2002). Hence, collaboration within integrated medical and mental health care models is particularly useful. If an individual presents with anxiety to the medical side of an integrated setting, the easier communication between medical and mental health providers allows physicians to facilitate referrals to a mental health therapist more efficiently. The collaboration ensures that clients are getting the best treatment for their diagnosis.

http://dx.doi.org/10.1037/0000069-009
An ICD–10–CM Casebook and Workbook for Students: Psychological and Behavioral Conditions, J. B. Schaffer and E. Rodolfa (Editors)

The Case

Imagine that you work as a psychologist at an integrated student health and counseling center. You have just had your first session with your client, Amy. She is a 19-year-old, single, Chinese American woman who is a chemistry-major college student and identifies as heterosexual. She was referred by her primary care provider (PCP) after she went to the Student Health Center with complaints of trembling, nervousness, muscle tension, inability to stop worrying about everything, stomach issues, and difficulty falling sleep. She explains that she worries all day long, typically about her studies. She spends many hours each day studying but feels her efforts are less efficient because she cannot concentrate. Amy's grades have dropped over the past two semesters. Socially, she is not spending as much time with friends because she is tired. She no longer enjoys being social and notices her mind is "somewhere else."

The client presents as somewhat nervous and fidgety. She offers vague responses to questions about her mental health concerns and is initially distant and guarded. Amy has difficulty expressing what brings her to meet with you. You hypothesize that her reluctance may relate to this being her first experience with psychotherapy, and perhaps she is unsure of what to say or expect.

As an only child from what she describes as a "traditional Asian family," Amy explains that her parents prioritize education and achievement. She acknowledges the unspoken expectation that she will provide for them when they are older and is aware of how much her parents have sacrificed for her. Amy identifies as a first-generation college student. Her father is a manager at a grocery store and her mother works in housekeeping at a hotel. Her parents live in a town an hour away from the university, and Amy lives in a dorm. While appreciative of their support, Amy experiences pressure to succeed and fears disappointing them if she does not excel academically. Growing up, she was often reprimanded for grades below an A. At the university, she also feels disappointed with herself when she earns any grade but an A.

Amy remembers that her anxiety began in 10th grade, when she started feeling stressed about her grades and university plans. Even though she was a straight-A student, she worried she might not get into the university of her choosing. While her friends were socializing on the weekends, Amy reported she had difficulty having fun and would often spend her leisure time ruminating about completing tasks on her to-do list. She acknowledges that she has been increasingly isolating herself and feels sad and lonely at times. Extracurricular activities include her role as the president of the premed student association, but outside of her responsibilities to the student organization, she rarely accepts invitations for social gatherings anymore because she just doesn't have the energy. She also notes that she is reacting with feelings of irritability and frustration to tasks that she normally would not have reacted to negatively in the past. Self-identified as an "overthinker," Amy states she worries about "everything and anything": grades, future career plans, finances and how people perceive her. She explains that she was raised to think about how her actions reflect not only on her but also on her family and community.

Although referred by her physician, she is ambivalent about committing to therapy because her family stigmatizes mental health treatment. She indicates that she would like to make changes in her life and is willing to meet for a few sessions to see if therapy will help. She states that a primary goal would be to learn coping skills to manage her anxiety.

Assessment Using the ICD–10–CM

ACTIVITY 8.1:

What additional information do you believe would be important to reach a diagnosis? How would you go about eliciting such information?

Before we can start considering diagnoses, it is important to make sure that we have accurate data. One of the ways to get helpful data from a clinical interview is to build good rapport with the client (Kinoshita & Hsu, 2006), especially with someone who is not familiar with psychotherapy and may have been taught not to divulge family information to strangers. In addition, a good alliance is essential for treatment and is considered one of the common factors for therapy (Tracey, Lichtenberg, Goodyear, Claiborn, & Wampold, 2003).

Given that the client indicated difficulty with anxiety and worries, it would be helpful to ask about other symptoms of anxiety, such as shortness of breath, muscular tension, and restlessness. Consider the fact that several symptoms overlap between depressive and anxiety disorders, and therefore, it is also helpful to ask if the client is exhibiting depressive symptoms, such as depressed mood, the duration of the depressed mood, as well as suicidal ideation. As the client starts denying or endorsing symptoms, you can start ruling out and ruling in diagnoses. Notice the content of the client's thoughts to clarify whether it is anxiety, depression, both, or something else. For instance, does Amy catastrophize about not meeting goals (suggesting anxiety) or harbor thoughts about being worthless (suggesting depression)?

ICD–10–CM Diagnosis

ACTIVITY 8.2:

What particular diagnoses seem appropriate at this point? Include all potential diagnoses that may be appropriate, given the information you have.

Early in the process, you want to get a sense of whether the symptoms are of a more long-standing nature rather than a reaction to a specific stressor. If they are a reaction to a specific change in her life, you might consider one of the Adjustment disorders (F43.2) with possible specifiers, such as Adjustment disorder with anxiety (F43.22) or Adjustment disorder with mixed anxiety and depressed mood (F43.23). However, the information you have gathered so far does not suggest a specific situation that led to the symptoms. One could argue that the anticipation of attending college, a major life change, was perhaps what caused the onset of anxiety in the 10th grade. However, symptoms for adjustment disorders typically do not last more than 6 months. Given that Amy has had symptoms for about 4 years, you can rule out adjustment disorders. Notice the use of the scientific method through the process of determining which diagnosis fits the client. First, set a hypothesis (e.g., Adjustment disorder). Then, look at the evidence to see which pieces of data are consistent with your hypothesis (e.g., anticipation of college as major life change) and which pieces of data might contradict it (e.g., duration more than 6 months). Finally, make a decision based on the data (in this case, ruling out adjustment disorders).

The next step is to determine whether her symptoms are more consistent with an anxiety disorder or a depressive disorder (e.g., Major depressive disorder, recurrent [F33]). Some symptoms you see in the client are listed as criteria for both anxiety and depressive disorders: reduced energy, concentration, and self-esteem, as well as disturbed sleep. It would be helpful to ask the client directly during the interview how central a role her sadness plays in her current life. Although she reports not spending as much time with friends, this appears to be secondary to fatigue rather than a loss of interest. Assuming her depression is not her major complaint and there is a lack of anhedonia (loss of pleasure), it seems that ruling out depression is reasonable.

Now that you are considering the realm of anxiety, it is necessary to determine whether the anxiety manifests in discrete periods of panic attacks or in a more generalized way. During the clinical interview, it is always helpful to ask the client whether the anxiety symptoms appear suddenly and are severe or are present most of the time. Asking about specific symptoms of anxiety is also important because clients often do not recognize a symptom as being caused by anxiety. This is particularly true of physiological symptoms, which the client may attribute to medical problems; for example, increased heart rate may be attributed to heart problems and not to anxiety. This could be particularly relevant in Amy's case because she went to a medical doctor first, who then referred her to you. She does not describe sudden onset of severe symptoms and instead worries "all day long." As a result, it appears that she does not suffer from panic attacks.

The next step is to look at whether the cause of the anxiety is specific or generalized. This question grows out of your hypothesis that she may be suffering from a specific phobia. Reflecting on the information you have, there are two references to reduced social interactions, and Amy worries about how other people perceive her. It is worth considering whether Social phobias (F40.1x) are an issue. This hypothesis should lead you to think about questions that you can ask that will ascertain whether the client's fear of scrutiny by others is the cause of avoidance of social situations. You already have some clues, such as the fact that she has been social in the past, sufficiently so to join a student organization and be elected its president. Further, she offered tiredness as the reason she does not engage socially more often. Also, her lack of enjoyment is related to worrying about tasks she has to complete rather than fear of judgment. Given her previous social functioning and her reasons for avoiding social interactions, it is likely that a specific phobia can be ruled out at this point.

If her anxiety is specific, another possible diagnosis is Obsessive-compulsive disorder (F42). Amy does report ruminating, and it is worth examining whether her ruminations fit criteria for obsessional thoughts. In her case, she has recurring thoughts of tasks she needs to accomplish, but she does not indicate that she strives to avoid the thought, a classic symptom of Obsessive-compulsive disorder. Amy has adopted these recurring thoughts almost as part of her identity, in describing herself as an "over-thinker." She also does not engage in compulsive stereotyped behaviors to avoid the thought. If she does engage in behaviors to reduce her anxiety, she tends to engage in productive behavior (attending to her to-do list). The *ICD–10 Classification of Mental and Behavioural Disorders: Clinical Descriptions and Diagnostic Guidelines* (*Blue Book*; World Health Organization, 1993) suggests that compulsive behaviors do not result in the completion of inherently useful tasks. In other words, she does not appear to meet criteria for Obsessive-compulsive disorder.

The next possible diagnosis is Generalized anxiety disorder (F41.1). Indeed, her anxiety is generalized to various fears and apprehension (about grades, judgment of others, "anything and everything"). She reports motor tension, specifically trembling and muscle tension. Her symptoms also present evidence of autonomic overactivity, such as stomach problems. Her symptoms have lasted several weeks or months, and there is evidence of past history of anxiety. Thus, the anxiety symptoms she presents are consistent with GAD (F41.1), the most likely the diagnosis, given the data you currently have. However, before drawing a firm conclusion, it is helpful to take into consideration three other possibilities: Neurasthenia (F48.0), Other mixed anxiety disorders (F41.3), and Other specified anxiety disorders (F41.8).

In the ICD–10–CM, a diagnosis of GAD (F41.1) lists a Type 2 exclusion for Neurasthenia (F48.8). This means Neurasthenia is not part of GAD, and a client could have both diagnoses. Therefore, it is helpful to examine the criteria for that disorder. Your client does complain of being tired, or decreased mental efficiency, which are symptoms of Neurasthenia. However, her primary concern is that she worries most of the day. She mentions the fatigue later and only when asked about social engagement. Neurasthenia is not often diagnosed in the United States, and in Amy's case, it appears more likely that her fatigue is a symptom of anxiety.

Second, Other mixed anxiety disorders (F41.3) is a possibility. If criteria for GAD (F41.1), as well as prominent features of other anxiety disorders, are present, you need to consider whether those other anxiety diagnoses might be a better fit. In Amy's case, she does not meet full criteria for Other mixed anxiety disorders (F41.3), such as phobias or panic attack. With no prominent features of other anxiety disorders, GAD appears to be a better fit.

Lastly, Other specified anxiety disorders (F41.8), such as mixed anxiety and depressive disorder, should be considered when both anxiety and depression are present but neither set of symptoms is sufficiently severe to meet criteria for a diagnosis. In her case, you have already established that her symptoms are severe enough to fit an anxiety disorder, and she lacks the depressed or irritable mood component of depressive disorders. Therefore, you can feel reasonably certain that the best diagnosis is a GAD (F41.1).

Ethical Considerations—Protecting Your Patient

ACTIVITY 8.3:

Refer to the American Psychological Association (APA; 2017) *Ethical Principles of Psychologists and Code of Conduct* (APA Ethics Code) or the Canadian Psychological Association (CPA; 2017) code of ethics and identify specific ethical dilemmas you might encounter in an integrated care setting. Would you share your diagnostic impressions with Amy? When might sharing diagnostic information be helpful or harmful to a client? What potential ethical concerns might arise when sharing diagnostic information?

Providing assessment and therapy that aligns with our professional Code of Ethics means that we provide clients with adequate informed consent. This includes sharing information with the client on the various procedures used in the assessment process and in psychotherapy, the nature and length of both, as well as the limits of confidentiality (APA [2017] Ethics Code, Standard 10.01, Informed Consent to Therapy; CPA [2017] Code of Ethics, Standard I.26). Given that Amy is new to therapy, it will be essential to explain clearly what therapy is and explore any expectations or assumptions she might have about therapy. Examining any cultural factors that may influence her adherence to therapy is also essential. Similarly, exploring any potential worries that may arise is encouraged, given that Amy's parents do not believe in psychotherapy. Please note that informed consent is a procedure conducted at the onset of the assessment and of therapy, and it is also an ongoing process throughout the course of treatment. So, throughout therapy, it is important to check in with the client to monitor the person's reactions and progress in therapy and to ensure that you have ongoing consent for the treatment being provided.

Another aspect of informed consent when working in a team setting is to inform Amy that medical and mental health information is shared, when appropriate for care (see also Chapter 1, this volume). However, there may be some situations when the client is uncomfortable with your speaking to her PCP about her symptoms. Although under the Health Insurance Portability and Accountability Act (1996) you are legally permitted to consult with the referring PCP for continuity of care purposes, checking with the client to determine whether she has any concerns with the sharing of her information is strongly suggested. Ongoing communication about who is involved in her treatment helps to ensure the client has trust in the therapeutic relationship.

For treatment, interdisciplinary consultation may expand beyond the health disciplines, such as consulting with the client's academic advisors. This could involve a more intrusive lack of privacy and so should be considered with great care. Clearly explaining to Amy how the sharing of information would occur, the potential benefits and risks, with the consent of the release of information is of utmost importance to ensure trust is maintained and that her privacy is protected to the maximum degree within the context of quality treatment.

In this case, you work in a clinic that uses a short-term treatment model, so it is important to assess whether Amy's goals are suited for short-term therapy and provide a referral, if needed. The goal of the initial assessment is to maximize the benefit and minimize harm for the client.

Competence is another integral ethical issue to consider in this case (APA Ethics Code, Standard 2.01, Boundaries of Competence; CPA Code of Ethics, Standard II.6, 9; see also Chapters 3 and 5, this volume). This means that you should have the relevant training and knowledge to provide the appropriate therapy for the client's diagnosis and related issues, including multicultural competence to ensure that "cultural and socioeconomic contexts become the basis for informed inquiry rather than the illusion of uniform group characteristics with which to stereotype the client" (Pope & Vasquez, 2007, p. 227). Low-income mothers are more likely to receive a diagnosis of GAD based on symptoms that are a natural reaction to lack of resources in the environment (Baer, Kim, & Wilkenfeld, 2012). Such a diagnostic label in this instance could lead to interventions targeted at individual change, when in fact interventions should target environmental change. Pope and Vasquez (2007) stressed the importance of therapists being aware of how their own cultural values and attitudes influence their work with clients of various cultural identities. Failure to attend to the cultural background results in not capturing the breadth of the client's experiences, leading to inadequate treatment. Being culturally competent could also help lower the high premature dropout rates for ethnic minorities (Barrett, Chua, Crits-Christoph, Gibbons, & Thompson, 2008).

Thus, being aware of cultural similarities and differences between you and the client can help you identify potential biases you may hold and how that may affect your work. Using cultural sensitivity to understand salient identities of the client is essential to implementing appropriate treatment to ensure that the primary issues are being addressed.

One controversial issue in the mental health field is whether one shares diagnostic information with the client. Assessing what emotions, behaviors, and thought patterns fit potential diagnostic criteria can inform the treatment process. Whether to share the diagnosis with a client can depend on a number of factors, including the therapist's beliefs about the purpose of a diagnosis. Some clients may feel empowered by having a diagnostic label to denote and identify what they have been experiencing. Other clients may feel pathologized or labeled and may do better without knowing whether their symptoms fit criteria for a particular mental disorder. We suggest you explore with clients what type of information they are looking for and what they hope to gain by knowing their diagnosis. If you believe the client's knowing the diagnostic label would be more negative than positive, an alternative is to inform the client of your assessment conclusions and clinical impressions, independent of the diagnostic label used, which is, after all, merely a hypothetical construct. Exploring the client's expectations of the diagnosis and assessment conclusions can assist in using the diagnostic information to help empower rather than harm the client.

Risk Management—Protecting Your Patient, Protecting Yourself

ACTIVITY 8.4:

What are the major risks for you and Amy? What might be ways at the onset of therapy to provide safeguards to maximize her safety?

Risk assessment is critical in minimizing harm for both therapist and client. A comprehensive and documented risk assessment reduces clinical liability. To assess for safety for the client, inquiring about suicidality and homicidality as part of the routine clinical interview is recommended (see also Chapter 6, this volume). By assessing for both of these issues, you are screening for safety of both the client and the public. Risk factors include the presence of any of the following: suicidality (intent, plan, preparation, history), environmental stressors such as one that causes severe loss or shame, lack of supports, depression, feelings of hopelessness, and alcohol or other substance abuse. Severe loss can include a difficult breakup or dealing with the loss of a loved one. If a loved one has died by suicide, this can also increase suicidal risk. Assessing for supports, such as determining whether the individual has someone in whom to confide, such as a friend, partner, therapist, or spiritual advisor, can also decrease feelings of isolation, thus creating a safety net that can support the client. The presence of substance abuse can decrease inhibition and increase impulsive tendencies, which can lead to increased risk. Suicidal ideations can be a fairly common occurrence, with 20% of students having at least one experience of suicidal ideation over the course of their university life (American College Health Association, 2015). Exploring the frequency and severity of the ideations and any history of suicide attempts, as well as increased specificity of the plan, can help assess imminent risk. If the client is endorsing suicidal ideation, assessing the factors described here can assist in determining what type of safety plan is necessary and what course of action may be appropriate to maximize safety for the client.

Discussing with clients the limitations of therapy is important because psychotherapy does not help everyone. Explain the potential course of treatment and share with clients that they may feel worse before they improve. In the case of anxious clients who are avoidant of their internal experiences, such as anxious thoughts and feelings, initially exposing themselves to their anxiety by verbalizing their anxious experiences may increase anxiety during and after sessions. If clients are not fully informed about potential experiences they may have, including the fact that they may experience anxiety more strongly in session, confusion, discouragement, and dropout may result. Keep in mind that informed consent maximizes benefits for the client and minimizes risk to the clinician. Risk to the clinician, especially in the absence of informed consent, can include a malpractice suit, a complaint to the licensing board, and perhaps most commonly, premature dropout before therapy goals are reached. If the clinician does not fully inform the client about the realistic nature of how progress is defined in therapy (e.g., that progress might differ depending on the person and the issue), the client may have unrealistic expectations. With unrealistic expectations for her presenting problem, she may feel that you did not deliver effective care even if she did show improvement in her symptoms and functioning.

Disposition

ACTIVITY 8.5:

On the basis of the current data, what particular treatment concerns do you have for Amy? When might you consider consulting with her PCP or another interdisciplinary professional for client's treatment?

Once you have gathered all the relevant data, it is time to create an appropriate treatment plan, whether you are in the role of assessor or therapist. We know the diagnosis, GAD (F41.1), and client's stated treatment goals, to reduce her worrying and to regain her energy.

In reviewing Amy's story and symptoms, it appears she is a good candidate for short-term psychotherapy, given her report of no history of trauma or long-term psychological issues other than the anxiety. Variables that can influence treatment progress include her motivation for treatment and external social supports. Amy's strengths that can be helpful in treatment include her work ethic, self-discipline, and ability to succeed at a university.

On the basis of the clinical literature, there are several empirically supported treatments for GAD. Cognitive behavior therapy (Szkodny, Newman, & Goldfried, 2014) and mindfulness-based and acceptance approaches (Baer, 2005) have been empirically supported to alleviate anxiety symptoms. Although cognitive behavioral approaches appear to be the most extensively validated for the treatment of anxiety, the common factors model suggests that other factors can be responsible for therapeutic change, including therapist characteristics, such as the ability to form a therapeutic relationship (e.g., being flexible, warm, trustworthy, interested, open, and demonstrating competence; Reisner, 2005). With that in mind, having established therapeutic rapport, and having familiarized yourself with the literature on which treatments are effective for her diagnosis, you can recommend the best treatment plan.

In Amy's case, you are considering the following treatment interventions and goals over eight sessions. First, you plan to have a discussion with her about her views of mental health treatment and provide psychoeducation about ways in which psychotherapy can help, as well as its limitations. It is important that Amy be aware at the onset of what type of treatment she is committing to, which can influence instillation of hope and clarify expectations of therapy.

An important goal is to build rapport with Amy and provide a supportive and empathic stance so she can begin to explore her emotional experience in a nonjudgmental and safe space, which can help to create a corrective experience for her by helping her learn new skills to deal more effectively with her anxiety.

Using a culturally sensitive approach, it is necessary to understand Amy's cultural identities (race, culture, gender, class) and how those are influencing expectations she has for herself (Sue, Zane, Nagayama Hall, & Berger, 2009), including her family's expectations related to her academics. This will involve the issue of how her own beliefs about success and failure are related to her parents' expectations (Yee, DeBaryshe, Yuen, Kim, & McCubbin, 2006). Given cultural expectations regarding relationships between parents and children, this obviously must be undertaken with great sensitivity. You do not want to exacerbate the dilemma Amy may feel in being caught between two sets of cultural expectations.

Given her specific symptoms, psychoeducation on how anxiety affects the body and mind, as well as the utility of implementing sleep hygiene and physical exercise to reduce anxiety, may be a useful intervention, which can include cultivating self-care practices such as relaxation strategies (e.g., progressive muscle relaxation, guided imagery, deep breathing) to reduce physiological arousal associated with anxiety symptoms. Related to increasing self-care practices, mindfulness skills are also recommended to bring attention to how often Amy is on autopilot worrying. Encouraging more present-centered thinking, as well as implementing self-compassion and a nonjudgmental attitude, would likely be helpful. Given her concerns with her persistent ruminations, using cognitive-behavioral interventions to challenge cognitive distortions and substitute healthier and realistic self-talk is also suggested.

Although Amy has identified having strong social supports, referring her to resources for first-generation college students can help connect her with other students who may have similar stressors, as well as increase her awareness of funding and study strategy resources. Another avenue that may be helpful in guiding her treatment plan is to consult with her PCP to share your assessment conclusions and for possible referral for a psychotropic medication trial. Stein (2006) identified first-line pharmacotherapy for GAD as selective serotonin reuptake inhibitors or serotonin-noradrenaline reuptake inhibitors.

A discussion of Amy's specific goals can help clarify what she values in her treatment, which can improve her motivation to commit to therapy. It is important to keep in mind that the treatment plan is an ongoing assessment of the client's progress. This includes having a discussion with her to inquire about what progress looks like for her, and how she feels she is progressing toward her goals. Depending on how the therapy unfolds, modifying the treatment plan should always be considered, as should consulting with your supervisor or a trusted colleague if you encounter roadblocks.

References

American College Health Association. (2015). *American College Health Association–National College Health Assessment II: Reference group executive summary fall 2014*. Hanover, MD: Author.

American Psychological Association. (2017). *Ethical principles of psychologists and code of conduct* (2002, Amended June 1, 2010 and January 1, 2017). Retrieved from http://www.apa.org/ethics/code/index.aspx

Baer, J. C., Kim, M. S., & Wilkenfeld, B. (2012). Is it generalized anxiety disorder or poverty? An examination of poor mothers and their children. *Child & Adolescent Social Work Journal, 29*, 345–355. http://dx.doi.org/10.1007/s10560-012-0263-3

Baer, R. A. (Ed.). (2005). *Mindfulness-based treatment approaches: Clinician's guide to evidence base and applications*. New York, NY: Academic Press.

Barrett, M. S., Chua, W.-J., Crits-Christoph, P., Gibbons, M. B., & Thompson, D. (2008). Early withdrawal from mental health treatment: Implications for psychotherapy practice. *Psychotherapy: Theory, Research, Practice, Training, 45*, 247–267. http://dx.doi.org/10.1037/0033-3204.45.2.247

Breslau, J., Aguilar-Gaxiola, S., Kendler, K. S., Su, M., Williams, D., & Kessler, R. C. (2006). Specifying race-ethnic differences in risk for psychiatric disorder in a USA national sample. *Psychological Medicine, 36*, 57–68. http://dx.doi.org/10.1017/S0033291705006161

Canadian Psychological Association. (2017). *Canadian code of ethics for psychologists* (4th ed.). Retrieved from http://www.cpa.ca/docs/File/Ethics/CPA_Code_2017_4thEd.pdf

Center for Collegiate Mental Health. (2015, January). *2014 Annual Report* (Publication No. STA 15-30). Retrieved from http://ct.counseling.org/2006/08/ct-online-ethics-update-6

Grant, B. F., Hasin, D. S., Stinson, F. S., Dawson, D. A., Ruan, W. J., Goldstein, R. B., . . . Huang, B. (2005). Prevalence, correlates, co-morbidity, and comparative disability of *DSM-IV* generalized anxiety disorder in the USA: Results from the National Epidemiologic Survey on Alcohol and Related Conditions. *Psychological Medicine, 35*, 1747–1759. http://dx.doi.org/10.1017/S0033291705006069

Health Insurance Portability and Accountability Act of 1996 (HIPAA), Public Law 104-191.

Kessler, R. C., Berglund, P., Demler, O., Jin, R., Merikangas, K. R., & Walters, E. E. (2005). Lifetime prevalence and age-of-onset distributions of *DSM–IV* disorders in the National Comorbidity Survey Replication [correction appears in *Archives of General Psychiatry, 62*, 768]. *Archives of General Psychiatry, 62*, 593–602. http://dx.doi.org/10.1001/archpsyc.62.6.593

Kinoshita, L. M., & Hsu, J. (2006). Assessment of Asian Americans: Fundamental issues and clinical applications. In F. T. L. Leong, A. G. Inman, A. Ebreo, L. H. Yang, L. Kinoshita, & M. Fu (Eds.), *Handbook of Asian American psychology* (2nd ed., pp. 409–428). Thousand Oaks, CA: Sage.

McLean, C. P., Asnaani, A., Litz, B. T., & Hofmann, S. G. (2011). Gender differences in anxiety disorders: Prevalence, course of illness, comorbidity and burden of illness. *Journal of Psychiatric Research, 45,* 1027–1035. http://dx.doi.org/10.1016/j.jpsychires.2011.03.006

Pope, K. S., & Vasquez, M. J. T. (2007). *Ethics in psychotherapy and counseling: A practical guide* (3rd ed.). San Francisco, CA: Jossey-Bass.

Reisner, A. (2005). The common factors, empirically validated treatments, and recovery models of therapeutic change. *The Psychological Record, 55,* 377–399.

Stein, D. J. (2006). Evidence-based treatment of anxiety disorders. *International Journal of Psychiatry in Clinical Practice, 10*(Suppl. 1), 16–21. http://dx.doi.org/10.1080/13651500600552487

Sue, S., Zane, N., Nagayama Hall, G. C., & Berger, L. K. (2009). The case for cultural competency in psychotherapeutic interventions. *Annual Review of Psychology, 60,* 525–548. http://dx.doi.org/10.1146/annurev.psych.60.110707.163651

Szkodny, L. E., Newman, M. G., & Goldfried, M. R. (2014). Clinical experiences in conducting empirically supported treatments for generalized anxiety disorder. *Behavior Therapy, 45,* 7–20.

Tracey, T. J. G., Lichtenberg, J. W., Goodyear, R. K., Claiborn, C., & Wampold, B. E. (2003). Concept mapping of therapeutic common factors. *Psychotherapy Research, 13,* 401–413. http://dx.doi.org/10.1093/ptr/kpg041

Wittchen, H. U. (2002). Generalized anxiety disorder: Prevalence, burden, and cost to society. *Depression and Anxiety, 16,* 162–171. http://dx.doi.org/10.1002/da.10065

World Health Organization. (1993). *ICD–10 classification of mental and behavioural disorders: Clinical descriptions and diagnostic guidelines.* Retrieved from http://www.who.int/classifications/icd/en/bluebook.pdf

Yee, B. W. K., DeBaryshe, B. D., Yuen, S., Kim, S. Y., & McCubbin, H. I. (2006). Asian American and Pacific Islander families: Resiliency and life-span socialization in a cultural context. In F. T. L. Leong, A. G. Inman, A. Ebreo, L. H. Yang, L. Kinoshita, & M. Fu (Eds.), *Handbook of Asian American psychology* (2nd ed., pp. 69–86). Thousand Oaks, CA: Sage.

Samantha S. Yard and Stephen R. McCutcheon

F43.1 Posttraumatic Stress Disorder

9

osttraumatic stress disorder (PTSD; F43.10) occurs in response to an exceptionally distressing life event (or multiple such events) and consists of
a complex array of debilitating symptoms across emotional, behavioral,
cognitive, and physiological domains. These symptoms can lead to functional impairments in almost every aspect of life, including productivity, interpersonal relationships, community involvement, physical health, and quality
of life. In conjunction with the *ICD–10 Classification of Mental and Behavioural
Disorders: Clinical Descriptions and Diagnostic Guidelines* (*Blue Book*; World Health
Organization [WHO], 1993), we recommend *Handbook of PTSD: Science and
Practice* (Friedman, Keane, & Resick, 2015) as a primary reference.

The traumatic events that can lead to PTSD (F43.10) include (but are not
limited to) sexual assault, combat, natural disasters, and life-threatening accidents and illnesses. Before 1980, pathological reactions to these types of events
were typically categorized according to the traumatic events themselves (e.g.,
battered woman syndrome, combat fatigue). When these phenomena were
grouped together in the third edition of the *Diagnostic and Statistical Manual of
Mental Disorders* (*DSM*), this syndrome was reconceptualized as an anxiety disorder and named PTSD (F43.10), which was defined as occurring in response
to events "outside the range of usual human experience." Over the course of
the next 3 decades, a wealth of research and changes in diagnostic criteria have

http://dx.doi.org/10.1037/0000069-010
An ICD–10–CM Casebook and Workbook for Students: Psychological and Behavioral Conditions, J. B. Schaffer
and E. Rodolfa (Editors)

continued to shift our conceptualization of PTSD, including a broader definition of what constitutes a traumatic event. Epidemiological research has shown that traumatic events are actually quite common, with about 10% of women and 5% of men experiencing PTSD at some point in their lives (National Center for PTSD, 2016). Among veterans of the Iraq and Afghanistan wars, the rate is almost 20% (Finley et al., 2017). Most people recover naturally and do not develop PTSD (Friedman et al., 2015). Furthermore, a number of extremely distressing experiences can lead to PTSD in conjunction with each individual's unique vulnerabilities and ways of coping (Friedman et al., 2015). Similarly, the specific symptoms that make up a PTSD diagnosis have developed over time. The most widely accepted current conceptualization of the disorder includes four symptom clusters: (a) intrusive reexperiencing of the traumatic event (through nightmares, flashbacks, or intrusive memories); (b) avoidance of internal and/or external reminders of the trauma; (c) hyperarousal and heightened reactivity to stimuli, including vigilance of potential dangers, sleep disturbances, and irritability; and (d) negative cognitions and mood related to the traumatic event(s) [Friedman et al., 2015].

The Case

A 35-year-old male patient (Max) has come to treatment at the request of his wife (Karen) primarily due to anger outbursts he has exhibited in front of their children. Karen has accompanied Max to an initial assessment at a PTSD specialty clinic. Max is a veteran of the Iraq War (Operation Iraqi Freedom) and was medically discharged from the Marines due to a severe injury sustained to his foot and leg and a concussion that occurred in 2009. Since discharge, Max has had trouble reintegrating into his family and community. He continues to behave as if he is still in Iraq. He is vigilant of his surroundings, distressing images from his time in Iraq come into his mind at least daily, and he is on edge and easily angered. There has also been increasing frequency and intensity of disagreements with Karen. Max views everything in a negative light, having a hard time mustering energy and enthusiasm for activities with the kids, and he describes an ongoing commentary in his head consisting of criticisms toward himself and others, particularly his wife. He presents as mistrustful and irritable. He reports rarely laughing or experiencing joy and describes feeling cut off from the people around him, as if he were in his own world and unable to feel intimate with anyone.

Karen confirms her husband's statements. She adds that sometimes he joins the family for games or outdoor activities, but when he does, he's distracted and she can tell that he is just "putting on a happy face." Karen also complains that Max is not willing to be in crowds with the kids, which makes family time at the park or beach impossible. He says that he finds these places intolerable; there's no way to protect the children, given the wide-open spaces and other people around.

Part of Max's irritability may stem from his chronic lack of sleep. He reports sleeping about 4 hours each night. He has trouble falling asleep, sometimes lying in bed for hours, and is then awakened by nightmares and has difficulty falling back to sleep. Karen corroborates and adds that sometimes she sleeps in the guest bedroom. He has tried some medications for sleep, but they leave him feeling groggy during the day, so he would rather not use them.

Drinking alcohol is his primary coping strategy. Max relies on having several drinks before any family event or social gathering; otherwise, he struggles to interact with others. His difficulties interacting are partly a result of having such a hard time concentrating on the conversation while staying vigilant of his surroundings. Also, he finds people's questions about his military service insensitive and disingenuous. Usually he keeps his drinking to about three drinks per evening, but every month or so he drinks six or seven drinks a night. These evenings usually end in an argument with his wife, who worries about his drunkenness around the children. For several days after, Max feels guilty and ashamed of his behavior and isolates from his family either by spending time in the garage or staying in bed. Max has been trying to reduce his alcohol use but has not been successful so far. He can usually abstain at home with the family, but in a social situation, he experiences "intolerable" anxiety without a few drinks.

In part, Max has been trying to cut down on alcohol because he read online that alcohol could impede recovery from his traumatic brain injury (TBI). He was exposed to several bomb blasts during his service in Iraq, including one that seemed "close enough to finish me" and resulted in him losing consciousness for a few minutes and feeling disoriented for an hour afterward. Max worries that exposure to these blasts had a significant effect on his thinking and health, including his difficulties concentrating and headaches. He tried taking some college classes after returning from deployment but found that it was difficult to stay focused on the content during class. He also didn't like being in large lecture halls and was able to tolerate his anxiety only by sitting at the back of the room close to the door. He believes his grades were lower than his intellectual capabilities, having been a strong student in high school (all A's and B's). Notes in Max's chart indicate that a neuropsychologist determined that he had had a mild TBI (S06.2X1A), which could be associated with some relatively minor long-term effects, but that any effects are likely static now, given how long ago the incident occurred.

Max has had difficulties confiding in his wife and friends about his symptoms given how mental distress was handled in his squad. His staff sergeant frequently harassed soldiers who expressed distress after combat missions. Furthermore, having grown up in a military family in which mental illness was seen as a weakness, Max was not accepting of his own symptoms, instead suppressing fears and doubts and using alcohol to get relief from tension and rumination. Similarly, Max has been reluctant to seek professional help for his symptoms. He met a few times with a psychiatrist for sleep aids while he was still in the service, but he never followed through with taking the prescribed medications. Max's intrusive symptoms have become so frequent and distressing over the past few months that he is willing to try medicine, but he remains doubtful that he can be helped.

Assessment Using the ICD–10–CM

> **ACTIVITY 9.1:**
>
> What are the key symptoms or targets that you would need to assess further? What are some additional sources of information that you could use to inform your assessment of Max?

MENTAL STATUS EXAM

Max came to the session on time, wearing clean clothes, with good grooming, and appearing alert, although he was fairly stiff in his posture. He was cooperative but somewhat guarded; he maintained good eye contact and showed no abnormal movements other than fidgeting. He demonstrated a normal rate, volume, and rhythm of speech, providing fluent content both in response to direct questioning and without prompting. When questioned about his mood, he replied that he feels "fine" but when pressed further, admitted he was "not great." His affect was stable throughout the interview, congruent with his mood, with a restricted range. His thought process was linear, coherent, and goal directed, with no homicidal or suicidal ideation, and he denied auditory or visual hallucinations. He appeared grossly within normal limits in memory (for recent and distant past events) and executive functioning during the interview. He demonstrated fair insight in that he understood his experiences in combat have contributed to feelings of fear and anxiety that have affected his ability to interact with others in a variety of important ways. His judgment appeared good, in that he was seeking treatment for his symptoms and described a sound decision-making process. Some limits in judgment appeared to reflect distorted safety beliefs and emotion dysregulation deficits, rather than poor judgment per se.

We can summarize a number of key targets for case conceptualization, further assessment, and treatment planning:

1. Nightmares and intrusive images related to combat experiences (F51.5);
2. Poor sleep with frequent waking and difficulty falling asleep (G47.9);
3. Cognitive concerns including concentration (R41.840), memory, and learning (G31.84);
4. Irritability and anger outbursts (R45.4);
5. Marital and parenting conflict (Z63.0 and Z62.820);
6. Alcohol abuse (F10.10);
7. Distorted beliefs related to a traumatic event, including moral injury (R41.82 or R45.82); and
8. Social problems: mental illness stigmatization (Z60.9), distress in social situations (Z73.4), and isolation (Z60.4).

It is worth noting that it is often helpful to have multiple sources of information, such as from Max's wife or other family members, friends, or professional colleagues, when gathering history and current functioning (Friedman et al., 2015). The most direct means of gathering such information is to do collateral interviews, which, however, raises ethical issues of its own (see Chapter 4, this volume).

ICD–10–CM Diagnosis

> **ACTIVITY 9.2:**
>
> Which of the preceding key targets are the most plausible primary diagnoses in this case? How do you distinguish PTSD from adjustment to a stressful life event?

A logical way to structure a diagnostic evaluation is to start with the most likely primary diagnosis, which in Max's case is PTSD (F43.10 when unspecified). The *Blue Book* allows for an unspecified categorization for all patients showing symptoms lasting at least 1 month. The PTSD specifier *acute* (F43.11) is appropriate when a patient's symptoms have lasted between 1 and 3 months. Most patients (like Max) will show symptoms for more than 3 months, in which case they receive a diagnosis code for the *chronic* specifier (F43.12). To determine whether Max's symptoms suggest a PTSD diagnosis, you must identify a traumatic event and clear examples of the core PTSD symptomatology.

A QUALIFYING TRAUMATIC EVENT

Did Max experience an exceptionally distressing life event? What counts as a traumatic event is a controversial issue in PTSD theory and research (Friedman et al., 2015). Experiences of life-threatening violence, accidental near-death, sexual assaults or abuse, and combat are common examples of events that can lead to PTSD. Current conceptualizations of traumatic events allow for other experiences, such as life-threatening illness, news of another's death, or sometimes indirect exposure to events if they are traumatic to the individual. It is rare for someone to develop PTSD without having reacted to the event with intense fear, horror, or helplessness (Friedman et al., 2015). Regardless, it is exceedingly important when you ask questions about past events to be sensitive to the fact that these memories may be highly distressing and may elicit intense shame and urges to avoid disclosure. Your goal is to acquire the information that you need without the experience being so traumatic that it jeopardizes the patient's willingness to participate in future mental health treatment. Clearly, Max's multiple blast exposures, especially when he lost consciousness and had his foot crushed, count as exceptionally distressing. Indeed, there is a dose–response aspect to PTSD, in that PTSD occurs more frequently with multiple traumatic events (Friedman et al., 2015). Given Max's military history, you would inquire about other trauma events experienced during war (e.g., military sexual trauma, contact with dead bodies, close quarters combat, prisoner of war) and then explore more generally events that occurred during his service, during childhood, and at any other time.

REPEATED AND INTRUSIVE RECOLLECTIONS

Does Max reexperience the traumatic event through nightmares, daytime intrusive images, or flashbacks (in which the memory may be so vivid that he loses awareness of present-day surroundings)? You would follow up on any indications of reexperiencing to get more details about the nature of these recollections—in particular, which memories are most common, which one(s) bother him the most, and how frequently and distressing they are for him. The key to identifying these symptoms is that they are involuntary and highly sensory, tending to occur for short periods and without context (Friedman et al., 2015).

AVOIDANCE OF TRAUMA REMINDERS

As for external reminders, in addition to crowds and open spaces, Max also avoids the smell of diesel gasoline (which reminds him of Iraq) and exposure to loud noises. It can be more difficult to assess internal avoidance, which may come up during treatment, but many with PTSD will describe trying to push images and thoughts out of their head or quiet them with substance use or distractions.

AUTONOMIC HYPERAROUSAL AND REACTIVITY

Max reports being on alert almost constantly. Every time he goes into a store or restaurant, walks out of the house, or comes home, he describes being acutely aware of and attentive to his surroundings, watching for and feeling as if dangers are around every corner. His sleep problems and anger outbursts are also indicators of hyperarousal and reactivity.

NEGATIVE COGNITIONS AND MOOD

Max describes having a hard time accessing or recognizing his own emotions, though he does acknowledge feeling and expressing anger. He also struggles to empathize with his wife; she confirms that he often seems uninterested or "cold." He experiences his wife and others, including his children, as if they are far away even when they are physically quite close and becomes uncomfortable and anxious when Karen makes efforts to understand his thoughts and emotions. He can't remember the last time he really enjoyed a good movie or a game on TV or any experience like he used to before deployment. PTSD manifests in a number of negative mood states—most commonly anger, guilt, shame, and anxiety (Friedman et al., 2015). Other examples of this negative state include feelings of isolation and estrangement from others, emotional numbing, and negative views about the traumatic event, the world, themselves, and their future.

ONSET

When did Max start developing symptoms? Typically, symptoms arise within 6 months after the event, except in rare cases of delayed onset (Goodwin et al., 2012). You might assess onset through open-ended questioning. Using collateral, Karen was able to pinpoint that his symptoms began almost immediately upon his return from Iraq while he was still in the hospital.

To feel confident about a diagnosis, it is best to differentiate PTSD from other disorders in the same family, which, in the F43 category, include Acute stress reaction (F43.0) and Adjustment disorder (F43.20). You can easily rule out Acute stress reaction given that Max's symptoms have lasted for quite some time—certainly longer than a few days. But could his symptoms be better conceptualized as an Adjustment disorder? Adjustment disorders are appropriate when there is an emotional disturbance that interferes with functioning and occurs following adaptation to a major life change or stressful event. Indeed, discharge from a well-structured military life and community reintegration could constitute a major life change. However, Max's symptoms have likely persisted longer than 6 months, which is the limit for an Adjustment disorder. Furthermore, in an Adjustment disorder, the symptoms should not be so severe that they would justify a more specific diagnosis (like PTSD) that involves intense distress and functional impairment. The best way to assess the severity of symptoms is with a standardized assessment instrument (e.g., the 20-item PTSD Checklist for *DSM–5* [PCL5]). Max's score of 68 on the PCL5 was significantly above the cutoff of 38, suggestive of a PTSD diagnosis according to psychometric research using this scale (Weathers et al., 2013). Furthermore, Max's descriptions of his functioning indicate high symptom severity. Thus, his symptoms rise above the level of an Adjustment disorder and are clearly appropriate for a PTSD diagnosis.

Many of the symptoms of PTSD overlap those of other mood and anxiety disorders, and ICD–10–CM should be used to identify as many disorders as are present for a patient. Furthermore, a number of problems often co-occur with PTSD, including excessive alcohol or drug use, anxiety and depression, and suicidal ideation. Complete guidance for assessment of these symptoms is available in other chapters of this volume, the application of each to the current case is briefly discussed next to augment your understanding of how co-occurring disorders might overlap with PTSD, especially given that it is extremely common for people with PTSD to meet criteria for another disorder (Friedman et al., 2015).

ALCOHOL ABUSE (F10.10)

It would be important for you to know how much alcohol Max typically uses per day and how frequently he is consuming it, as well as the frequency of hazardous (binge) drinking, especially because of the potential for alcohol use to interfere with PTSD treatment. See also Chapter 2 of this volume.

SUICIDAL IDEATION (R45.851)

Max has not reported suicidal ideation. However, given the stigma about suicide, a military culture that favors stoicism and resilience, and Max's personal difficulties with emotional disclosure, he may have simply chosen not to disclose it. People with PTSD are more likely to attempt suicide (compared with a community sample; Sareen, Houlahan, Cox, & Asmundson, 2005), so it is essential that this be explored. In addition, a population health approach, as well as VA policy, recommends screening for suicide ideation and history in any population known to be at risk by virtue of demographic variables or risk exposure. Suicide risk is not static; it can change based on life circumstances and must be periodically reevaluated, especially given that Max has some chronic risk factors for suicide, including his PTSD diagnosis and his access to firearms. See also Chapter 6 of this volume. (For more information on R codes, see Schaffer & Rodolfa, 2016, Chapter 1).

ANXIETY DISORDERS (F41.9)

Many of the symptoms described could be evidence of another anxiety disorder, including Panic disorder (F41.0), Generalized anxiety disorder (F41.1; see Chapter 8, this volume), or Social phobia (F40.1; see Chapter 7, this volume). Although Max clearly has elevated anxiety symptoms in the context of social interactions, his anxiety is not restricted to these situations because he can easily feel anxious at home as well, while driving alone in his car, and while watching action movies. Thus, social phobia does not adequately explain our observations. Similarly, although he sometimes has panic-like symptoms, they are not unpredictable. He suffers them when specifically thinking about or being confronted with situations that trigger memories of his traumatic experiences. For Max, PTSD appears to be the "primary" diagnosis because it accounts for the main reasons that he is seeking treatment at this time.

DEPRESSIVE DISORDERS (F32.9)

Given Max's negative beliefs, anhedonia (R45.84), irritability (R45.4), sleep problems (G47.9), difficulty concentrating (R41.840), self-criticism, and hopelessness, it should seem plausible that he is in the midst of a depressive episode (F32.9). We refer the reader to Chapters 5 and 6 of this volume to consider the assessment of depressive disorders.

Ethical Considerations—Protecting Your Patient

ACTIVITY 9.3:

What specific ethical issues does PTSD raise? What strategies can you implement to ensure ethical practice with Max? How might you communicate with him during assessment and treatment to promote his engagement and well-being throughout the process?

First, in addition to informing a patient about the procedures that you are about to follow and their choices in participation, you must always be cautious about the potential harm of the procedures themselves (American Psychological Association, 2017, *Ethical Principles of Psychologists and Code of Conduct* [APA Ethics Code], Principle A: Beneficence and Nonmaleficence). As noted earlier, questioning someone about his or her trauma history must be undertaken with sensitivity. Given that one of the core components of PTSD is trauma avoidance, explicit assessment of the trauma is inevitably going to increase anxiety and may even elicit highly distressing reexperiencing symptoms that could occur long after you are no longer present to provide support or soothing. Sadly, the individual may not receive symptom relief through intervention for some time. In fact, the initiation of treatment might increase distress in the short term (Foa, Zoellner, Feeny, Hembree, & Alvarez-Conrad, 2002). To mitigate the potential harm of this assessment, providing clear expectations about what information you are looking for when asking questions about a trauma, protecting against unnecessary self-disclosure about traumatic events, and assessing how the person might cope with increased symptoms after the interview are all important components of an ethical assessment of PTSD. Furthermore, if the patient does not appear to have adequate coping skills, it may be necessary, even as part of the assessment process, to provide a few quick and straightforward strategies for tolerating distress effectively (see APA, 2010, 2013). So, have some strategies prepared! Furthermore, you want to make sure that the patient has phone numbers to call in the case of increased symptoms or crisis situations, especially in the period before a firm relationship with a treatment provider has been established.

At the conclusion of an evaluation process, discussion of reasonable treatment options is another crucial component of ethical practice. Not every patient who receives treatment improves, and many patients drop out of treatment early (Steenkamp, Litz, Hoge, & Marmar, 2015). Ultimately, relaying accurate information about the advantages and limitations of treatment, in a supportive and encouraging manner, is an important step in adhering to the ethical principles of justice, integrity and respect for the patient's right to self-determination (APA Ethics Code, Principle C: Integrity, Principle D: Justice, Principle E: Respect for People's Rights and Dignity). Clearly discussing the treatment process is also an important factor in promoting initial engagement in treatment. To best prepare the patient to make an educated decision about where to go next, prepare him for what is involved, and warn him about potential pitfalls, you will need to have educated yourself on the research evidence supporting particular treatments, as well as the tasks and expectations of these treatments. Doing your best to encourage engagement in care despite potential drawbacks is critical because active treatment offers the best chance of improving life over the long term. Finally, discussing the low likelihood that symptoms will resolve on their own and contrasting this with what life might look like if meaningful symptom reduction were to occur might encourage engagement.

Risk Management—Protecting Your Patient, Protecting Yourself

ACTIVITY 9.4:

What specific risk issues are present among individuals with PTSD (F43.10)? Do you have any ethical responsibilities to ensure the well-being of Max's wife and children?

Ethical principles also have to be considered in the context of legal requirements for the profession. These can be especially challenging to manage when legal concerns are not in alignment with ethical obligations. For example, mandated reporting laws (see Schaffer & Rodolfa, 2016, pp. 115–116) could damage rapport and jeopardize engaging a patient in treatment. How can you balance the ethical demands of patient confidentiality, informed consent, protection of vulnerable populations, and legal obligations? To raise the stakes further in these matters, new legal precedents indicate that mandated reporters can be found liable for not disclosing to authorities when they have knowledge that a child could be at risk of abuse (Child Welfare Information Gateway, 2014). As a mental health provider, psychologists not only have responsibilities in child abuse situations, they also have potential reporting responsibilities in any life- or well-being-threatening situation, including the risk of suicide. As a result, you should begin your contact with patients by informing them of the exceptions to confidentiality, which include the statement that information provided by them regarding current or past child abuse or behaviors that are a risk to others or themselves might be reported to authorities, depending on the legal requirements in your jurisdiction. You may want to add that any necessary reporting would be conducted with the patient's involvement whenever possible.

Disposition

> **ACTIVITY 9.5:**
>
> What do you think is the most efficacious plan to treat this patient? What are the issues that you may confront as you decide on the patient's disposition?

So far, we have discussed various different treatment targets: Chronic PTSD (F43.10), Depression (F32.9), Alcohol abuse (F10.10), Insomnia (G47.9), and Marital distress (Z63.0). When PTSD is identified as the primary disorder, this puts it at the top of the list for treatment. Furthermore, the severity of some co-occurring disorders or problems has been shown to decrease in line with treatment for PTSD (Bisson, Roberts, Andrew, Cooper, & Lewis, 2013). Thus, given limited resources and the demands of treatment, you may decide in collaboration with the patient to observe how symptoms change after a course of treatment for PTSD rather than aim to address co-occurring symptoms at the same time, depending on the severity of the other symptoms and the likelihood that they would be affected by PTSD treatment. For example, if substance use is at a high severity level or preceded PTSD, you may look at other options for substance abuse treatment before or in conjunction with PTSD treatment (Saxon & Simpson, 2015). Numerous psychotherapeutic, pharmacological, and somatic interventions are efficacious for PTSD, with separate meta-analyses, systematic reviews, and comprehensive textbooks agreeing that cognitive and exposure-based psychotherapies have the strongest empirical support (for reviews, see, e.g., Finley et al., 2017; Foa, Keane, Friedman, & Cohen, 2009; Haagen,

Smid, Knipscheer, & Kleber, 2015; Steenkamp et al., 2015; Watts et al., 2013). However, some of these treatments also have relatively higher dropout rates (Steenkamp et al., 2015), so it may be worth discussing alternative treatments that have more limited empirical support but higher retention rates (the preceding reviews provide extensive lists of such treatments and their effects).

References

American Psychological Association. (2010). *Stress in America*. Retrieved from http://www.apa.org/helpcenter/managing-stress.aspx

American Psychological Association. (2013). *Road to resilience*. Retrieved from http://www.uis.edu/counselingcenter/wp-content/uploads/sites/87/2013/04/the_road_to_resilience.pdf

American Psychological Association. (2017). *Ethical principles of psychologists and code of conduct* (2002, Amended June 1, 2010 and January 1, 2017). Retrieved from http://www.apa.org/ethics/code/index.aspx

Bisson, J. I., Roberts, N. P., Andrew, M., Cooper, R., & Lewis, C. (2013). Psychological therapies for chronic post-traumatic stress disorder (PTSD) in adults. *Cochrane Database of Systematic Reviews, 12*, CD003388. http://dx.doi.org/10.1002/14651858.CD003388.pub4

Child Welfare Information Gateway. (2014). *Penalties for failure to report and false reporting of child abuse and neglect*. Washington, DC: Children's Bureau, U.S. Department of Health and Human Services. Retrieved from https://www.childwelfare.gov/topics/systemwide/laws-policies/statutes/report

Finley, E. P., Noël, P. H., Lee, S., Haro, E., Garcia, H., Rosen, C., & Pugh, J. A. (2017, March 16). Psychotherapy practices for veterans with PTSD among community-based providers in Texas. *Psychological Services*. Advance online publication. http://dx.doi.org/10.1037/ser0000143

Foa, E. B., Keane, T. M., Friedman, M. J., & Cohen, J. A. (2009). *Effective treatments for PTSD: Practice guidelines from the International Society for Traumatic Stress Studies* (2nd ed.). New York, NY: Guilford Press.

Foa, E. B., Zoellner, L. A., Feeny, N. C., Hembree, E. A., & Alvarez-Conrad, J. (2002). Does imaginal exposure exacerbate PTSD symptoms? *Journal of Consulting and Clinical Psychology, 70*, 1022–1028. http://dx.doi.org/10.1037/0022-006X.70.4.1022

Friedman, M. J., Keane, T. M., & Resick, P. A. (2015). *Handbook of PTSD: Science and practice* (2nd ed.). New York, NY: Guilford Press.

Goodwin, L., Jones, M., Rona, R. J., Sundin, J., Wessely, S., & Fear, N. T. (2012). Prevalence of delayed-onset posttraumatic stress disorder in military personnel: Is there evidence for this disorder? Results of a prospective UK cohort study. *Journal of Nervous and Mental Disease, 200*, 429–437. http://dx.doi.org/10.1097/NMD.0b013e31825322fe

Haagen, J. F., Smid, G. E., Knipscheer, J. W., & Kleber, R. J. (2015). The efficacy of recommended treatments for veterans with PTSD: A metaregression analysis. *Clinical Psychology Review, 40*, 184–194. http://dx.doi.org/10.1016/j.cpr.2015.06.008

National Center for PTSD. (2016). Facts about PTSD. *Psych Central.* Retrieved from https://psychcentral.com/lib/facts-about-ptsd

Sareen, J., Houlahan, T., Cox, B. J., & Asmundson, G. J. G. (2005). Anxiety disorders associated with suicidal ideation and suicide attempts in the National Comorbidity Survey. *Journal of Nervous and Mental Disease, 193,* 450–454. http://dx.doi.org/10.1097/01.nmd.0000168263.89652.6b

Saxon, A. J., & Simpson, T. L. (2015). Co-occurring substance use disorders and PTSD. In N. C. Bernardy & M. J. Friedman (Eds.), *A practical guide to PTSD treatment: Pharmacological and psychotherapeutic approaches* (pp. 135–150). Washington, DC: American Psychological Association.

Schaffer, J., & Rodolfa, E. (2016). *A student's guide to assessment and diagnosis using the ICD–10–CM: Psychological and behavioral conditions.* Washington, DC: American Psychological Association.

Steenkamp, M. M., Litz, B. T., Hoge, C. W., & Marmar, C. R. (2015). Psychotherapy for military-related PTSD: A review of randomized clinical trials. *JAMA, 314,* 489–500. http://dx.doi.org/10.1001/jama.2015.8370

Watts, B. V., Schnurr, P. P., Mayo, L., Young-Xu, Y., Weeks, W. B., & Friedman, M. J. (2013). Meta-analysis of the efficacy of treatments for posttraumatic stress disorder. *The Journal of Clinical Psychiatry, 74,* e541–e550. http://dx.doi.org/10.4088/JCP.12r08225

Weathers, F. W., Litz, B. T., Keane, T. M., Palmieri, P. A., Marx, B. P., & Schnurr, P. P. (2013). *The PTSD Checklist for DSM–5 (PCL–5).* Retrieved from the National Center for PTSD website: https://www.ptsd.va.gov/professional/assessment/adult-sr/ptsd-checklist.asp

World Health Organization. (1993). *ICD–10 classification of mental and behavioural disorders: Clinical descriptions and diagnostic guidelines.* Geneva, Switzerland: World Health Organization. Retrieved from http://www.who.int/classifications/icd/en/bluebook.pdf

Gregory A. Hinrichsen and Aliza Romirowsky

F43.2 Adjustment Disorders

10

An adjustment disorder is a condition of subjective emotional distress, typically involving depression, anxiety, or both, that follows a significant life change or stressful life event that interferes with a person's ability to function effectively. Because many older adults contend with life issues to which they are challenged to adjust, this chapter on adjustment reaction disorder focuses on this age group.

Each day about 10,000 members of the so-called baby boomer generation turn 65 years of age. By 2030, about 20% of the U.S. population will be 65 years of age or older (Karel, Gatz, & Smyer, 2012). Many European nations and Japan will also have historically high proportions of older adults. Surprisingly to many, the rates of almost all mental disorders, including depression, are lower in older adults than in younger adults. Furthermore, surveys show that older adults are happier than younger adults (Carstensen, Fung, & Charles, 2003). The one mental disorder that is more common in older versus younger adults is dementia, a progressive loss of mental abilities. The most common ICD–10–CM mental disorders related to cognitive decline in older adults are Alzheimer's disease (G30.0 and F02.8) and Vascular dementia (F01.5).

Among older people seeking psychological services, depression and anxiety are frequently expressed concerns. Often depression or anxiety is preceded

http://dx.doi.org/10.1037/0000069-011
An ICD–10–CM Casebook and Workbook for Students: Psychological and Behavioral Conditions, J. B. Schaffer and E. Rodolfa (Editors)

by ongoing or emerging life issues, many of which are health related. As we age, we are more likely to have medical problems, particularly chronic medical problems. Adjustment disorders related to health problems, care for someone with health or cognitive problems, or death of an important person are commonly seen in clinical practice with older adults.

The Case

You work in a geriatric primary care medical clinic. One of the geriatricians (medical doctors who specialize in work with older people) told you that her patient, Mr. Brooks, a 77-year-old White man, appeared to be depressed and having problems dealing with the death of his wife. The geriatrician said that Mr. Brooks's daughter called and stated that her father "needed to be on an antidepressant." The geriatrician was reluctant to add another medication to the many Mr. Brooks was already taking and asked you to evaluate him for psychological services. The geriatrician's reluctance likely reflected broader concerns in the field of geriatric medicine about the possible adverse effects of older adults taking many medications—often called *polypharmacy* (Arnold, 2008).

You set up a first appointment with Mr. Brooks to gather information. Mr. Brooks tells you that he had been providing care for his wife for about ten years because she was diagnosed with early onset Alzheimer's disease (without behavioral disturbance; G30.0, F02.80). At first his wife was merely forgetful, but problems grew increasingly worse over the years. She had died about five months before this first appointment. He feels that he has been coping with things the best he could and is annoyed that his daughter had called the geriatrician to say he needed to see a mental health care provider. "She should stay out of my business," he remarks with some irritation. Mr. Brooks agreed to see you only because he liked and trusted his geriatrician. Mr. Brooks immediately impresses you as a very independent person.

Mr. Brooks acknowledges that in the past 5 months, he has experienced grief over the loss of his wife. "That's normal, right, doc?" He also says he has been feeling sad, "down in the dumps," not as interested in things as he was before, and discouraged. There are some "good days," but he wishes there were more. He doesn't function as well as he used to but says he doesn't have much to do anyway. He has begun to worry about his own health and the well-being of his grandchildren ("I'm turning into some sort of worry wart").

He acknowledges that the years of providing help to his wife had been stressful for him. "It turned into a full-time job," he remarks. He catalogues the many things he needed to do for his wife as her dementia worsened: taking her to doctors, making sure she took her medications, managing the bills, and doing the lion's share of meal preparation. As time went on, the list of his "job" responsibilities increased: help with bathing and toileting and managing his wife's confusion and occasional emotional agitation. When his wife became bedbound, he got part-time assistance at home. "Then the next part of my job was an employer of home health aides," he says. The year before his wife died, she resided in a nursing home. He visited his wife daily to make sure she received the care he felt she deserved. Despite these many responsibilities, Mr. Brooks speaks with pride that he had taken care of his wife. "Family takes care of family." Despite his wife's increasing cognitive impairment, a new kind of closeness developed in their relationship during this time. He believes that he did well in the many tasks of being a caregiver. He says it was surprising that, in many ways, he found care for his wife rewarding. He thinks a lot about their years together and, despite the ups and downs of their relationship, believes that he was lucky to have shared his life with such a good companion.

Notably, Mr. Brooks took an active role in his local chapter of the Alzheimer's Association, a national support and advocacy group. At one point, he was vice president of the group and organized fundraising events for it. Mr. Brooks said he was good at organizing and running things. In fact, he had run his own successful accounting firm for many years and at one time had 30 employees. He worked part-time during the early years of his wife's dementia but then retired to "my other job" in providing help to his wife. His daughter offered to help with her mother's care, but Mr. Brooks felt he could manage much of it by himself. With the exception of his involvement with the Alzheimer's Association, he lost contact with friends and family. Previously, he had been an avid racquetball player, a member of the Rotary Club (a service organization), and a member of his church. Over the course of providing care to his wife, he stopped doing all of these activities.

In the month after his wife's death, Mr. Brooks kept busy with the many practical responsibilities that often follow the death of a spouse. Then "I ran out of things to do," he recalls. He stopped visiting his wife's grave every week because he believed he was coming to terms with her loss. Now that he was no longer a caregiver, he found involvement in the Alzheimer's Association less helpful. He has increased visits to his daughter, but her now-grown children have less interest in spending time with him than they did when they were younger. He feels he has to push himself to get out of the house. "But once I'm out, I don't have much to do. How much time can you spend at the grocery store?" Feeling "down in the dumps" worried, discouraged, and lacking motivation are new and perplexing experiences for him. He describes feeling confused by how he had been such a good caregiver but now had difficulty taking care of himself. "I don't know what to do. And I'm not going to have my daughter run my life either."

Assessment and Diagnosis Using the ICD–10–CM

ACTIVITY 10.1:

What seems to be the apparent precipitant(s) of the patient's depressive and anxiety symptoms? Do you have any initial thoughts about his relationship with his daughter?

As with an assessment of younger adults, you gather basic factual information (e.g., age, marital/partner status, education, ethnic/racial/gender identification, sexual orientation), past and current mental health history, medical status, current medications, history of current problems, past life history, and assessment of risk for harm to self or others. These data provide a foundation for making an accurate diagnosis and subsequently a treatment plan. Given the increased prevalence of health and cognitive problems in older adults, it is important to devote more time to assessment of those issues than is often the case with younger adults (American Psychological Association [APA], 2014; Edelstein, Martin, & Gerolimatos, 2013). For Mr. Brooks, you would want to know his current medical problems and current medications. Even when other professionals work in the same agency, you want to obtain informed consent—and often written permission—to contact the other professional to verify or augment information provided by the patient. In medical circumstances, this information may be important because sometimes medical problems or medications prescribed for the patient are the cause of mental health symptoms. Also, you would do a brief screen of the patient's cognitive functioning, given an increased risk for cognitive difficulties in older adults. Several brief psychometrically sound cognitive screening instruments exist, including the Montreal Cognitive Assessment and the Mini-Mental State Examination (Nasreddine et al., 2005; Tombaugh, McDowell, Kristjansson, & Hubley, 1996). Cognitive screening instruments sometimes reveal mild cognitive problems that are not otherwise evident. If the cognitive screen suggested problems, the patient would be more formally evaluated for possible cognitive disorders or referred to a neuropsychologist for such an evaluation.

ICD–10–CM Diagnosis

ACTIVITY 10.2:

Given this information, what are the possible ICD–10–CM diagnoses? How would input from Mr. Brooks's geriatrician inform your diagnosis? What additional information might you seek from his geriatrician?

A first diagnostic question is whether Mr. Brooks has a medical condition (including polypharmacy) that might explain or partially explain the onset of symptoms of depression and anxiety. Although it is likely his geriatrician would have ruled this out as an explanation, further consultation with the geriatrician might be indicated, both to clarify questions about any medical conditions or medications and to gain her perspective of his past functioning, view of self and others, response to stress, and usual emotional state. There is, for example, the possibility of ICD–10–CM Mood disorder due to known physiological condition (F06.3x) and Anxiety disorder due to known physiological condition (F06.4). If a medical explanation for Mr. Brooks's symptoms of depression and anxiety is ruled out, the next step is to characterize the nature and severity of his depressive symptoms.

Were Mr. Brooks's depressive symptoms severe and persistent enough to meet ICD–10–CM criteria for a Major depressive disorder (F32.x)? If so, were the symptoms consistent with a mild, moderate, or severe depressive episode with or without psychotic symptoms (F32.0, F32.1, F32.2, F32.3)? If he had past depressive episodes, Major depressive disorder, recurrent (F33.x) of relevant severity might also be indicated. Furthermore, has there been one or more manic episode (F30.x) in the past (see Chapter 4, this volume), in which case, Bipolar disorder (F31.xx) would be considered? For Mr. Brooks, there was no evidence of a past history of any mental disorder, nor did he describe or exhibit any psychotic symptoms.

As Mr. Brooks reported, he has feelings of grief, sadness, feeling "down in the dumps," discouragement, and loss of interest in things. He reports doing less than he did before. But he does say he has "good days." ICD–10–CM does not consider grief to be a mental disorder because the experience of grief is considered a normal and expected response to the loss of an important person. Would being "sad" and "down in the dumps" be considered the equivalent of depressed mood? It would be helpful to clarify further with Mr. Brooks the meaning of these descriptors. If "sad" meant for him feelings similar to grief, it would not be considered a depression equivalent, but people use different language to characterize affective states, including what mental health professionals would consider "depression." Each cohort of adults has its own generational language to describe emotional states, as well as comfort with sharing feelings of emotional distress. Efforts to clarify further the meaning of "down in the dumps" might include providing alternative ways of describing depression, such as: "Do you feel hopeless?" "Do you feel helpless to change things?" "Do you feel happy?" "Are you in good spirits?" Questions like these are included in the Geriatric Depression Rating Scale (Yesavage et al., 1982), which has been normed on older adults. On the basis of Mr. Brooks's report, you conclude that he indeed has depressive symptoms.

The duration of his symptoms is additional information that is important in making a diagnosis in the ICD–10–CM. Depressive symptoms appeared to begin in the month after his wife died and have continued into the present for a total duration of about 4 months. This duration of depressive symptoms would rule out Dysthymic disorder (F34.1) because this diagnosis requires a 2-year period of ongoing depressive symptoms. To meet even the mildest form of Major depressive disorder, Mr. Brooks would have had to experience at least two of the following symptoms for at least 2 weeks: daily depressed mood for most of the day, loss of interest in activities he used to enjoy, and decreased energy. He would also need to have experienced at least two of the following symptoms, for a combined total of four or more symptoms: low self-esteem, excessive feelings of guilt, suicidal thinking, difficulty concentrating, psychomotor disturbance, and changes in sleep (World Health Organization, 1993). Although Mr. Brooks evidences some depressive symptoms, he does not have a sufficient number of sustained symptoms to meet criteria for mild (F32.0), moderate (F.32.1), or a nonpsychotic (F32.2) severe Major depressive episode.

Mr. Brooks reports increased worrying, so let's consider the possibility of an anxiety disorder. Does he have symptoms of anxiety that might be consistent with an anxiety disorder? Of most interest would be whether he meets criteria for Generalized anxiety disorder (F41.1), which involves excessive worry about numerous topics and the experience of distressing physical symptoms of anxiety (e.g., excessive sweating, racing heart) that last for at least 6 months. If no additional symptoms of anxiety were present, the person would not meet criteria for generalized anxiety disorder, which appears to be the case with Mr. Brooks.

At this point in the diagnostic process, two diagnoses appeared to be the best candidates to characterize his symptom picture: Other mixed anxiety disorder (F41.3) and Adjustment disorders (F43.2). The patient does have mixed anxiety and depression. However, he clearly indicates that anxiety and depressive symptoms were preceded by a psychosocial stressor, the death of his wife. Therefore, an adjustment disorder appears to be the best diagnostic category to consider.

ICD–10–CM adjustment disorders require that there is a psychosocial stressor within a month of the onset of symptoms. As noted earlier, Mr. Brooks has subthreshold symptoms of depression and anxiety and evidences change in his behavior: He is less interested and less engaged in activities and, in fact, is doing less than usual. Therefore, two subtypes of adjustment disorder seem relevant: Adjustment disorder with mixed anxiety and depressed mood (F43.23) and Adjustment disorder with mixed disturbance of emotions and conduct (F43.25). Mixed disturbance of emotions and conduct includes "both emotional symptoms and disturbances of conduct," which commonly refers to aggressive or dissocial behaviors. Anxiety and depression would be considered "emotional symptoms." Would Mr. Brooks's difficulties with functioning be considered a disturbance of conduct? This would be a clinical judgment. For the purposes of this discussion, let us assume that you have concluded that Mr. Brooks's current functioning, compared with his previous high level of functioning, would be considered significant enough to be characterized as a "disturbance of conduct." Therefore, the final diagnosis for Mr. Brooks would be Adjustment disorder with mixed disturbance of emotions and conduct (F43.25).

Sometimes you believe you need more information than was gleaned in an initial interview to confidently make an ICD–10–CM diagnosis. As stated earlier, consultation with the referring geriatrician may provide useful information. When appropriate, and with the patient's consent, family members may have useful perspectives to offer. One diagnostic challenge for evaluating patients who have experienced a recent (or even more remote) loss is disentanglement of "normal" feelings of grief from symptoms of depression, about which there is ongoing discussion in the mental health field (Shear et al., 2011).

Ethical Considerations—Protecting Your Patient

In addition to the laws and statutes that govern practice in individual states, APA's (2017) *Ethical Principles of Psychologists and Code of Conduct* (APA Ethics Code) guides your professional activities. In working with older adults, it is also helpful to consider APA's (2014) "Guidelines for Psychological Practice With Older Adults" and *Ethical Practice in Geropsychology* by Bush, Allen, and Molinari (2017). The APA Guidelines are intended to assist psychologists in evaluating their own readiness for working with older adults and in seeking and using appropriate education and training to increase their knowledge, skills, and experience relevant to this area of practice. Most relevant to ethical issues is Guideline 19: "Psychologists strive to understand the special ethical and/or legal issues entailed in providing services to older adults." Several of the principles are worth discussing in this case.

BOUNDARIES OF COMPETENCE

With the growing numbers of older adults in the U.S. population, psychologists are more likely to be referred older adults than in the past. Psychologists generally trained to work with adults will likely possess the requisite skills to assess and treat many of the issues brought by older adults, but in complicated cases the patient may require the services of or consultation with a professional geropsychologist (see APA Ethics Code, Standard 2.01b, Boundaries of Competence). APA's (2014) "Guidelines for Psychological Practice With Older Adults" provides an overview of the domains of attitudes, knowledge, and skills that best prepare psychologists to provide professional services to older adults. Psychologists who serve older adults will benefit from a review of these guidelines. Because in this scenario you are considered a geropsychologist, you possess the needed skills. However, if Mr. Brooks had evidenced significant cognitive deficits and you did not have experience in use of neuropsychological measures, you would best refer the patient to a neuropsychologist (and also likely a neurologist) for further evaluation.

ACTIVITY 10.3:

After your first appointment with Mr. Brooks, his daughter called you and gave you information about her father that she thought would be helpful and asked for your assessment. What information can you provide?

MAINTAINING CONFIDENTIALITY AND DISCLOSURE OF INFORMATION

Older adults often seek psychological services at the behest of another person. A common scenario is that an adult child urges the older person to see a psychologist because of concerns about his or her emotional or cognitive well-being. Even when the patient is in your office because of a concerned adult child, however, for you to share any information with that adult child, you must obtain permission from the patient. Sometimes providers casually speak with adult children or other providers without getting formal consent from the patient. The clinician may assume that the family member has the patient's best interests in mind, which may or may not be the case. The patient still has a right to consent or deny consent to sharing of information (see APA Ethics Code Standards 4.01, Maintaining Confidentiality, and 4.05, Disclosures). Without a formal consent for sharing information, the health care provider is breaching confidentiality, which can create legal, regulatory, and ethical problems for the psychologist. Nonetheless, family members can provide helpful information about the patient's current and past strengths and problems; they are often allies in effective treatment of the older patient. When a patient does not want to give consent for sharing information or coordinating care with a concerned family member, it is helpful to understand the reasons for that. For example, a patient may have long-standing conflict with the family member that could be a focus of treatment. This complex issue shows how discussions regarding informed consent and other ethical issues often involve broader relational and treatment considerations.

USE OF ASSESSMENT INSTRUMENTS

A challenge for psychologists assessing older adults is using instruments that are valid and reliable for that group. Formal psychometric data do not exist for many instruments for older adults. A growing body of professional work has identified some assessment instruments and procedures for older persons that are valid and reliable. A psychologist who provides assessment services to older adults on a regular basis needs to be familiar with those instruments. When using instruments that have not been validated for older adults, conclusions drawn should take into account the possible limitations of the validity of such data (see APA Ethics Code, Standard 9.02, Use of Assessments).

CAPACITY TO GIVE CONSENT

It should be assumed that older adults have the capacity to give consent for evaluation, treatment, and sharing of information. However, this is sometimes not the case. Psychologists are periodically called on to evaluate one or more aspects of capacity in older people, for example, whether the individual is capable of managing his or her own medical, financial, or legal affairs. For some patients, questions of capacity arise in the course of doing an assessment for reasons other than cognitive ability (e.g., depression, anxiety, sleep problems). When working with individuals for whom there are questions about capacity to give consent, it is important to provide an explanation to the patient of the assessment process, obtain the individual's assent to that process (which is generally a verbal and positive agreement), take into consideration the individual's best interests and preferences, and follow any legal requirements (see APA Ethics Code Standard 3.10; APA, 2017).

Risk Management—Protecting Your Client, Protecting Yourself

ACTIVITY 10.4:

What are your thoughts about working with an older patient like Mr. Brooks? Does the case prompt thoughts about the aging of your parents or your own aging? If you are younger, might you feel any discomfort helping someone much older than yourself?

Bush et al. (2017, Chapter 2) pointed out that everyone has some preconceptions, whether positive or negative, about the aging process. Psychologists are not immune from ageist beliefs that might influence how we interact with older patients. Positive experiences with older relatives can facilitate rapport building with older patients, whereas negative perceptions of aging can impair clinical judgment (Bush et al., 2017). Allowing biases or your own personal issues or problems to influence your practice can expose you to an accusation of unethical and incompetent practice (see APA Ethics Code, Standards 2.06, Personal Problems and Conflicts, and 3.01, Unfair Discrimination). To ensure that psychologists assess and treat older patients in an ethical and competent manner, it is imperative to develop an awareness of our ageist beliefs, including how those beliefs might influence our work. Proper education, training, and supervised experience when practicing with older patients is one important mechanism of risk management (see APA Ethics Code, Standard 2.01a).

DOCUMENTATION OF PRIVACY AND CONSENT

In addition to regulatory and ethical considerations, the Health Insurance Portability and Accountability Act of 1996 (HIPAA), a U.S. federal law, sets standards for safeguarding patients' confidential information. Institutions typically have processes in place for educating providers about those provisions and following requirements. Independent practitioners who are "covered entities" are also required to follow HIPAA provisions. For example, providers are required to create written privacy protections and document that a copy of these protections has been offered to new patients. HIPAA rules govern what the practitioner is required to do if privacy protections are breached.

CLINICAL DOCUMENTATION

Complete clinical documentation is not only ethical but also reduces the likelihood of denial of insurance claims and the occurrence of legal or regulatory problems. For example, for psychologists, Medicare requires that patients be asked whether the primary medical provider may be contacted. The rationale is that this coordination of care benefits the patients. Whether or not the patient gives permission, this effort must be documented. Patient visits must be documented each time. A record of release of patient records and documentation of consent must be maintained. Requirements for what information must be documented are informed by APA ethics, state regulations, and requirements of those entities that pay for services. Making sure you understand such requirements and remain informed about any changes is one important way of protecting yourself from legal or regulatory action.

REPORTING REQUIREMENTS

In some states, psychologists are legally mandated to report concerns about possible elder abuse, neglect, or maltreatment. This can create a tricky balance between requirements to maintain confidentiality and requirements to report. Careful consultation, including with an attorney knowledgeable in health care law, can be helpful.

Disposition

ACTIVITY 10.5:

What treatment models would be useful to you as you develop intervention plans for Mr. Brooks? Do you think antidepressant medication might help relieve Mr. Brooks's symptoms?

You judged that Mr. Brooks would benefit by time-limited psychotherapy to facilitate better adaptation to his new life circumstances because clinical research studies have found that most older people respond as well to psychotherapy as younger people (Scogin & Shah, 2012). In most instances of such an adjustment disorder, antidepressant medication does not appear to be indicated.

In a feedback session, you told the patient you believed he had difficulties adjusting not only to the loss of his wife but to the loss of his long-standing role as a caregiver. Often, individuals providing care to an infirm family member for years reduce involvement with others and limit engagement in previously enjoyable activities and become full-time caregivers—a phenomenon sometimes called *role engulfment*. The death of the family member may then leave the caregiver with the challenge of reclaiming former involvements ("roles") or establishing new involvements (Skaff & Pearlin, 1992). Mr. Brooks had normal and expected feelings of grief about his wife's loss. Feelings of depression, anxiety, discouragement, and having to push himself to get things done were part of a condition that the mental health professional calls an "adjustment disorder." He was in a transition in his life and in some ways was getting stuck—and depression and anxiety were making it more difficult for him to move on in his life.

You proposed that the patient take part in a time-limited psychotherapy called interpersonal psychotherapy (IPT; Hinrichsen & Clougherty, 2006). IPT is based on the idea that life problems sometimes result in depression and that depression itself becomes its own problem because depressed people often feel "down," do less, think more negatively, and have other emotional and behavioral problems. Almost 40 years of research has found that IPT is useful in the treatment of depression in adults (Cuijpers et al., 2011). In recent years, research has also found IPT to be helpful for older adults (Hinrichsen & Iselin, 2014; van Schaik et al., 2006). In the treatment of depression, IPT is typically conducted over 16 sessions. The goal of the treatment to reduce depression and improve the patient's ability to contend with the life issue or issues tied to the depression. The four IPT problem areas include interpersonal role disputes (conflict with others), role transitions (life changes), grief (complicated bereavement), and interpersonal deficits (individuals who have problems initiating and/or sustaining relationships). IPT outlines goals and strategies for each of these problem areas and uses a variety of techniques to implement them. The role of the therapist is active, collaborative, and supportive. The therapist helps the patient to understand better the interpersonally relevant problem(s) tied to the depression, generate options address the problem, and then make efforts to improve the problem. Unlike cognitive behavior therapy, IPT does not use written structured worksheets and specific homework assignments, nor does it facilitate the identification of negative cognitions and change of those cognitions. IPT often focuses on improvement of current relationships that are tied to the onset or exacerbation of depression and on expression of affect tied to life changes. IPT is especially well-suited to the problems often seen with depressed older adults in clinical practice (Hinrichsen & Clougherty, 2006).

References

American Psychological Association. (2014). Guidelines for psychological practice with older adults. *American Psychologist, 69*, 34–65. http://dx.doi.org/10.1037/a0035063

American Psychological Association. (2017). *Ethical principles of psychologists and code of conduct* (2002, Amended June 1, 2010 and January 1, 2017). Retrieved from http://www.apa.org/ethics/code/index.aspx

Arnold, M. (2008). Polypharmacy and older adults: A role for psychology and psychologists. *Professional Psychology: Research and Practice, 39*, 283–289. http://dx.doi.org/10.1037/0735-7028.39.3.283

Bush, S. S., Allen, R. S., & Molinari, V. A. (2017). *Ethical practice in geropsychology*. http://dx.doi.org/10.1037/0000010-000

Carstensen, L. L., Fung, H. H., & Charles, S. T. (2003). Socioemotional selectivity theory and the regulation of emotion in the second half of life. *Motivation and Emotion, 27*, 103–123. http://dx.doi.org/10.1023/A:1024569803230

Cuijpers, P., Geraedts, A. S., van Oppen, P., Andersson, G., Markowitz, J. C., & van Straten, A. (2011). Interpersonal psychotherapy for depression: A meta-analysis. *The American Journal of Psychiatry, 168*, 581–592. http://dx.doi.org/10.1176/appi.ajp.2010.10101411

Edelstein, B. A., Martin, R. R., & Gerolimatos, L. A. (2013). Assessment in geriatric settings. In J. R. Graham, J. A. Naglieri, & I. B. Weiner (Eds.), *Handbook of psychology: Vol. 10. Assessment psychology* (2nd ed., pp. 425–447). Hoboken, NJ: Wiley.

Health Insurance Portability and Accountability Act of 1996 (HIPAA), Public Law 104-191.

Hinrichsen, G. A., & Clougherty, K. F. (2006). *Interpersonal psychotherapy for depressed older adults.* http://dx.doi.org/10.1037/11429-000

Hinrichsen, G. A., & Iselin, M.-G. (2014). Interpersonal psychotherapy. In N. A. Pachana & K. Laidlaw (Eds.), *Oxford handbook of geropsychology* (pp. 622–636). Oxford, England: Oxford University Press.

Karel, M. J., Gatz, M., & Smyer, M. A. (2012). Aging and mental health in the decade ahead: What psychologists need to know. *American Psychologist, 67*, 184–198. http://dx.doi.org/10.1037/a0025393

Nasreddine, Z. S., Phillips, N. A., Bédirian, V., Charbonneau, S., Whitehead, V., Collin, I., . . . Chertkow, H. (2005). The Montreal Cognitive Assessment, MoCA: A brief screening tool for mild cognitive impairment. *Journal of the American Geriatrics Society, 53,* 695–699. http://dx.doi.org/10.1111/j.1532-5415.2005.53221.x

Scogin, F., & Shah, A. (Eds.). (2012). *Making evidence-based psychological treatments work with older adults.* http://dx.doi.org/10.1037/13753-000

Shear, M. K., Simon, N., Wall, M., Zisook, S., Neimeyer, R., Duan, N., . . . Keshaviah, A. (2011). Complicated grief and related bereavement issues for *DSM–5. Depression and Anxiety, 28,* 103–117. http://dx.doi.org/10.1002/da.20780

Skaff, M. M., & Pearlin, L. I. (1992). Caregiving: Role engulfment and the loss of self. *The Gerontologist, 32,* 656–664. http://dx.doi.org/10.1093/geront/32.5.656

Tombaugh, T. N., McDowell, I., Kristjansson, B., & Hubley, A. M. (1996). Mini-Mental State Examination (MMSE) and the Modified MMSE (3MS): A psychometric comparison and normative data. *Psychological Assessment, 8,* 48–59. http://dx.doi.org/10.1037/1040-3590.8.1.48

van Schaik, A., van Marwijk, H., Adèr, H., van Dyck, R., de Haan, M., Penninx, B., . . . Beekman, A. (2006). Interpersonal psychotherapy for elderly patients in primary care. *The American Journal of Geriatric Psychiatry, 14,* 777–786. http://dx.doi.org/10.1097/01.JGP.0000199341.25431.4b

World Health Organization. (1993). *ICD–10 classification of mental and behavioural disorders: Clinical descriptions and diagnostic guidelines.* Geneva, Switzerland: Author. Retrieved from http://www.who.int/classifications/icd/en/bluebook.pdf

Yesavage, J. A., Brink, T. L., Rose, T. L., Lum, O., Huang, V., Adey, M., & Leirer, V. O. (1982). Development and validation of a geriatric depression screening scale: A preliminary report. *Journal of Psychiatric Research, 17,* 37–49. http://dx.doi.org/10.1016/0022-3956(82)90033-4

Lauren Bigham and Ryan E. Breshears

F45 Somatoform Disorder

11

S omatoform disorders (F45.0–45.9) are characterized by a presentation of multiple physical symptoms, typically recurring and often changing, with significant functional impairment, including social dysfunction and occupational difficulties. These symptoms occur in the absence of objective positive medical findings or medical findings insufficient to account for them. Because of increased primary care and specialty visits, emergency department visits, hospital admissions, and higher inpatient and outpatient costs, researchers estimate that somatization alone results in $256 billion a year in medical care costs (Barsky, Orav, & Bates, 2005). Patients with somatization are more likely to be female, non-White, and less educated (Allen & Woolfolk, 2010), with comorbidity with anxiety and depressive disorders 3.3 times more likely than expected by chance (de Waal, Arnold, Eekhof, & van Hemert, 2004).

Few psychiatric conditions perpetuate the level of diagnostic confusion as much as those subsumed under this diagnostic category, with reported prevalence rates ranging between 16% and 29% (de Waal et al., 2004; Fink, Sørensen, Engberg, Holm, & Munk-Jørgensen, 1999; Roca et al., 2009). The term *somatoform* is derived from the root word *soma*, Greek for body, and *forma*, or Latin for form. Somatoform conveys the notion that a psychological concern can guise itself in the form of bodily complaints (Kirmayer, 1996). As neuropsychology and clinical health psychology subspecialties continue to

http://dx.doi.org/10.1037/0000069-012
An ICD–10–CM Casebook and Workbook for Students: Psychological and Behavioral Conditions, J. B. Schaffer and E. Rodolfa (Editors)

grow and as psychologists continue to increase their presence in medical settings, accurate identification of somatoform disorders is of increased importance.

The Case

Working as a psychologist in private practice and specializing in clinical health psychology, you receive a referral from a primary care physician (PCP), Dr. Thomas. Referred for treatment of depression, Mary is a 26-year-old, married, White woman with 16 years of education and no children. At the onset of her first visit, you clarify the patient's presenting concerns and her expectations of the visit. Mary describes her perspective as follows.

Mary: My health is declining, and none of my doctors know why. I've been to all kinds of specialists, and I'm just so tired of it all. This has been going on for 2 years now, and it's frustrating for me, my husband, everyone. I hardly have a life anymore. My whole life has become focused on solving this problem. I just don't know what to do, but I want answers. I'm not sure why I'm even here, and Dr. Thomas didn't really explain, but he said I'm depressed and told me to come see you. I know you think I sound crazy, but I'm not.

You: I can appreciate the frustration and stress of this uncertainty over the past 2 years. I can also empathize with how confusing it is to have been referred to a psychologist when you're having these physical problems. Maybe it would be helpful if I first clarified what I do. As a clinical health psychologist, with board certification, I specialize in working with people who have medical conditions, health-related problems, or even stress that is affecting their physical health. So, this might be different from what would normally come to mind when you hear the term *psychologist*. The fact that you're here despite your confusion about the purpose is a testament to your commitment to improving your quality of life. At the end of today's visit, I would like us to talk about the ways in which I might be able to help you, as well as my limitations. My goals are to help make your world bigger and improve your quality of life. Does that give you a better sense of what I do and how I might be helpful to you?

Mary: Yes.

You: Since you've given me a glimpse into some of what has been going on, I think we need to focus more attention on the health problems you've experienced over the past couple of years. It would, however, also be helpful for me to get a better sense of who you are, so I would like to ask some general questions about your background before we hone in on recent events.

You proceed with the clinical interview and learn the following from Mary. She is the youngest of three children. Describing her childhood as favorable and denying any traumatic experiences, she acknowledges that her parents' divorce when she was 12 years old was "tough." After the divorce, Mary was raised by her mother (whom she describes as "direct and rule-oriented"), and contact with her father was limited. Her mother's commitment to the custodial arrangement, her father's remarriage shortly after the divorce, and his occupational demands were identified barriers to contact. Despite limited time with him, Mary notes that her father "has always been someone I can go to for help."

Outside of her parents' divorce, Mary reports an unremarkable (not contributory) childhood or developmental history. After high school, Mary enrolled in a state university where she earned an undergraduate degree in business and accounting. Since college, Mary has worked as an entry-level accountant for a small health care company. Despite two attempts, she has not passed her certified public accounting exam, which she describes as "embarrassing." Mary also reports that she is stressed about the recent buyout of her company and worries that her lack of certification will make her vulnerable to job loss. Given her perceived lack of professional achievement, Mary acknowledges that she feels inferior to her siblings and parents.

Mary's father is an attorney in a large and distinguished law firm, and her mother is a certified public accountant and business owner. Mary's brother, 6 years older than she, is a medical resident in orthopedics. Her other brother, 4 years her senior, is employed in pharmaceutical sales. Mary notes that her most significant achievement to date is her marriage to John, whom she met in college. Currently employed as an emergency medical technician, John is in the process of applying to medical school. Mary explains that John is often preoccupied with work and studying and indicates that her health problems have resulted in increased stress in their relationship.

Apart from migraines, Mary reports a relatively unremarkable medical history throughout childhood and adolescence. With onset around age 11, the migraines have persisted with variable frequency, intensity, and functional impact for 15 years. Although menstruation is a chronic trigger, Mary's migraines have historically intensified during times of stress (e.g., during the months before graduating from college). In consultation with her PCP, neurology established a preventive and acute pharmacotherapy regimen, which Mary has followed for 8 years.

Mary reports experiencing recurrent and poorly managed migraine symptoms, debilitating nausea, and generalized fatigue over the past 24 months, symptoms that have had an impact on her ability to function effectively. She misses work frequently, struggles to complete chores around the house, and has become more disengaged from social activities and former hobbies, such as attending aerobics classes. Despite seeking medical treatment on numerous occasions, Mary explains that she has not found a treatment that successfully mitigates her nausea or fatigue. Exasperated, she notes that instead of improvement, she has experienced other physical symptoms, none of which have been traced to a singular cause. During her most recent primary care visit, Mary reports that she became tearful with frustration and sadness. As a result, Dr. Thomas prescribed her 10 mg of escitalopram (Lexapro) for depression and referred her to you.

When reflecting on her medical experiences to date, Mary remarks that she has "lost track" and cannot remember the number of times that she has sought out medical treatment. Despite marked frustration stemming from the perceived failure of medical providers to diagnose and treat her condition, Mary states that she refuses to concede and remains motivated to find a cure. She denies any personal or family history of depression, anxiety, suicidal ideation, alcohol abuse, use of illicit substances, or misuse of prescribed medications. On further inquiry regarding depressive or anxious symptomatology, Mary normalizes her reaction in Dr. Thomas's office, stating, "I felt so frustrated, and I just had a meltdown. Anyone who has been through what I've been through would have done the same thing in that situation." Upon further inquiry, Mary admits that she has felt more down, and even depressed, as a result of her health concerns.

Assessment Using the ICD–10–CM

ACTIVITY 11.1:

Do you have enough information from her medical history to confidently diagnose Mary? What other information would you need, and which assessments would be helpful in collecting it? When performing a medical record review with Mary, what questions would you ask to develop further diagnostic hypotheses and conclusions?

By the end of the intake interview, you question the diagnostic validity of depression as the primary problem. It appears that Mary's presenting concern and corresponding distress stem from her physical ailments, particularly her headaches, nausea, and fatigue, and the functional capacities that she has lost due to her perception of their severity. However, you are also hesitant to take Mary's stated background information as sufficient to render a conclusive diagnosis. As Mary acknowledged an incomplete description of her medical history, you are uncertain of the etiology of her symptomatology and whether is it secondary to a primary medical condition, an underlying psychiatric problem, or both.

To ensure diagnostic accuracy, you begin by identifying important elements and major themes. You note Mary's insistence on the physical cause of her problems, her frustration with the inadequacy of her health care providers, her perceived status degradation compared with her siblings and parents, her perceived vulnerability to further status degradation via possible loss of employment, and her psychological needs for order, understanding, and shame avoidance. You appraise other sources of information from the clinical interview, including Mary's emotional valence (characterized by frustration and exasperation), the well-organized structure of her thoughts, and the extent of rumination and obsession about her physical health and symptoms.

Using these initial impressions and observations, you hypothesize that Mary could be manifesting symptomatology consistent with a Somatoform disorder (F45.x). To be able to confirm or rule out Somatoform disorder, you recognize the need for a more complete understanding of Mary's medical history. Before the conclusion of the intake, you and Mary discuss the need to gather more information. You discuss with her the value and potential disadvantages of your consulting other professionals, and she agrees to sign a release of information (ROI) to allow you and Dr. Thomas to consult, both to share and receive information relevant to her case. Mary also agrees to bring in her medical record for review during her next appointment. You are inclined to administer a brief psychological testing battery to corroborate or objectively dispute your subjective impressions of Mary's psychological and personality functioning.

CONSULTATION

During your brief consultation with Dr. Thomas, he expresses his concerns and provides an overview of the past 2 years. He notes Mary's seeming inability to focus on anything other than her health symptoms and the need to find an efficacious medical treatment. Moreover, Dr. Thomas reports that he has "exhausted every conceivable possibility" to determine a physiological cause for Mary's symptoms.

RECORD REVIEW

Mary's medical record reveals the following sequence. Two years ago, her headache frequency increased over the time span of 1 month. Mary saw her neurologist, who increased her beta-blocker to limit the frequency of such migraines. One month later, Mary saw her PCP with the complaint of unremitting nausea and fatigue. Surmising that her symptoms could be side effects of her increased beta-blocker, Dr. Thomas prescribed ondansetron (Zofran) to help treat the nausea. Over the subsequent 6 weeks, Mary sought out medical treatment twice more. She returned to Dr. Thomas and reported continued symptoms of nausea and fatigue. She described the Zofran as unhelpful and discontinued the medication after 2 days. Appropriate and routine testing performed by Dr. Thomas identified no cause to explain Mary's symptoms. Mary then presented to the hospital emergency department with reports of abdominal pain and vomiting. Again, after appropriate and routine testing, no cause for these symptoms was identified.

Approximately 12 months after Mary's initial visit to Dr. Thomas, she presented again to her PCP. Her nausea remained, and she reported concerns of chest pain, breathlessness without exertion, as well as numbness and tingling in her upper extremities. Dr. Thomas referred Mary to a cardiologist for further evaluation. Unable to determine a cause for Mary's reported symptomology, the cardiologist referred her back to her PCP. During the past 10 months, Mary saw Dr. Thomas an additional six times with unremitting yet variable symptoms lacking convergence.

PSYCHOLOGICAL TESTING

The importance of forethought regarding the sequencing of diagnostic tests is sometimes overlooked or minimized. In cases in which somatic complaints are identified as proximal to diagnosis, the use of biofeedback tools can assist in the establishment of buy-in, helping patients understand the brain–body connection. Therefore, after Mary's second visit, you perform a brief biofeedback "stress test" using physiological measurements of Mary's galvanic skin response (GSR), finger temperature, respiration, and blood volume pulse.

During that assessment, Mary is exposed to alternating stress and relaxation conditions. Upon completion, Mary expresses surprise to see the marked reductions in hand temperature, increases in GSR, and shallow breathing rates that accompanied each of the stress conditions. You provide psychoeducation regarding the autonomic nervous system and open dialogue on the Cartesian myth (where the mind is considered separate from and having little impact on the body). Moreover, you introduce the hypothesis that Mary's physical conditions could be bidirectional, with her emotions affecting her physical symptoms and her physical symptoms affecting her emotions more than she estimates.

Because Mary feels her symptoms physically, she is inclined to attribute the cause to the only explanation she has ever considered: that something is wrong with her body. To consider a psychological explanation would suggest that she is "crazy"—to her, an unthinkable notion. The implication of which she is not aware is that the mind and body may be working together to generate the unpleasant symptoms she has experienced. You suggest that a brief testing battery may help improve her and your understanding of the psychological and physiological contributors to her health problems.

Mary's third visit entails administration of the Patient Health Questionnaire—15 (PHQ–15) and the Personality Assessment Inventory (PAI). Mary's PHQ–15 score falls within the upper range of medium severity, with symptom manifestations compatible with her self-report and Dr. Thomas's medical records. On the PAI, her profile demonstrates elevations on several clinical scales, including Somatization, Depression, and Stress. The Alcohol, Drug Use, and Suicidal Ideation scales are not excessive, but Mary's Interpersonal Dominance scale is significantly depressed, suggesting that her internal locus of control is lacking. Furthermore, subscale analysis further elucidates the potential of Somatization and Health Concerns.

ICD–10–CM Diagnosis

ACTIVITY 11.2:

What are your initial diagnostic impressions of Mary? Other than a Somatoform disorder (F45.x), what are the diagnostic possibilities for this case?

Before proceeding, it is important to note that in addition to the ICD–10–CM (Centers for Medicare and Medicaid Services, 2016), we have opted to use the *ICD–10 Diagnostic Criteria for Research* (World Health Organization [WHO], 1993b), given that it offers a higher level of criterion specificity compared with the *ICD–10 Classification of Mental and*

Behavioural Disorders: Clinical Descriptions and Diagnostic Guidelines (the *Blue Book*; WHO, 1993a). Available for download from the WHO (http://www.who.int/classifications/icd/en/GRNBOOK.pdf), the *ICD–10 Diagnostic Criteria for Research* (WHO, 1993b) also offers criteria that are more consistent with current thinking concerning Somatization disorder (F45.x).

When reflecting on Mary's case, what are the diagnostic possibilities? Before consulting with Dr. Thomas or completing the medical record review, you could still consider Mary a candidate for a primary medical diagnosis—that is, a diagnosis centered on Mary's continued reports of nausea and fatigue. However, with the support of the consultation and medical record review, you are now privy to the various efforts of Mary's physicians to rule out potential medical diagnoses. Therefore, it is important to consider whether, and to what extent, psychological factors are contributing to Mary's physical concerns.

Understanding that depression can manifest as physical symptoms, it was reasonable for Dr. Thomas to consider depression as a potential diagnosis. A diagnosis of depression (Major depressive disorder, single episode [F32.x] or Major depressive disorder, recurrent [F33.x]) is contingent, however, on the convergence of symptom presentation, duration, and severity. Because Mary only reports two out of the three symptoms in Criterion B (i.e., depressed mood and decreased energy/increased fatigue), the diagnosis is restricted to either mild (F32.x or F33.x) or moderate (F32.1 or F33.1) depression.

It is noted that Mary only meets one of the additional symptoms (i.e., reduced self-esteem and self-confidence) required to make a diagnosis of mild depression. As such, there is an insufficient number of aggregate symptoms to corroborate the diagnosis (F32.x or F33.x). Emphasizing a mixture of somatic depressive symptoms and the possibility that her mood symptoms have manifested secondary to health-related stress, a diagnosis of Other depressive episodes (F32.8) or Adjustment disorder with depressed mood (F43.21) may be likely. However, further assessment will be required to substantiate these diagnoses.

Commonly associated with marked depression, the more likely primary diagnosis includes Somatization disorder (F45.x). Having (a) identified clinical elevations for Somatization and Health Concerns on the PAI, (b) consulted with Dr. Thomas, and (c) reviewed the patient's history of complaints (which encompass three of the four systems—gastrointestinal, cardiovascular, and pain), it becomes evident to you that Mary meets the criteria for Somatization disorder. Importantly, conceptualizing the diagnosis in this way is more central to Mary's presentation than would be the diagnoses of Other depressive episodes (F32.8) or Adjustment disorder with depressed mood (F43.21).

When reviewing the criteria for Somatization disorder (F45.x) as outlined in the *ICD–10 Diagnostic Criteria for Research*, Mary meets Criterion A by reporting at least 2 years of multiple and variable physical symptoms. Additionally, as stated by Dr. Thomas, such symptoms cannot be unequivocally associated with a primary physical explanation. Meeting Criterion B, Mary demonstrates an elevated degree of preoccupation with her symptoms, which then leads to persistent distress and more than three consultations with her PCP and other specialists.

In accordance with Criterion C, Mary is reluctant to accept her doctors' reassurance that there is no probable physical explanation for her symptoms. Last, as outlined by Criteria D, Mary reports a total of six symptoms, including nausea, abdominal pain, complaints of vomiting, chest pains, breathlessness without exertion, and unpleasant numbness or tingling sensations. By noting a significant impact on her ability to go to work, perform household chores, and engage in once-loved group workout classes, Mary demonstrates a significant degree of impairment in her everyday functioning as a result of the reported symptoms.

Ethical Considerations—Protecting Your Patient

ACTIVITY 11.3:

Would you be competent to provide the psychological service being requested, that is, do you have the requisite knowledge and skills? If you are not competent to provide these psychological services, what would it take for you to become and remain competent?

In accordance with the American Psychological Association (APA; 2017) *Ethical Principles of Psychologists and Code of Conduct* (APA Ethics Code) Principle A: Beneficence and Nonmaleficence and Standard 3.04, Avoiding Harm, psychologists must strive to benefit patients and take reasonable steps to avoid harming patients. Thus, the first question that needs to be addressed is whether you are competent to provide services to Mary (APA Ethics Code, Standard 2.01, Boundaries of Competence). As a licensed psychologist with a specialization in health psychology, meaning that you have specialized training in understanding medical conditions and how to manage the psychological components of such conditions, it is likely you have the education, supervised training, study, and professional experience that would enable you to diagnose Mary. Being board certified, you have gone to even greater lengths to attain and demonstrate the expertise needed to treat patients of Mary's complexity. Even with your described credentials, the varying presentations of patients with health-related problems require ongoing reeducation via continuing education seminars, participation in hospital grand rounds, or peer consultation with other health psychologists, as well as medical providers. In addition, to avoid harm to Mary and given your conclusion that she is not suffering from a primary depression, contacting her PCP to recommend consideration of stopping her prescription for escitalopram is warranted.

To protect Mary while upholding your primary obligations of beneficence and nonmaleficence, it is imperative that you also consider the concept of Integrity found in Principle C of the APA Ethics Code and the scientific basis of your practice (APA Ethics Code, Standard 2.04, Bases for Scientific and Professional Judgments). These speak to the importance of accuracy, for example, the importance of ensuring an accurate understanding and knowledge of the empirical basis of somatoform disorders before rendering a diagnosis and corresponding treatment.

Working with somatoform disorders requires both a foundational knowledge of health-related conditions and an elevated understanding of somatization. Without such, providers may be prone to making diagnostic deductions that perpetuate Cartesian mythology, erring on either side of the medical versus psychological dialectic. By acquiring foundational knowledge of health-related conditions and by keeping up with the scientific literature on somatization, you ensure that your work is based on established scientific and professional knowledge.

Given the emergent science that is helping us to understand better the complex relationships between the mind and body, psychologists may elect to use a battery of assessments that assist in diagnosis and treatment. While helping to provide a methodological check and balance to ensure diagnostic accuracy, risk or harm are possible if assessments are not used appropriately. Therefore, the assessment battery must include instruments that are most appropriate for the individual case, referral question, or presenting concern (APA Ethics Code, Standard 9.02a, Use of Assessments), including ensuring that tests and measures are objective measurements that have been validated with patients with Somatization disorder (APA Ethics Code, Standard 9.02b). Moreover, it is necessary to determine whether the assessment methods correspond with the individual's language and reading preference (APA Ethics Code, Standard 9.02c).

Risk Management—Protecting Your Patient, Protecting Yourself

ACTIVITY 11.4:

What specific risks does Mary present, and how would you best protect yourself? What risks might you encounter in an integrated care context in which you are working with Mary's PCP, Dr. Thomas?

When discussing risk management, it is good practice to talk in detail about informed consent and confidentiality. One of the best ways to protect yourself is by being honest, cautious, and transparent in your dealing with your patients, including protecting the patient's confidentiality (APA Ethics Code, Standard 4.01, Maintaining Confidentiality). However, in this case study, you identified the need to go outside the confines of the practitioner–patient relationship to collect missing but necessary information. By obtaining Mary's informed consent to an ROI, you honored her privacy and confidentiality while also protecting yourself against potential risk. More than just a formality of signing a piece of paper, it is important to note that a process needs to occur leading up to the attainment of an ROI. To be truly informed, an appropriate explanation should be provided, and the advantages and disadvantages must be discussed in a manner that is understandable to the patient. Furthermore, when requesting the ROI, you acted with prudence by specifying the terms of the ROI where you could both share and receive information from Mary's PCP. By doing so, you may consult and cooperate with Mary's PCP for her benefit (APA Ethics Code, Standards 3.09, Cooperation With Other Professionals, and 4.06, Consultations). Such measures can be extremely helpful as the gap between psychology and medicine continues to close with increases in integration.

Disposition

> **ACTIVITY 11.5:**
>
> Given what you know about Mary and Somatization disorder (F45.x), what factors should you consider when developing her treatment plan? How might you keep her engaged in treatment if she is resistant?

Before initiating treatment with Mary, you must direct your attention to several pretreatment mandates. Without a proper foundation leading up to treatment, your efforts may be fruitless with Mary, given the challenging nature of Somatization disorder. Pretreatment mandates include fostering a strong provider–patient relationship, communicating the diagnosis, and offering continued psychoeducation.

Because there appears to be no clear and primary physical cause for the reported symptomatology, patients with Somatization disorder are often considered taxing to the health care system in both health-service burden and economic cost (Janca, Isaac, & Ventouras, 2006). Often reporting extreme frustration, patients with Somatization disorder can feel invisible to and even patronized by health care providers. Keeping in mind such hardships, it is imperative to recognize the importance of the working alliance. By validating Mary's subjective experiences, you aligned yourself with Mary and supported the development of a working alliance. Without a working alliance built on an empathic patient-centered approach, Mary may discontinue seeking psychological services when presented with the diagnosis and corresponding treatment goals.

To help ensure that clinical practices, including diagnostic assessments and tests, are evidence based, it is necessary for you to talk with Mary about her diagnosis before engaging in treatment. Considered one of the most important steps in caring for an individual with Somatization disorder, delivery of the diagnosis deserves significant forethought and practice (Oyama, Paltoo, & Greengold, 2007). When communicating the diagnosis, it is imperative that you maintain an empathic and nonjudgmental approach while acknowledging Mary's lived experience. The suffering and distress that Mary experiences as a result of her diagnosis are real and not willfully adopted or contrived. While validating her subjective experiences, you may then introduce the diagnosis and review the criteria.

Given Mary's strong belief that her symptoms have a medical cause, it will not be easy for her to receive the diagnosis of somatization disorder and then immediately consider possible treatment options. Without an adequate understanding of the mind–body connection, Mary's medically oriented framework may provoke her to disengage prematurely from psychological services while insisting that there is a medical cause to her problems. With biofeedback and other experiential exercises, it may be helpful to develop further Mary's understanding of the mind–body connection and the benefits associated with psychological services.

In review, as a psychologist working with an individual with Somatization disorder (F45.0), you need to be attuned to the importance of validating Mary's subjective experience as "real." You also must recognize a foundational imperative, that your buy-in with Mary is largely contingent on your ability to appraise her psychological needs and abilities via the establishment of a true working alliance. With regard to these important considerations, your messaging to Mary is derived from two pretheoretical and descriptive concepts (Ossorio, 2006):

1. By nature of being a person, Mary makes sense. That she has not yet made sense to herself or to her medical providers does not suggest that she is somehow mysterious but that certain concepts have been missing to elucidate the reasons for her symptoms.
2. Change is contingent on helping a person do what she can do as opposed to what she cannot do. Mary's ability to see the problems that derive from her physical health is a strength, in contrast to the difficulty she has appreciating emotional correlates. Your initial challenge is to form an alliance with Mary on what you both agree is a problem.

When choosing specific treatment interventions, the treatments that have been shown to have efficacy in the treatment of Somatization disorder include cognitive behavior therapy (Allen & Woolfolk, 2010; Kroenke, 2007), with greater decrease in health care costs, improved functioning, and a reduction in somatic symptoms in comparison with standard medical care (Allen, Woolfolk, Escobar, Gara, & Hamer, 2006). In addition, a meta-analysis of mindfulness-based therapy suggested a small to moderate positive treatment effect in improving quality of life and reducing pain, symptom severity, depression, and anxiety associated with somatization disorders (Lakhan & Schofield, 2013).

References

Allen, L. A., & Woolfolk, R. L. (2010). Cognitive behavioral therapy for somatoform disorders. *Psychiatric Clinics of North America, 33*, 579–593. http://dx.doi.org/10.1016/j.psc.2010.04.014

Allen, L. A., Woolfolk, R. L., Escobar, J. I., Gara, M. A., & Hamer, R. M. (2006). Cognitive-behavioral therapy for somatization disorder: A randomized controlled trial. *Archives of Internal Medicine, 166*, 1512–1518. http://dx.doi.org/10.1001/archinte.166.14.1512

American Psychological Association. (2017). *Ethical principles of psychologists and code of conduct* (2002, Amended June 1, 2010 and January 1, 2017). Retrieved from http://www.apa.org/ethics/code/index.aspx

Barsky, A. J., Orav, E. J., & Bates, D. W. (2005). Somatization increases medical utilization and costs independent of psychiatric and medical comorbidity. *Archives of General Psychiatry, 62,* 903–910. http://dx.doi.org/10.1001/archpsyc.62.8.903

Centers for Medicare and Medicaid Services. (2016). *ICD–10–CM.* Retrieved from http://www.cdc.gov/nchs/icd/icd10cm.htm

de Waal, M. W., Arnold, I. A., Eekhof, J. A., & van Hemert, A. M. (2004). Somatoform disorders in general practice: Prevalence, functional impairment and comorbidity with anxiety and depressive disorders. *The British Journal of Psychiatry, 184,* 470–476. http://dx.doi.org/10.1192/bjp.184.6.470

Fink, P., Sørensen, L., Engberg, M., Holm, M., & Munk-Jørgensen, P. (1999). Somatization in primary care. Prevalence, health care utilization, and general practitioner recognition. *Psychosomatics: Journal of Consultation and Liaison Psychiatry, 40,* 330–338. http://dx.doi.org/10.1016/S0033-3182(99)71228-4

Janca, A., Isaac, M., & Ventouras, J. (2006). Towards better understanding and management of somatoform disorders. *International Review of Psychiatry, 18,* 5–12. http://dx.doi.org/10.1080/09540260500466766

Kirmayer, L. J. (1996). Cultural notes and somatoform and dissociative disorders. In J. E. Mezzich, A. Kleinman, H. Fabrega, Jr., & D. L. Parron (Eds.), *Culture and psychiatric diagnoses: A DSM–IV perspective* (pp. 151–158). Washington, DC: American Psychiatric Press.

Kroenke, K. (2007). Efficacy of treatment for somatoform disorders: A review of randomized controlled trials. *Psychosomatic Medicine, 69,* 881–888. http://dx.doi.org/10.1097/PSY.0b013e31815b00c4

Lakhan, S. E., & Schofield, K. L. (2013). Mindfulness-based therapies in the treatment of somatization disorders: A systematic review and meta-analysis. *PLoS One, 8,* e71834. http://dx.doi.org/10.1371/journal.pone.0071834

Ossorio, P. G. (2006). *The behavior of persons* [eBook]. Retrieved from https://openlibrary.org/works/OL6702488W/The_Behavior_of_Persons

Oyama, O., Paltoo, C., & Greengold, J. (2007). Somatoform disorders. *American Family Physician, 76,* 1333–1338.

Roca, M., Gili, M., Garcia-Garcia, M., Salva, J., Vives, M., Garcia Campayo, J., & Comas, A. (2009). Prevalence and comorbidity of common mental disorders in primary care. *Journal of Affective Disorders, 119,* 52–58. http://dx.doi.org/10.1016/j.jad.2009.03.014

World Health Organization. (1993a). *ICD–10 classification of mental and behavioural disorders: Clinical descriptions and diagnostic guidelines.* Retrieved from http://www.who.int/classifications/icd/en/bluebook.pdf

World Health Organization. (1993b). *ICD–10 classification of mental and behavioral disorders: Diagnostic criteria for research.* Geneva, Switzerland: World Health Organization. Retrieved from http://www.who.int/classifications/icd/en/GRNBOOK.pdf

Carol B. Peterson and Emily M. Pisetsky

F50 Eating Disorders

12

An eating disorder can consist of (a) deliberate attempts to lose weight to the degree of significant undernourishment, typically accompanied by disturbances in body image; (b) repeated episodes of overeating, with or without compensatory behaviors like self-induced vomiting; and (c) some combination of these symptoms. Prevalence estimates of eating disorders in adolescents and adults range from 0.3% to 4.3% of the population, depending on the type and definition of eating disorder symptoms (Smink, van Hoeken, & Hoek, 2012; Swanson, Crow, Le Grange, Swendsen, & Merikangas, 2011), with eating disorders, in general, more common in females than males (Smink et al., 2012). The onset of eating disorder symptoms typically occurs in adolescence or early adulthood (Swanson et al., 2011) and the short- and long-term course is highly variable (Steinhausen, 2009). Causal and maintenance factors of eating disorders involve a complex combination of genetic, sociocultural, psychological, developmental, and biological risk factors (Culbert, Racine, & Klump, 2015). Eating disorders are characterized by high rates of comorbid psychopathology, particularly mood, anxiety, and substance use disorders, as well as suicidal behavior (Hudson, Hiripi, Pope, & Kessler, 2007; Swanson et al., 2011). Mortality risk is increased for all types of eating disorders as a result of medical problems (e.g., electrolyte disturbance,

http://dx.doi.org/10.1037/0000069-013
An ICD–10–CM Casebook and Workbook for Students: Psychological and Behavioral Conditions, J. B. Schaffer and E. Rodolfa (Editors)

cardiac complications) and suicide (American Psychiatric Association, 2013; Smink et al., 2012; Steinhausen, 2009). Eating disorders are also associated with reduced quality of life in most domains, including social, emotional, role-related functioning, and general health (Winkler et al., 2014). Although evidence-based approaches, particularly psychotherapy, have been identified for the treatment of eating disorders in adolescents and adults (Kass, Kolko, & Wilfley, 2013; National Institute for Clinical Excellence, 2004), the majority of individuals with eating disorders in the community do not receive treatment that directly targets their eating disorder symptoms (Hudson et al., 2007; Swanson et al., 2011).

The Case

As an advanced clinical trainee in a university-based integrated health and counseling center, you have been assigned this case by your supervisor and are responsible for conducting a comprehensive diagnostic interview. With limited experience working with eating disorders clinically, you are conducting the evaluation alone, with a plan to meet later that day with your supervisor.

Sarah is a 21-year-old White woman entering her senior year at the university and states that her primary reason for seeking treatment is that she "can't stop eating, and I really want to stop," with particularly uncontrollable urges to eat in the evenings. Although she is occasionally able to distract herself until the urges pass, her typical pattern is to purchase large amounts of food from one of the local grocery stores and eat all of it before leaving the grocery store parking lot. During these episodes, she reports that her eating feels "completely out of control" and that she can't stop herself from eating once she starts. Initially after these overeating episodes occur, she feels a sense of relief; however, she then becomes extremely worried and even feels "panic" about the possibility of weight gain and will self-induce vomiting.

To determine her ICD–10–CM diagnosis (World Health Organization, 1993), you ask her to describe several of these recent overeating episodes to determine whether the amount she has eaten is objectively large by clinical standards (Fairburn, 2008). Sarah reports that she typically eats foods that she would not let herself consume outside of these bulimic episodes, as she tries to maintain strict rules about her eating in an attempt to lose weight. For example, during the evening prior to the appointment, she ate two pints of ice cream and 25 cookies in a 20-minute period. Four nights earlier, her overeating episode consisted of two extra-large pizzas in 30 minutes. Outside of these overeating episodes, she usually restricts the overall amount of calories she eats to less than 1,200 calories (kilocalories) per day and avoids eating carbohydrates, refined sugar, and dairy products. Sarah reports that in the past 6 months, these overeating episodes accompanied by self-induced vomiting occurred, on average, two to three times each week. Throughout the interview, you note that Sarah is intermittently tearful while she speaks but is able and willing to describe her eating patterns in detail. She states,

I was nervous about coming here today, but as soon as I started talking it felt like kind of a relief to tell you about it. I mean, it's disgusting, but you don't seem to be judging me or anything. Also, I have tried to stop on my own before and couldn't, and I want to be honest about it with you because I really need help.

Sarah reports that she is 5 feet 5 inches tall and weighs 135 pounds, which indicates that her body mass index (BMI; i.e., kg/m^2) of 22.5 is in the normal range. These numbers were confirmed when she agreed to allow her height and weight to be measured, as long as she did not "have to look at that awful number on the scale." Sarah states that she is extremely unhappy with her weight and shape, and that she "feels fat" all of the time. She often avoids looking at herself in the mirror, but when she does, she often finds herself crying about her "obese body." She maintains that her ideal weight is 120 but admits that she would be "happy if it were even lower." She describes constantly ruminating about this particular number and believes that she would feel happier and be more accepted by her peers at that weight. Sarah reports feeling particularly distressed by the size of her legs and stomach and states that she is preoccupied with how big she looks. She notes feeling scared that other people might be thinking negatively about her appearance (e.g., that she looks overweight), although she denies experiencing any criticism for her weight or appearance. She also states that her weight and shape are among the main factors that influence her feelings about herself as a person, along with her grades at school.

To assess other compensatory behaviors, you ask Sarah if she has ever used laxatives, diuretics, or diet pills, which she denies. Sarah reports that she used to fast for 24 hours at a time at least once a week when she was a young teenager, but she no longer "is able" to go for long periods of time without eating. Currently, Sarah exercises an hour each day, including yoga, running, and/or dance classes. She states that although "sometimes" she feels driven or compelled to exercise to compensate for what she has eaten or in the context of weight loss, "most of the time" she exercises because it improves her mood and body image.

When she was younger (from ages 14 to 15), she exercised for several hours a day at a high level of intensity (e.g., 100 sit-ups followed by a 10-mile run) in an attempt to lose weight. In addition to weekly fasting, she would restrict her calorie intake to 500 calories a day and limit her food intake to fruit, vegetables, and rice. At that time, she had already reached her adult height of 5 feet, 5 inches, but her weight dropped from 125 to 104 pounds (i.e., BMI = 17.3) over the course of 5 months. Nevertheless, she continued to perceive herself as "disgusting and obese," in spite of the fact that her friends expressed concern about her weight loss. Sarah also stopped menstruating for 6 months. She reports that she was extremely depressed and anxious during that time. Eventually, her pediatrician referred her to an outpatient eating disorder treatment program, where she followed the eating recommendations of her dietician and therapist in order to avoid being hospitalized, not because she was motivated to gain weight. In fact, she reports that the process of weight regain was extremely upsetting and made her feel "more fat and depressed." During the course of being underweight and gradually weight restored to 130 pounds by age 15, Sarah claims that she did not self-induce vomiting or have overeating episodes similar to the ones that she is currently experiencing. She would occasionally experience a driven compulsion to eat smaller amounts of food during that time, such as a piece of bread or a handful of nuts (which have been described as subjective bulimic episodes, characterized by a sense of loss of control in the context of eating an amount of food that is not objectively large; Fairburn, 2008) but never any larger episodes accompanied by a sense of loss of control (i.e., objective bulimic or binge eating episodes; Fairburn, 2008).

Between ages 15 and 18, Sarah describes maintaining a weight between 120 and 130 pounds, feeling extremely preoccupied with her weight and shape, restricting her food intake to 1,000 to 2,000 calories a day, and thinking about self-induced vomiting but not actually engaging in the behavior. Upon her arrival at college, Sarah found the social transition and the increased academic demands stressful. Later that fall, she began to experience overeating episodes in the dining hall involving eating multiple desserts. Concerned about a 3-pound weight gain, Sarah began to self-induce vomiting after eating dinner, which brought her an immediate sense of relief from both the fear of weight gain and of the experience of feeling overly full. Over the course of her freshman year, she found herself overeating in secret and consuming an increasingly large amount of food prior to purging. She also reported experiencing a worsening of depressive symptoms, including persistent dysphoria, anhedonia, persistent feelings of guilt and worthlessness, sleep disturbance, suicidal ideation, and concentration impairment, which have persisted, including suicidal ideation with thoughts of jumping off a nearby bridge. She denies any suicidal intent or a past history of suicide attempts or self-injurious behavior. Sarah states that she drinks alcohol occasionally with friends but generally avoids it "because alcohol is high in calories" and denied use of drugs. She denies symptoms of anxiety although admits that she is "told by everyone that I am too much of a perfectionist."

Sarah grew up in a different state and feels far away from her family and friends. Both of her parents are professionals, and she has a younger brother who is in his final year of high school. Sarah describes her relationships with her family members as "good." Her parents believe that she is in full remission and are unaware of her current eating disorder symptoms. Sarah has several close friends at college and has had boyfriends in the past but is not currently dating anyone, in part because she believes that she is "too fat too date." She has not told anyone about her bulimic symptoms. She is a high-achieving student and is in the process of applying for graduate school. One reason for her decision to seek treatment is "so that I don't have to go on to another school with this secret life."

When asked about her health status, Sarah reports that she has not seen a physician in several years. She states that she often experiences dizziness (although she has not fainted since she was age 14) and stomach pain, especially after vomiting. She also notices that she occasionally vomits blood, although not in the past month.

Assessment Using the ICD–10–CM

ACTIVITY 12.1:

How would you gather additional information from Sarah? What additional questions would you ask to determine whether you need to request help from your supervisor or are comfortable continuing this assessment alone?

As described in Berg, Peterson, and Frazier (2012) and Peterson (2005), establishing rapport is especially important in the context of conducting a diagnostic interview with individuals with eating disorders, given the likelihood that patients experience shame, fear, and reluctance in discussing eating disorder behaviors and symptoms. In addition, patients with eating disorders may be inclined to minimize or, occasionally, exaggerate symptoms, for example, denying symptoms because of fearing forced hospitalization or exaggerating to make sure their cry for help is heard. Asking questions, such as the following, that convey both empathy and expertise can be reassuring to patients. "What kind of rules do you try to follow about what to eat and what not to eat?" "When you said you eat a bagel for breakfast, how much of the bagel do you eat?" "Are there specific parts of your body that you find particularly upsetting?" "Do you find that your body image seems to fluctuate, so that if you have just eaten something or are having strong feelings that you feel or look bigger to yourself?" (see Berg et al., 2012; Peterson, 2005). Detailed and specific questions are particularly helpful. In addition, an objective measure of height and weight along with a thorough medical evaluation are essential for diagnostic, treatment planning, and patient care purposes.

A physical examination may be important to rule out medical causes of bulimic symptoms (e.g., gastrointestinal conditions resulting in Vomiting, R11.10), although these types of cases are not typically accompanied by the psychological symptoms that characterize eating disorders (e.g., fear of weight gain, overvaluation of weight and shape). A medical evaluation is an important aspect of a comprehensive diagnostic evaluation in order to consider medical conditions that may be the cause or a result of the presenting eating disorder symptoms.

You also decide to administer some self-report questionnaires. Sarah's score on the Beck Depression Inventory (Beck, Ward, Mendelson, Mock, & Erbaugh, 1961) is 22, indicative of significant depressive symptoms. Her score on the Eating Disorder Examination Questionnaire global scale (Fairburn, 2008; available in the public domain: http://www.credo-oxford.com/6.2.html) is 4.2, suggesting clinically significant eating disorder psychopathology.

There are times when you may feel that you need immediate input from your supervisor. You may have had limited experience assessing and intervening with a client who presents with imminent risk, which makes the presence of your supervisor crucial. In this case, the most likely risks are of self-harm or a medical event, given her unhealthy eating behaviors. Therefore, conducting a careful evaluation of her intention to self-harm will be essential (see Introduction, this volume), given that she admitted to suicidal ideation. In addition, depending on the nature of the medical risk, an immediate referral to a physician may be indicated. Your supervisor's involvement may occur during your supervision time, or if the risk is high, your supervisor may need to be included immediately in the clinical session with your patient to ensure an optimal level of care and as a risk management strategy for you in your role as a trainee.

ICD–10–CM Diagnoses

ACTIVITY 12.2:

Which types of eating disorders do you think Sarah might have, and what specific information from Sarah leads you to these possible diagnoses? Are depression or anxiety possible diagnoses?

One of the notable, and not uncommon, features of this case is that this patient met criteria for a different eating disorder in the past than the diagnostic criteria she meets currently. One can rule out current Anorexia nervosa (F50.0) in Sarah's case, an important consideration in determining an eating disorder, because her current BMI is in the normal range. However, based on her self-reported BMI of 17.3 at age 14, which would place her in the underweight range (defined in the ICD–10–CM as less than 17.5), along with her reported severe dietary restriction and food avoidance, body image distortion, and amenorrhea, it appears that the diagnosis of Anorexia nervosa, restricting type (F50.01) would have been assigned to Sarah as a younger adolescent. She also described significant symptoms of anxiety (e.g., worry about the onset of negative events; physical symptoms, including headaches and heart palpitations) suggesting that an anxiety disorder, such as Anxiety disorder, unspecified (F41.9), should be considered (Emmelkamp & Ehring, 2014). In addition, she described a number of symptoms of Major depressive disorder, recurrent, mild (F33.0; e.g., persistent dysphoria, sleep disturbance, thoughts of death, loss of interest in pleasurable activities), which may warrant a separate diagnosis or may be secondary to the effects of semistarvation. Despite improvement in her weight status, Sarah remained weight preoccupied with occasional subjective binge eating episodes (Fairburn, 2008), although the amount of food that she consumed was not objectively large. These episodes often occur in the context of anorexia nervosa and bulimia nervosa as well as other types of eating disorders (Fairburn, 2008).

Given that Sarah does not meet criteria for current anorexia nervosa, the next diagnostic consideration is Bulimia nervosa (F50.2) due to her subjective experience of loss of control over eating (i.e., feeling unable to resist eating or stop eating once started, feeling driven or compelled to eat) accompanying the consumption of an objectively large amount of food (Fairburn, 2008). The second consideration in the diagnosis of bulimia nervosa is the occurrence of compensatory behaviors aimed to prevent weight gain, including self-induced vomiting, laxative or diuretic misuse, fasting, and/or use of drugs, including thyroid medication, or insulin omission among diabetic individuals (Crow & Brandenburg, 2010; Fairburn, 2008). As Sarah reported during the interview, her current overeating episodes are always accompanied by self-induced vomiting.

Although the behavioral features of eating disorder symptoms are important in assigning an ICD–10–CM diagnosis, psychological aspects of eating disorder psychopathology, particularly attitudes and feelings related to weight, shape, and eating, are also essential considerations (Crow & Brandenburg, 2010; Fairburn, 2008). Sarah reported being preoccupied with weight loss, along with having a specific weight loss goal and feeling distressed and self-conscious about her current size and shape. In addition, she reported overvaluing weight and shape in the context of her self-esteem, all of which are characteristic of eating disorders in general, including Bulimia nervosa. The longitudinal course of Sarah's eating disorder symptoms, characterized by the onset of anorexia nervosa followed by the later occurrence of bulimia nervosa occurs in approximately 30% of cases (Eddy et al., 2008). As Sarah described this progression, it appears that, although her behavioral symptoms improved in terms of severe dietary restriction and her associated weight status, her preoccupation with weight loss and distress about weight and shape have been continuous since age 14. Although her reported weight goal is 120 pounds, the fact that Sarah was weight-restored to 130 pounds in order to resume menstruation in the past suggests that her goal weight would be too low, particularly in terms of endocrine functioning.

Another diagnostic consideration is a current or past diagnosis of Body dysmorphic disorder (F45.22) given Sarah's preoccupation with and distress about her appearance, along with the likelihood that she engages in shape and weight checking, a common feature of eating disorders (Fairburn, 2008). Although these types of appearance preoccupations and checking behaviors are prominent in Body dysmorphic disorder, a separate diagnosis is not given when these symptoms occur in the context of an eating disorder.

An additional diagnostic question is whether these symptoms are better accounted for by a mood disorder, particularly depression. Sarah clearly meets criteria for a mood disorder (and based on her self-reported history, her most likely diagnosis is Major depressive disorder, recurrent, mild [F33.0]), as well as Bulimia nervosa (F50.2). Although the trajectory of the co-occurrence of depression and bulimic symptoms is heterogeneous, with some patients experiencing the onset of depression first, some experiencing bulimic symptoms first, and others experiencing the onset of both types of symptoms simultaneously, a comorbid depressive disorder diagnosis is often indicated, as it is for Sarah. Although Sarah describes some symptoms of anxiety, including Social phobia (F40.1), the fact that the content is circumscribed to fears related to weight, shape, and eating, as well as self-consciousness about appearance, suggests that she would not be given a separate anxiety disorder diagnosis because the content of her anxiety is circumscribed within the eating disorder.

Given these considerations, Sarah is assigned a primary diagnosis of Bulimia nervosa (F50.2), with a secondary diagnosis of Major depressive disorder, recurrent, moderate (F33.1).

Ethical Considerations—Protecting Your Patient

ACTIVITY 12.3:

Given the complications of this case, do you think it was ethical for your supervisor not to be immediately available during the intake interview? When might you invite your supervisor to become directly involved as your evaluation of Sarah continues? What other type of professional could you consult with as part of a comprehensive assessment?

The first ethical question is whether you as the trainee are competent to assess this patient. You do have experience in conducting interviews, but your experience working with eating disorders is limited. The American Psychological Association's (APA's; 2017) *Ethical Principles of Psychologists and Code of Conduct* (APA Ethics Code) stipulates that psychologists only provide services in areas of competence or when they are undertaking the appropriate "education, training, supervised experience, consultation, or study" necessary to obtain that competence (APA Ethics Code, Standards 2.01a, 2.01c, Boundaries of Competence). In addition, the patient raised a number of concerns regarding potential risks. The first and most imminent concern is that Sarah reported Suicidal ideations (R45.851) with plan (e.g., thoughts of jumping from a bridge). Although she assured you that she was safe and denied any intention to act on her suicidal ideation, the risk of suicide is critically important to evaluate in eating disorder assessment. Indeed, an examination of her responses on the Beck Depression Inventory was made while Sarah was still present and corroborated the information she had provided in the interview, an especially important consideration with thoughts and behaviors related to suicide and self-injury. Although written self-report information can be useful corroborating data, discussing suicide and safety risks comprehensively in the context of a full evaluation is imperative. In addition, consultation and supervision, along with careful documentation, are essential.

Sarah's reports of dizziness and a past history of vomiting blood constitute a second area of risk. Given the medical risks associated with eating disorder symptoms, particularly electrolyte disturbance caused by repeated vomiting episodes (Mehler, Birmingham, Crow, & Jahraus, 2010), Sarah's medical status is an important consideration along with her suicide risk. Given the potential medical and suicide risks involved, ethical practice would warrant an opportunity for immediate consultation regarding steps to take with your supervisor, potentially by stepping out for consultation during the interview.

After describing the case to your supervisor, you considered various options and, considering the significant risks involved, you decided to invite the supervisor in for the final portion of Sarah's evaluation. In the interim, your supervisor was able to contact the clinic medical director, who was able to arrange for Sarah's medical evaluation immediately following the conclusion of your diagnostic interview. The potential medical risks of eating disorder symptoms warrant timely evaluation by a physician or nurse. The primary reasons for the decision to meet jointly with Sarah at the end of the interview were to conduct a more thorough evaluation of suicide risk and to establish a safety plan along with a treatment plan.

The diagnosis and treatment of eating disorders involves a number of ethical considerations. Although Sarah was self-referred to the clinic and agreed to meet with the physician for a medical evaluation, some individuals with eating disorders refuse treatment and may or may not be able to demonstrate capacity to consent. Clinician responses to these types of ethical situations require complex decision making and considerations of client needs and legal issues (Matusek & Wright, 2010). Supervisor and peer consultation is especially important in these types of situations, including legal consultation. Consultation and supervision can also be especially helpful for clinicians who have a personal history of an eating disorder themselves, in order to manage boundaries, make decisions about self-disclosure, monitor relapse risk, and countertransference (APA Ethics Code, Standard 2.06, Personal Problems and Conflicts). Such a circumstance can be potentially advantageous for the client but problematic if the clinician continues to struggle with these symptoms and endorses eating disorder beliefs in the context of treatment (Williams & Haverkamp, 2015).

Risk Management—Protecting Your Patient, Protecting Yourself

ACTIVITY 12.4:

Other than consulting your supervisor, what steps do you need to take to minimize the suicide and health risks that you identified above?

From a risk management perspective, the decision to consult with the supervisor during Sarah's evaluation was indicated considering the potential suicide and medical risks. The decision to refer Sarah for immediate medical evaluation also minimized risk, along with having the supervisor conduct a second, thorough suicide assessment. These steps, referrals (e.g., medical, as well as providing Sarah with crisis resources should her suicidality intensify), and treatment recommendations will be reviewed with Sarah and documented in the medical record. In addition, Sarah should be asked to sign a release of information in order to obtain the medical records from her previous eating disorder treatment that she received as a younger adolescent. Obtaining previous medical records would be useful in confirming Sarah's diagnostic history, as well as in getting more detailed information about her potential suicide risk (e.g., if, in spite of her denial, she had actually made a previous suicide attempt). In addition, because Sarah will be asked to sign a release of information for you to communicate with her current medical provider, discussing issues of interdisciplinary communication and obtaining informed consent will be imperative. In this context, discussing issues of confidentiality and consultation with Sarah will be especially important (APA Ethics Code, Standard 4, Privacy and Confidentiality).

Disposition

ACTIVITY 12.5:

Given what you know about Sarah, what factors do you think will be important in selecting treatment recommendations? What strategies would you use to engage her in treatment? What strengths of Sarah's would you hope to build on?

Although Sarah's case is challenging, her presentation is representative of many eating disorder patient diagnostic interviews in several ways. First, she presented with a 7-year history of eating disorder symptoms. Indeed, many patients with eating disorders do not seek treatment for many years once they are symptomatic, and some never seek treatment at all (Hudson et al., 2007; Swanson et al., 2011). Second, like many patients with eating disorders, Sarah had one type of eating disorder (Anorexia nervosa, restricting type [F50.01]), partially recovered for several years although remaining shape and weight focused, then developed another type of eating disorder, which was assigned as her current diagnosis (Bulimia nervosa [F50.2]), separate but related to the initial one. Third, Sarah had significant depressive symptoms, an important consideration in her diagnosis and treatment. Finally, she presented with significant risk for both suicide and medical complications. This case highlights the importance of risk assessment and risk management in the context of diagnostic interviewing, in general, and eating disorder diagnostic procedures, in particular. It also emphasizes the importance of rapport and empathy in conducting diagnostic interviews with eating disorder patients, as well as the value of collaboration and consultation between trainees and supervisors.

Fortunately, several evidence-based treatments have been found to be helpful for patients like Sarah with bulimia nervosa (Kass et al., 2013). Psychotherapy treatments, including cognitive–behavioral therapy (Fairburn, 2008), interpersonal therapy (Tanofsky-Kraff & Wilfley, 2010), and dialectical behavior therapy (Safer, Telch, & Chen, 2009), have all been found to be efficacious in the treatment of bulimia nervosa in research trials. Given that these various treatments are associated with comparable long-term outcomes in bulimia nervosa (Kass et al., 2013), psychotherapy selection can be made collaboratively between the patient and the clinician. In addition to psychotherapy, adjunctive medication can be helpful for treating bulimia nervosa and comorbid psychiatric symptoms, including depression (Fairburn, 2008; Kass et al., 2013; National Institute for Clinical Excellence, 2004). A more intensive treatment program may be useful as well, although bulimia nervosa can generally be treated on an outpatient basis. Although future research and clinical development are needed to broaden treatment efficacy for bulimia nervosa, existing and future treatments for patients like Sarah can serve to shift their trajectory toward short- and long-term recovery.

References

American Psychiatric Association. (2013). *Diagnostic and statistical manual of mental disorders* (5th ed.). Arlington, VA: American Psychiatric Association.

American Psychological Association. (2017). *Ethical principles of psychologists and code of conduct* (2002, Amended June 1, 2010 and January 1, 2017). Retrieved from http://www.apa.org/ethics/code/index.aspx

Beck, A. T., Ward, C. H., Mendelson, M., Mock, J., & Erbaugh, J. (1961). An inventory for measuring depression. *Archives of General Psychiatry, 4*, 561–571. http://dx.doi.org/10.1001/archpsyc.1961.01710120031004

Berg, K. C., Peterson, C. B., & Frazier, P. (2012). Assessment and diagnosis of eating disorders: A guide for professional counselors. *Journal of Counseling & Development, 90*, 262–269. http://dx.doi.org/10.1002/j.1556-6676.2012.00033.x

Crow, S. J., & Brandenburg, B. (2010). Diagnosis, assessment and treatment planning for bulimia nervosa. In C. M. Grilo & J. E. Mitchell (Eds.), *The treatment of eating disorders: A clinical handbook* (pp. 28–43). New York, NY: Guilford Press.

Culbert, K. M., Racine, S. E., & Klump, K. L. (2015). Research review: What we have learned about the causes of eating disorders—A synthesis of sociocultural, psychological, and biological research. *Journal of Child Psychology and Psychiatry, 56*, 1141–1164. http://dx.doi.org/10.1111/jcpp.12441

Eddy, K. T., Dorer, D. J., Franko, D. L., Tahilani, K., Thompson-Brenner, H., & Herzog, D. B. (2008). Diagnostic crossover in anorexia nervosa and bulimia nervosa: Implications for *DSM–V*. *The American Journal of Psychiatry, 165*, 245–250. http://dx.doi.org/10.1176/appi.ajp.2007.07060951

Emmelkamp, P., & Ehring, T. (Eds.). (2014). *The Wiley handbook of anxiety disorders*. http://dx.doi.org/10.1002/9781118775349

Fairburn, C. G. (2008). *Cognitive behavior therapy and eating disorders*. New York, NY: Guilford Press.

Hudson, J. I., Hiripi, E., Pope, H. G., Jr., & Kessler, R. C. (2007). The prevalence and correlates of eating disorders in the National Comorbidity Survey Replication. *Biological Psychiatry, 61*, 348–358. http://dx.doi.org/10.1016/j.biopsych.2006.03.040

Kass, A. E., Kolko, R. P., & Wilfley, D. E. (2013). Psychological treatments for eating disorders. *Current Opinion in Psychiatry, 26*, 549–555. http://dx.doi.org/10.1097/YCO.0b013e328365a30e

Matusek, J. A., & Wright, M. O. (2010). Ethical dilemmas in treating clients with eating disorders: A review and application of an integrative ethical decision-making model. *European Eating Disorders Review, 18,* 434–452. http://dx.doi.org/10.1002/erv.1036

Mehler, P. S., Birmingham, C. L., Crow, S. J., & Jahraus, J. P. (2010). Medical complications of eating disorders. In C. M. Grilo & J. E. Mitchell (Eds.), *The treatment of eating disorders: A clinical handbook* (pp. 66–80). New York, NY: Guilford Press.

National Institute for Clinical Excellence. (2004). Eating disorders—Core interventions in the treatment and management of anorexia nervosa, bulimia nervosa, and related eating disorders. *NICE Clinical Guideline No. 9.* London, England: Author.

Peterson, C. B. (2005). Conducting the diagnostic interview. In J. E. Mitchell & C. B. Peterson (Eds.), *Assessment of eating disorders* (pp. 32–58). New York, NY: Guilford Press.

Safer, D. L., Telch, C. F., & Chen, E. Y. (2009). *Dialectical behavior therapy for binge eating and bulimia.* New York, NY: Guilford Press.

Smink, F. R. E., van Hoeken, D., & Hoek, H. W. (2012). Epidemiology of eating disorders: Incidence, prevalence and mortality rates. *Current Psychiatry Reports, 14,* 406–414. http://dx.doi.org/10.1007/s11920-012-0282-y

Steinhausen, H. C. (2009). Outcome of eating disorders. *Child and Adolescent Psychiatric Clinics of North America, 18,* 225–242. http://dx.doi.org/10.1016/j.chc.2008.07.013

Swanson, S. A., Crow, S. J., Le Grange, D., Swendsen, J., & Merikangas, K. R. (2011). Prevalence and correlates of eating disorders in adolescents: Results from the national comorbidity survey replication adolescent supplement. *Archives of General Psychiatry, 68,* 714–723. http://dx.doi.org/10.1001/archgenpsychiatry.2011.22

Tanofsky-Kraff, M., & Wilfley, D. E. (2010). Interpersonal therapy for bulimia nervosa and binge eating disorder. In C. M. Grilo & J. E. Mitchell (Eds.), *The treatment of eating disorders: A clinical handbook* (pp. 271–293). New York, NY: Guilford Press.

Williams, M., & Haverkamp, B. E. (2015). Eating disorder therapists' personal eating disorder history and professional ethics: An interpretive description. *Eating Disorders: The Journal of Treatment & Prevention, 23,* 393–410. http://dx.doi.org/10.1080/10640266.2015.1013393

Winkler, L. A., Christiansen, E., Lichtenstein, M. B., Hansen, N. B., Bilenberg, N., & Støving, R. K. (2014). Quality of life in eating disorders: A meta-analysis. *Psychiatry Research, 219,* 1–9. http://dx.doi.org/10.1016/j.psychres.2014.05.002

World Health Organization. (1993). *The ICD–10 classification of mental and behavioural disorders: Clinical descriptions and diagnostic guidelines.* Retrieved from http://www.who.int/classifications/icd/en/bluebook.pdf

Jennifer A. Vencill and Eli Coleman

F52.0 Sexual Dysfunction

13

S exual dysfunctions represent a heterogeneous group of disorders distinguished by difficulty participating in sexual encounters and behaviors and associated distress (National Center for Health Statistics, 2014). Sexual functioning involves a complex interaction of physiology, sociocultural factors, psychological functioning, and, often, interpersonal relationships. Disruption of any of these components can have a negative impact on the sexual experience, and as such, individuals may present with co-occurring sexual dysfunctions, each of which must be thoroughly assessed and diagnosed to provide effective treatment. In the United States, prevalence rates for each sexual dysfunction have been difficult to obtain due to the paucity of large-scale epidemiologic data. Research suggests, however, that sexual dysfunctions, as a whole, may be among the more prevalent psychological concerns in the general population (Simons & Carey, 2001).

The Case

Erin, a 26-year-old, married, heterosexual, Caucasian woman, recently completed an intake with your colleague, Dr. Hawkins, at the community mental health clinic where you both work as psychologists. Erin was assigned to your

http://dx.doi.org/10.1037/0000069-014

An ICD–10–CM Casebook and Workbook for Students: Psychological and Behavioral Conditions, J. B. Schaffer and E. Rodolfa (Editors)

caseload and is scheduled to begin therapy with you next week. In reading the intake report and consulting with Dr. Hawkins about the case, you learn the following information: Erin was referred to your clinic by her obstetrics and gynecology provider and shared that, since marrying her husband, Matt, 5 years ago, she has largely been unable to "be with him" without experiencing pain. Regarding social history, Erin has both undergraduate and master's degrees in communications and reported that, although often stressful, she finds her job at a local nonprofit organization to be very rewarding. Erin is an only child and reportedly has a positive relationship with both of her parents, who have been married for more than 30 years.

Dr. Hawkins noted that Erin was tearful during her intake, which she attended alone. Erin reported that neither she nor her husband has previously been married and, although Matt had some previous sexual partners, she had been "a virgin" before marriage. She indicated that she often experiences feelings of uncertainty and a lack of confidence during sexual encounters with Matt, sensing that she has disappointed him sexually. She reported that she is a generally happy, confident person and that sex is the only area of her life where she feels completely inadequate and "not myself." During the intake with Dr. Hawkins, Erin also shared that she and Matt would like to have a child. She indicated feeling "guilty" that she is unable to have pain-free penetrative sex with Matt and blames herself for the couple's inability to have intercourse and, thus, become pregnant in this manner. Dr. Hawkins described Erin as a genuine and kind person, who seems to care deeply for her spouse and feels at fault for the couple's current sexual and fertility concerns.

In exploring Erin's use of the term *virgin*, Dr. Hawkins discovered that Erin had not had penetrative, penile–vaginal sex before marriage. However, she was sexually intimate with one of her college boyfriends, reporting that the couple mostly engaged in heavy petting "over the clothes" and "hand stuff." None of these behaviors were reportedly painful to Erin, including digital penetration. In fact, she noted how pleasurable these early sexual encounters felt, stating that she could often "climax" when she was with this particular partner. Erin expressed disbelief and frustration that what once had felt "really good" to her has become painful and distressing.

Erin informed Dr. Hawkins that her first experience with penile–vaginal sexual activity occurred during her honeymoon with Matt. She shared that, although "uncomfortable," penile–vaginal penetration was not initially painful. She reported, however, that it has become "excruciating" over the past few years of the marital relationship. Erin stated that Matt typically initiates sexual activity one or two times per week, although the couple no longer engages in penetrative sex. Erin also reported that she has been unable to achieve orgasm during sexual activity with her husband, although she can do so "when I'm with myself." She stated that she feels unable to speak to her friends about these sexual concerns in her marriage because she perceives them as experiencing positive and pleasurable sex lives with their own partners.

As part of your clinic's standard intake process, Dr. Hawkins administered several psychological screens to Erin. The results of these measures indicated few to no symptoms of anxiety or depression, and raised no concerns about substance use or abuse. Dr. Hawkins also informed you that Erin denied any history of sexual abuse, assault, or trauma.

Assessment Using the ICD–10–CM

ACTIVITY 13.1:

List additional information that you believe would be important to gather from Erin about her presenting concerns, background, personal history, and the like. What is your comfort level in inquiring about matters such as sexual frequency, specific partnered sexual acts (e.g., oral sex, anal sex, penile–vaginal sex), masturbation habits, genital lubrication, erectile functioning, orgasm, ejaculation, sexual attractions, fidelity, polyamory, and so on?

Although clients commonly have sexual concerns, they often feel embarrassed, ashamed, and reluctant to discuss them. As in Erin's case, many will struggle with sexual difficulties for months, even years, before seeking professional help. As with any presenting concern, it is helpful for the therapist to gather as much information as possible by means of a thorough assessment to arrive at an accurate diagnosis. However, health care providers report that they are often uncomfortable discussing sex and feel inadequately trained to address sexuality concerns in a clinical context (Miller & Byers, 2008; Wittenberg & Gerber, 2009). When both client and provider find discussing sexual matters embarrassing and unnerving, the result is a very difficult assessment!

As we discuss later in this chapter, it is important for you as a health care provider to obtain training and education about sexual health concerns, as well as to gain confidence in speaking about sexuality-related topics in a professional manner. This becomes particularly critical for assessment and diagnosis because clients are likely to speak about sexual behaviors and beliefs using imprecise language and (a lot of) euphemisms. As we see in Erin's case, *virgin* means something very specific to her in terms of sexual activity, and Dr. Hawkins's initial evaluation was strengthened by further exploration of this term. We advocate strongly for using precise and unambiguous language when assessing clients' sexual concerns, including asking them to clarify their statements, experiences, and behaviors, as needed. For example, Erin used the phrase "when I'm with myself," suggesting that she likely engages in solo masturbation, a topic that will be important to discuss further to arrive at an accurate diagnosis. Do not assume you know what she means unless you ask. You might clarify by asking something such as "When you say 'with myself,' what exactly do you mean?" In addition to assessment, this is also an opportunity for you to educate and help desensitize clients to discussions of sex and sexuality. Using a medically correct term, such as *masturbation*, can normalize such conversations, which will likely be uncomfortable for many clients.

Although it is critical for the provider to have a solid understanding of medically accurate language and to use this knowledge for assessment, you are also encouraged to align with the client by adopting her or his own language *after you have clarified meaning*. Our experience has shown that this most often seems to arise around language for genitalia and sexual positions, in which slang or the use of euphemisms is a cultural norm (e.g., using the term *doggy style* when referring to penile–vaginal penetration from behind). You are encouraged to consider using the client's own language in asking follow-up questions (e.g., "When you and your husband have sex doggy style, where do you feel pain?"). Although treatment may ultimately involve providing education about accurate language (e.g., learning terms for one's genital anatomy), such verbal alignment with clients, especially early on in therapy, can help to put them at ease in discussing sexuality concerns with you because it communicates validation and a nonjudgmental approach.

ICD–10–CM Diagnosis

ACTIVITY 13.2:

List all the potential diagnoses that may be applicable, given the case information you have at this point in time. Would you consider a mood or anxiety disorder?

The most recent edition of the *Diagnostic and Statistical Manual of Mental Disorders* (*DSM*; American Psychiatric Association, 2013), the *DSM–5*, on which many mental health professionals, especially in the United States, have been trained, features a significant departure from previous editions in terms of how sexual dysfunctions are defined and categorized. For example, the *DSM–5* collapsed sexual pain diagnoses from previous editions of the manual (i.e., vaginismus, dyspareunia in the *DSM–IV–TR*) into a single diagnosis, labeled *genito-pelvic pain/penetration disorder*. The ICD–10–CM is not well aligned with the "Sexual Dysfunctions" chapter of the *DSM–5* but is more congruent with the previous *DSM–IV–TR* sexual dysfunction classifications. Hence, those trained using the *DSM–5* will likely notice significant discrepancies in sexual dysfunction diagnoses between that manual and the ICD–10–CM, which is required for use in billing third-party payors in the United States. This may require a slight shift in processing as you are learning to use the latter effectively for assessment and diagnosis of sexual concerns.

Let us consider the diagnostic possibilities with Erin. Although sexual dysfunctions are often comorbid with and related to anxiety and mood disorders, it is also important to remember that clients present with many emotions about their sexual functioning (e.g., guilt, shame, frustration) that do not necessarily constitute a mental health diagnosis. These feelings may, in fact, be natural and predictable reactions to sexual difficulties. Erin reported few symptoms of general anxiety or depression on the psychological screens administered at intake, providing evidence for rule-out of these diagnoses. That said, however, we encourage ongoing assessment of anxiety and mood, such as Other specified anxiety disorders (F41.8) or Adjustment disorder with mixed anxiety and depressed mood (F42.23) because such symptoms can arise during the course of treatment for sexuality-related concerns. Our focus here is on

Erin's pain during penile–vaginal penetration and seemingly inconsistent orgasmic capability.

In the case of sexual pain, the most obvious potential diagnoses are perhaps Vaginismus not due to a substance or known physiological condition (F52.5) or Dyspareunia not due to a substance or known physiological condition (F52.6). *Dyspareunia* is a general term for pain during intercourse and can be caused by a number of factors, including vaginismus, a spasm of the muscles surrounding the vagina that can prevent penetration, but also by a number of other organic concerns, such as inadequate lubrication; a sexually transmitted or other infection (e.g., yeast infections); pelvic and/or spinal injuries; irritation from a number of items, such as soap, feminine hygiene products, spermicide, and condoms; and even common skin conditions that can affect the genitalia (e.g., eczema, psoriasis). As is often the case, such considerations illuminate the need to obtain additional information from your client that would allow you to discuss and evaluate each of these issues. This may require referral to a physician, preferably someone specializing in sexual medicine, who can perform a physical examination to rule out or confirm physical causes that history-taking cannot always address. You will want to get a signed release of information that will allow you to review the results of this examination.

Because a diagnosis of Dyspareunia not due to a substance or known physiological condition (F52.6) refers to sexual pain in which no obvious physical cause is apparent or a case in which emotional factors may play a role, this would not be diagnosed if any of the preceding organic conditions were found to be the primary cause of Erin's sexual pain. For example, if you learned that Erin had developed herniated disks in her spine before experiencing sexual pain, and a physician confirmed that musculature spasms that occlude the vaginal opening are secondary to a client's back injury, such sexual pain would likely be classified as organic—that is, Dyspareunia due to a known physiological condition (N94.1) or Vaginismus due to a known physiological condition (N94.2)—rather than Vaginismus not due to a substance or known physiological condition (F52.5). Sometimes such diagnostic criteria are not clear. For example, the involuntary muscle contractions of vaginismus caused by back injury may be treated effectively via pelvic physical therapy, but despite physical improvement, the client could continue to experience pain during intercourse due to stress, anxiety, relationship factors, and so on. It is common to encounter sexual dysfunction that involves both organic and nonorganic underpinnings, so both diagnoses may be appropriate. This also affirms the importance of an interdisciplinary team approach when diagnosing and treating sexual functioning concerns. In the case of Erin, we are unfortunately provided little in the way of medical history, so including this on your list of additional information to gather is important.

Another potential ICD–10–CM diagnosis for Erin was alluded to earlier: Female sexual arousal disorder (F52.22). This diagnosis is made when the primary difficulty is vaginal dryness or lack of lubrication (which is likely to contribute to, or cause, sexual discomfort or pain). Origins of vaginal dryness can be both psychogenic (e.g., stress, anger, anxiety) and/or organic (e.g., estrogen deficiency, infection) in nature, again highlighting the critical importance of taking a thorough history and referring Erin for a physical examination. To gather evidence for or against a Female sexual arousal disorder (F52.22) diagnosis, you are encouraged to assess specifically the client's perception of her lubrication and genital "wetness," as well as the use of any store-bought lubricants during sexual activity, remembering, of course, that sometimes these can cause irritation or pain in and of themselves. You should also assess whether adequate foreplay typically occurs in the client's partnered sexual activity, providing time and space for vaginal lubrication to occur naturally. For some clients, education about the use of lubricants and the need to extend foreplay activities with their sexual partners can be enough to address this concern and alleviate experiences of sexual pain in the process.

One might also speculate that diagnoses such as Hypoactive sexual desire disorder (F52.0) or Sexual aversion disorder (F52.1) could apply to Erin. On the basis of the intake, we do not have sufficient evidence to support fully either diagnosis, but they raise crucial questions to consider asking the client. For example, does Erin experience desire for sexual activity or sexual thoughts? If so, how often? Are her husband's sexual advances welcome? Are they avoided? Given that Erin alluded to masturbating when alone, you may feel that a sexual aversion diagnosis is unlikely. However, Sexual aversion disorder (F52.1) is related specifically to avoidance of *partnered* sexual activity due to strong negative feelings, anxiety, or fear about such a sexual interaction. Perhaps this fits with Erin's reported experience of guilt and feelings of inadequacy when it comes to partnered sexual activity?

The ICD–10–CM offers only one option for diagnosing orgasmic concerns: Orgasmic disorder (F52.3) or, in this case, Female orgasmic disorder (F52.31). Orgasmic concerns are often identified as *situational* or *generalized*, respectively, referring to whether the problem occurs only in certain situations or is generalized to all sexual encounters. According to the intake report, Erin seems to be experiencing situational difficulty with orgasm in that she appears able to climax when masturbating alone. This information needs to be more fully evaluated, however, given that Erin did not specifically talk about masturbation during her intake, alluding only to "when I'm with myself." Of note, it is possible that Erin's difficulties with orgasm may be alleviated once the sexual pain is addressed. In this situation, even if problems with orgasm are linked to sexual pain, both diagnoses would still be made to capture fully the clinical picture and Erin's presenting concerns.

Although diagnoses related to concerns such as sexual trauma were ruled out at intake, others related to Erin's experiences might also be considered, including Problems related to social environment (Z60.8) or Problems in relationship with spouse or partner (Z63.0). Of note, third-party payers often do not reimburse for services based on such "Z code" diagnoses unless they are secondary to another concern (e.g., Female orgasmic disorder [F52.31]). If a Z code is the primary diagnosis, providers are ethically bound to discuss with their clients the implications of proceeding with treatment when it may not be financially covered.

Given the limited information that we currently have from Erin's intake, the most appropriate diagnoses at this point would likely be Dyspareunia not due to a substance or known physiological condition (F52.6) and Female orgasmic disorder (F52.31). It is important to remember that diagnoses can, and should, be changed as additional information is obtained. In Erin's case, this would entail further assessment of her medical history, current physical health, and sexual behaviors and functioning to rule out other potential diagnoses.

Ethical Considerations—Protecting Your Patient

> **ACTIVITY 13.3:**
>
> What are the specific ethical issues you see in this case? Are there any ethical concerns related to discomfort and embarrassment that can be associated with sexual dysfunction? What unique ethical issues could arise from couples therapy with Erin and her husband, rather than seeing Erin alone?

Perhaps the most important ethical consideration in Erin's case involves boundaries to clinical competence. Both the American Psychological Association (APA; 2017) *Ethical Principles of Psychologists and Code of Conduct* (APA Ethics Code) and the *Canadian Code of Ethics for Psychologists* (Canadian Psychological Association [CPA], 2017) explicitly address the importance of practicing within the scope of one's competence (APA Ethics Code, Standard 2.01, Boundaries of Competence; CPA Code of Ethics, Standard II.6, 9). The APA Ethics Code states: "Psychologists provide services . . . with populations and in areas only within the boundaries of their competence, based on their education, training, supervised experience, consultation, study, or professional experience." This is a critical concern that we return to in the next section.

Maintaining the privacy and confidentiality (APA Ethics Code, Section 4: Privacy and Confidentiality) of clients is an essential foundation on which psychotherapy is built, with an ethical obligation to minimize any potential intrusions to client privacy. Issues related to the maintenance and limitations of confidentiality must be discussed with all clients capable of providing informed consent or with their legal representative. Given the delicate and sensitive nature of sexual health information, including potential therapeutic discussions about sexual functioning, HIV status, partnered sexual activities, among others, it becomes even more critical to discuss thoroughly with clients how their privacy and confidentiality will be maintained, as well as how they may be limited. For example, in the era of electronic medical records and large health care systems, clients may not be aware that their other medical providers could potentially view diagnoses, therapy notes, or evaluation reports. It is incumbent on you, as the therapist, to ensure the client is fully aware and has provided informed consent regarding what information will become part of their medical record. Minimizing violations of privacy entails that written reports and progress notes include "only information that is germane to the purpose" of the communication. When it comes to documenting information regarding sexual history and sexual functioning, the provider is faced with a significant decision around which details are necessary for evaluation and treatment and which can be excluded to protect the client's privacy.

If you intend to move forward with conjoint or couples therapy sessions involving both Erin and Matt, you will need to consider carefully another ethical concern: the creation of multiple roles. Opinions in the field vary as to the therapist's role, for example, in seeing a client for individual therapy while also seeing her with her partner for couples/family therapy. Many believe that this is a situation better suited to two therapists: one for individual work and another for couples/family therapy, although it may depend on presenting concerns, availability of providers, and other circumstances (Corey, Corey, & Callanan, 2011). Alternatively, you may decide to bring Matt in as a collateral source, meaning that he is there to support Erin in her individual therapy rather than to engage in couples/family treatment. In either case, it is important to clarify your role and the role of the people you are working with (APA Ethics Code, Section 10: Therapy). You will need to consider carefully your role in the therapeutic process and be explicit in discussing this with both partners, including clarification around Matt's role as a collateral source or a couples/family therapy client and why. These are complex issues related specifically to therapeutic work with couples and families. As such, relevant resources (e.g., family therapy textbooks and journals, expert supervisors) should be consulted in addition to the ethics codes.

Risk Management—Protecting Your Patient, Protecting Yourself

ACTIVITY 13.4:

What potential risks do you see in working therapeutically with Erin? Are you concerned about any risks associated with you feeling uncomfortable or unqualified when addressing Erin or her husband's sexual concerns? How could you mitigate those risks?

In many ways, protecting one's clients also serves to protect oneself. In what is perhaps the largest potential risk in this case, we again turn to the question of competence. As a clinician, one of the most important ethical decisions related to client care (and excellent practice for your own protection) is ongoing self-evaluation as to your areas and levels of competence. What are your areas of clinical strength? What are your clinical weaknesses? We all have strengths and areas for continued growth. However, to see a client with a presenting problem or from a group or cultural identity that you have no experience with is inappropriate at best and dangerous at worst. If you are not competent in working clinically with a particular presenting concern or population, referral to another provider is likely to be the best (and most ethical) way to protect and serve both the client and yourself. Another option, as previously noted, is to enlist assistance via supervision or consultation.

With regard to Erin's case, and sexual dysfunctions in general, protecting oneself should also come in the form of specific education and training about sex and sexuality topics. We believe that working clinically with sexual functioning concerns represents a specialty within the mental health profession and, as such, requires specific training. We recognize, however, that many budding therapists are not provided options for such specialized training in sexual health. As you have read, this has resulted in a great number of providers who are inadequately trained to work with clients such as Erin or who feel quite uncomfortable doing so given that the concerns are sexual in nature. Thankfully, there are a number of resources for further education, training, and supervision of sexuality-related therapeutic care. You are encouraged to contact relevant professional organizations (e.g., the American Association of Sexuality Educators, Counselors, and Therapists) and to familiarize yourself with journals focused on sexuality concerns and treatment (e.g., the *Journal of Sex & Marital Therapy, Relationship and Sexual Therapy*). Exhibit 13.1 features a selection of excellent books for further reading.

EXHIBIT 13.1

Learning More: Addressing Sexual Concerns in Therapy

Binik, Y. M., & Hall, K. S. K. (Eds.). (2014). *Principles and practice of sex therapy* (5th ed.). New York, NY: Guilford Press.

Levine, S. B., Risen, C. B., & Althof, S. E. (Eds.). (2016). *Handbook of clinical sexuality for mental health professionals* (3rd ed.). New York, NY: Routledge.

Maurice, W. L. (1999). Talking about sexual issues: History-taking and interviewing. In E. M. Fathman (Ed.), *Sexual medicine in primary care* (pp. 6–24). St. Louis, MO: Mosby, Inc. [Available free of charge at: http://www.kinseyinstitute.org/resources/maurice.html]

Wincze, J. P., & Weisberg, R. B. (Eds.). (2015). *Sexual dysfunction: A guide for assessment and treatment* (3rd ed.). New York, NY: Guilford Press.

Disposition

ACTIVITY 13.5:

What thoughts do you have about how to be most effective in working with Erin? Would you treat her individually or with her partner? What might be some of your initial treatment goals for Erin? Would you make any referrals?

Our initial approach to evaluating sexual functioning concerns is fairly consistent across clients. First, a thorough assessment is conducted, which includes a detailed sexual and relationship history. Taking a sexual history is a unique skill and, for the reasons we have outlined in this chapter, one we feel is required to work effectively with clients who have sexual functioning concerns. For guidance on taking a sexual history, we refer you to the list of resources provided in Exhibit 13.1, particularly Maurice's (1999) chapter on this topic. Second, it is common practice for us to refer clients presenting with sexual functioning concerns to a physician specializing in sexual medicine to assess and rule out (as much as possible) any organic factors that may be contributing to the problem. This is true regardless of whether the client presents with sexual pain, arousal difficulties, problems with orgasm, or other issues and even when the concerns seem to us to be mostly psychological in nature.

In Erin's case, an initial diagnosis of Dyspareunia not due to a substance or known physiological condition (F52.6) was made to account for sexual pain. A rule-out for Vaginismus not due to a substance or known physiological condition (F52.5) was also included, and she was referred for a sexual medicine examination to clarify this diagnosis. During the physical examination, it was discovered that Erin did indeed exhibit involuntary pelvic muscle contractions (vaginismus). These contractions were found to be "mild" enough to still allow for some vaginal penetration, although with significant pain as penetrative objects increased in size. No organic factors were found on examination or within Erin's medical history to account for this symptom. As a result, Erin was referred by the physician to pelvic physical therapy and concurrently to attend psychotherapy for treatment of Vaginismus not due to a substance or known physiological condition (F52.5) and situational Female orgasmic disorder (F52.31).

Sexual dysfunctions represent an overlapping but heterogeneous group of disorders. As such, empirically supported treatment varies significantly by the dysfunction under consideration. For example, the behavioral "stop–start method," originally described by Kaplan (1989), is the gold standard for treating premature ejaculation in sex therapy. Further, although there is no medication approved specifically for the treatment of premature ejaculation, selective serotonin reuptake inhibitors (which have a known side effect of delayed ejaculation) are often successfully used off-label and in conjunction with therapy to address this concern. In this, as in the treatment of most (if not all) sexual dysfunctions, integrated clinical care is of upmost importance. A number of handbooks provide descriptions of empirically supported treatments across a variety of sexual dysfunctions (Binik & Hall, 2014; Hertlein, Weeks, & Gambescia, 2015; Levine, Risen, & Althof, 2016).

In the initial stages of treatment for sexual functioning concerns, therapy often primarily involves individual counseling. This allows you to establish a safe space with clients in which they can explore and talk about their sexuality, perhaps for the first time. Treatment is typically designed to help clients gain a greater understanding of their own anatomy, sexual beliefs, values, and desires. This includes helping clients learn to express openly their sexual likes, dislikes, and desires and, eventually, working to incorporate these skills into any partnered sexual encounters. Common techniques include exploring fantasy, self-touch exercises, and at-home genital looking and exploration. Beginning treatment with individual therapy also allows you to provide general support to your clients, who may present feeling quite isolated and unable to use their typical social support networks when it comes to discussing matters of sexuality. Furthermore, individual counseling is an important place for clients to explore and process feelings—including embarrassment, guilt, shame, and uncertainty—that often arise around sex and sexuality.

As previously noted, treatment for sexual dysfunctions may also necessitate involving partners in some way. Depending on your client's particular concerns and treatment goals, this may happen in the form of couples/family therapy or conjoint sessions, in which the partner is invited to join your client's sessions for support and education. In either scenario, it is common to assist partners in beginning to speak more honestly about their sexual needs, wants, and desires, bringing in learned skills from individual counseling. In the case of sexual pain, the therapist would likely recommend that partners not attempt to engage in penetrative sex while the client completes pelvic physical therapy. This opens up an opportunity for the couple to explore other sexual activities without pressure or fear of pain and can significantly increase sexual confidence and the expansion of a couple's sexual repertoire far beyond penetrative sex. Gradually, penetrative sex can be reintroduced with guidance by the clinician in a prescribed and systematic fashion.

Sometimes sexual dysfunction occurs in the presence of current, ongoing abuse in the relationship. In such a circumstance, safety must be addressed first and foremost, just as in other diagnoses. When there are active trauma symptoms, treating those before treating the sexual problems is typically indicated. Of course, case-by-case assessment is critical (e.g., a client who presents with nonsexual trauma related to war zone or military experience may be able to engage in treatment for a sexual dysfunction more immediately).

References

American Psychiatric Association. (2013). *Diagnostic and statistical manual of mental disorders* (5th ed.). Washington, DC: Author.

American Psychological Association. (2017). *Ethical principles of psychologists and code of conduct* (2002, Amended June 1, 2010 and January 1, 2017). Retrieved from http://www.apa.org/ethics/code/index.aspx

Binik, Y. M., & Hall, K. S. K. (Eds.). (2014). *Principles and practice of sex therapy* (5th ed.). New York, NY: Guilford Press.

Canadian Psychological Association. (2017). *Canadian code of ethics for psychologists* (4th ed.). Retrieved from http://www.cpa.ca/docs/File/Ethics/CPA_Code_2017_4thEd.pdf

Corey, G., Corey, M. S., & Callanan, P. (2011). *Issues and ethics in the helping professions* (8th ed.). Belmont, CA: Brooks/Cole.

Hertlein, K. M., Weeks, G. R., & Gambescia, N. (Eds.). (2015). *Systemic sex therapy* (2nd ed.). New York, NY: Routledge.

Kaplan, H. S. (1989). *PE: How to overcome premature ejaculation.* New York, NY: Brunner/Mazel.

Levine, S. B., Risen, C. B., & Althof, S. E. (Eds.). (2016). *Handbook of clinical sexuality for mental health professionals* (3rd ed.). New York, NY: Routledge.

Maurice, W. L. (1999). Talking about sexual issues: History-taking and interviewing. In E. M. Fathman (Ed.), *Sexual medicine in primary care* (pp. 6–24). St. Louis, MO: Mosby, Inc.

Miller, S. A., & Byers, E. S. (2008). An exploratory examination of the sexual intervention self-efficacy of clinical psychology graduate students. *Training and Education in Professional Psychology, 2,* 137–144. http://dx.doi.org/10.1037/1931-3918.2.3.137

National Center for Health Statistics. (2014). *International classification of diseases and related health problems—Tenth revision, clinical modification.* Washington, DC: United States Government. Retrieved from http://www.cdc.gov/nchs/icd/icd10cm.htm#icd2014

Simons, J. S., & Carey, M. P. (2001). Prevalence of sexual dysfunctions: Results from a decade of research. *Archives of Sexual Behavior, 30,* 177–219. http://dx.doi.org/10.1023/A:1002729318254

Wittenberg, A., & Gerber, J. (2009). Recommendations for improving sexual health curricula in medical schools: Results from a two-arm study collecting data from patients and medical students. *Journal of Sexual Medicine, 6,* 362–368. http://dx.doi.org/10.1111/j.1743-6109.2008.01046.x

Chelsea E. Sleep and Martin Sellbom

F60.6 Avoidant Personality Disorder/F60.0 Paranoid Personality Disorder

Categorical and Dimensional Approaches

14

P ersonality disorders generally reflect persistent patterns of inner experience and behavior that are considered to be maladaptive or culturally infrequent (World Health Organization [WHO], 1993). Specifically, they affect individuals' thinking, emotional regulation, behavioral control, and interpersonal relationships and cause significant distress or impairment. These dysfunctions are inflexible, pervasive across situations, and can generally be traced back to adolescence. Personality disorders are commonly found in all medical settings (Tyrer, Reed, & Crawford, 2015); therefore, given the enduring pattern and the distress they cause for the individual and society, they are important to identify and classify.

The assessment of personality disorders tends to be one of the most challenging tasks in clinical practice, most notably due to their pervasive nature and general lack of biological or independent markers to assist with identification (Tyrer et al., 2015). Unfortunately, we find that such assessment is all too often ignored or deemphasized in clinical training. In the second author's experience, many university clinics (across two continents) often refuse to treat patients with personality pathology, with the most frequent rationalization being that it is too difficult for student clinicians. The severity of the dysfunction, as well as inherent deficits in interpersonal functioning, obviously contribute to this difficulty. There is also a considerable debate among scholarly

http://dx.doi.org/10.1037/0000069-015
An ICD–10–CM Casebook and Workbook for Students: Psychological and Behavioral Conditions, J. B. Schaffer and E. Rodolfa (Editors)

experts regarding the classification of personality disorders, and that debate likely contributes to the confusion. Historically, a categorical model of classification has been used in our diagnostic manuals, influenced by the traditional medical model, which suggests that all mental disorders are distinct constructs. Psychopathology has been similarly described through defining sets of diagnostic criteria in the *International Classification of Diseases* (ICD) and the *Diagnostic and Statistical Manual for Mental Disorders* (DSM). The categorical classification of personality psychopathology has been plagued with conceptual and empirical limitations (see, e.g., Krueger, Hopwood, Wright, & Markon, 2014; Skodol, 2012; Widiger & Trull, 2007, for reviews). In particular, excessive symptom overlap produces high rates of comorbidity among supposedly distinct conditions. *Polythetic* criterion sets (i.e., a patient needs X out of Y symptoms to meet criteria for a diagnosis) create arbitrary boundaries between normal and maladaptive functioning, as well as a large number of different symptom manifestations for patients with the same diagnosis (in some cases, patients might not share a single symptom). These criterion sets can also result in valuable information loss due to arbitrary thresholds. For instance, if an individual does not have the required number of symptoms to be diagnosed with a disorder, then even if experiencing impairment, that person would not receive a diagnosis. Additionally, there is a loss of utility in clinical practice because you lose a way to describe the patient using common diagnostic labels. Furthermore, Peter Tyrer, the chair of the WHO's section on personality disorders for the upcoming 11th edition of the ICD (ICD–11), has asserted that traditional classification systems lack satisfactory empirical support. As a result, the categorical classification, particularly in terms of personality disorders, has little utility in clinical practice (Tyrer, 2013).

You may be relieved to learn that the field of personality disorder research is progressing. Indeed, in response to many of the limitations just mentioned, recent developments through assessment and psychopathology research have emphasized dimensional models, which maintain that personality psychopathology occurs along a continuum from normal functioning to severe dysfunction (Krueger et al., 2014). Such models are based on personality trait theories, which assert that all individuals have unique personalities comprising higher order and secondary traits (Tyrer, 2013). These models use not only a trait-based approach to assess and describe psychopathology but also a system for examining the individual's level of impairment. Research has indicated that a dimensional model of classification that focuses on dimensional personality traits can address most, if not all, of the limitations inherent in the categorical conceptualization (Widiger & Trull, 2007). This means that instead of diagnosing an individual with multiple personality disorders, you would describe an individual's personality through a constellation of elevations on maladaptive personality traits (Krueger & Markon, 2014). Dimensional models are also able to provide a greater coverage of maladaptive personality functioning without the inclusion of redundant diagnoses (Widiger & Trull, 2007). This is accomplished by organizing traits into a hierarchical structure, with higher order traits (e.g., neuroticism) at one level and more specific facets (e.g., anxiousness, separation insecurity) at the lower level. Overall, dimensional models have much more empirical support than the traditional categorical classification (Krueger et al., 2014; Widiger, 2011).

A new model for personality disorder diagnosis is set to be implemented in the ICD–11. The ICD–11 Work Group in charge of reclassifying personality disorders has recognized the aforementioned complications and opted to remove distinct personality disorder categories. Specifically, personality disorders will be considered through dimensional personality traits, which are still in the process of being selected (Tyrer et al., 2014). The primary classification will use one disorder with four levels of severity: Personality Difficulty (classified as a Z-code), Mild Personality Disorder, Moderate Personality Disorder, and Severe Personality Disorder. Note that in this proposed system, personality disorders will be viewed as a continuum. Additionally, severity is of chief importance in reaching a diagnosis and will be measured in various domains of functioning (Tyrer et al., 2014). The *DSM–5* has also moved away from a categorical model by proposing an alternative model of personality disorders in its Section III (American Psychiatric Association, 2013). Similarly, this alternative model reduces personality disorder categories and evaluates personality disorders in terms of personality traits and functional impairment.

A major question in the current literature regarding dimensional approaches to diagnosis is that of *clinical utility*. Some opponents to dimensional approaches will argue that there is no intuitive use of dimensions in practice. However, we and many others contend that the use of severity dimensions rather than polythetic criterion sets can only improve decision-making and classification (Livesley, 2012). Indeed, diagnostic manuals already have an example: intellectual disability. Here, we have a normally distributed, individual-differences construct—namely, intelligence. Extremely low standing (typically two standard deviations below the mean) on this construct is considered sufficiently abnormal, and, when coupled with adaptive deficits (i.e., functional impairment), a diagnosis is made. A similarly useful approach can be applied to the combination of dimensional personality traits and impairment, as well in diagnostic decision-making (Crawford, Koldobsky, Mulder, & Tyrer, 2011).

In this chapter, we analyze one case from both traditional (categorical; ICD–10) and dimensional perspectives. In particular, for the purpose of this chapter, we illustrate how to formulate personality disorders in terms of personality traits and functional impairment that are rooted in the empirical literature. Our evaluation of impairment is inspired by what is proposed to appear in ICD–11 as described by Tyrer and colleagues (2015). We hope this discussion will help you use the ICD–10–CM now and also help you look to the future in the diagnosis of personality disorders.

The Case

Anne is a 33-year-old White woman who requested a psychological evaluation for diagnosis and treatment recommendations. She contacted a local psychology clinic because she was diagnosed with "borderline personality disorder" by a previous psychologist and was hoping for an evaluation to confirm the accuracy of this diagnosis. Anne initially explains that she struggles with her "whole self" and is having "crazy thoughts." She has been trying to get help for years but to no avail. She describes every day as "overwhelming" and states that she doesn't have relationships with others, which is "clearly not how it's supposed to be." During the past 12 months, things have gotten particularly "out of hand" as she feels that she "just wants everyone to go away." She feels overwhelmed by stress and anxiety and as a result "loses it . . . and becomes really nasty . . . especially with the children." She admits to verbally and physically abusing them because she cannot cope with her own emotions and their acting out at the same time. She indicated that the verbal abuse is frequent, whereas the physical abuse happens about once every 2 or 3 months. As a result, Anne is experiencing significant emotional distress and problems in various areas of functioning.

In addition to her inability to control her emotions, Anne also reports severe social difficulties. She says she doesn't trust others, that the process of maintaining friendships with others scares her, and she believes that her significant others will not be faithful. She expresses reluctance to confide in others and believes people will exploit her if given the opportunity. She typically has "extreme hate" for others; indeed she "loves" to hate others because then "I am not the only scumbag around." It also becomes clear that feelings of inadequacy and self-loathing contribute to Anne's avoidance of social situations, as she is unwilling to socialize with others unless she is certain that she will be not be rejected. Indeed, she states several times that she is hypersensitive to criticism and hates to feel embarrassed. Nevertheless, Anne emphasizes (rather paradoxically) that she desires personal relationships and does not want to be alone. In fact, she has engaged in frantic efforts to avoid abandonment by a significant other, calling herself a "crazy lady" in this respect. This paradox is consistent with having an unstable or even nonexistent identity, which Anne expresses as, "I don't even know who I am." Anne also described an ongoing struggle with eating. She is underweight and will often starve herself, especially when feeling angry with herself. She is terrified of gaining weight and is self-conscious about her appearance. However, she also notes that she doesn't want to get "too skinny" again, supporting her rather unstable identity. Finally, Anne often experiences states of "dissociation" in which she "feels just not there . . . like a dream state . . . my whole body tingles; I am not on earth," which occurs frequently when she is in social situations.

This is not the first time Anne has sought help. She first saw a school counselor in Grade 5 or 6 due to behavior problems. At age 14, it was recommended that she "get cognitive behavior therapy," but she did not want to go through with it. Later, at age 18, she was hospitalized after a "breakdown." She describes a "suicide attempt" some months later, when she took 36 Effexor (venlafaxin, a selective serotonin reuptake inhibitor) pills, but she characterizes it as a "cry for help" more than a suicide attempt because she "wanted everyone to see how much I was struggling." Nonetheless, she states that she didn't really care if she died or not. She reports that she was taken to the "neuro ward" because she had three seizures from her overdose. At age 20, she sought rape crisis counseling, as she was the victim of a sexual assault. Subsequently, she received treatment from various psychologists "on and off" with little to no self-reported improvement.

A key element of diagnostic formulation is placing a client's presenting symptoms and problems within the context of her general background. Anne cannot remember much from her childhood, but she does state that growing up was at times chaotic because her mother was a "stress-head, but a good person." Her father had behavioral difficulties subsequent to a head trauma and used "emotional blackmail," when he would imply that if she did not do as he wished, he would disown her. She mentions that she witnessed her father physically abuse her older brothers but he did not do this to Anne because she was a girl. He was also more affectionate toward her, which created jealousy among the boys, who used to tease her and call her "princess." She recalls one specific instance in which they tried to smother her with a pillow "to scare me, not kill me." Anne also recalls that when she was young (between 3 and 5 years old), her oldest brother engaged in sexual play with her. She reports feeling very confused at the time, but she had forgotten it for a long time until her own daughter was sexually victimized. Anne also reports that in the sixth grade, she was pinned down by a group of boys who threatened to rape her. At age 20, she was drugged (flunitrazepam) in a bar and woke up to a stranger digitally penetrating her. These types of experiences can of course be quite formative with respect to later symptom development, especially emotional regulation.

Anne also reports that when growing up, she rarely had friends and did not fit in. She behaved in a very "sexualized" manner in early adolescence, which included exposing herself to boys because she thought it would make them like her. She also began drinking alcohol at age 13 because she "wanted to be cool and have friends." At age 17, she had her first boyfriend; he was 20 at the time. He pressured her to have sex, and she consented: "I would shut my eyes and pretend I wasn't there." He was also physically abusive to her, and she eventually managed to leave the relationship. A few years later, she met the father of her children. Their relationship was tumultuous, in part due to his methamphetamine addiction, and eventually ended. Anne reports having significant difficulties with her children. Her daughter (age 11) has "chronic PTSD" [posttraumatic stress disorder] as a result of being sexually victimized and "dissociates all the time." Her son (age 8) also has "trauma-based anxiety" and exhibits major behavioral problems in school and at home.

For the past 3.5 years, Anne has been dating a man who is in the Navy and has not been home much. She describes the relationship as "weird," and they often break up because of her emotional outbursts. However, they remain together. He has been very supportive of her, and "the kids love him." Anne loves him and has been completely faithful to him for the duration of the relationship, adding, "I fall in love very easily, so I wouldn't want to sleep with someone else and develop feelings." Unfortunately, he is about to be deployed to Antarctica for at least 6 months, which is stressful for her.

Assessment Using the ICD–10–CM

ACTIVITY 14.1:

What do you make of this complex symptom constellation? In terms of diagnosis, which behaviors and emotions are most relevant? What additional information do you think would be helpful?

Multiple sources of information are imperative in the diagnosis of personality pathology, as pervasive and complex patterns of behavior across adulthood are expected, which is not easily articulated through a single source (e.g., clinical interview). Moreover, evidence-based psychological assessment guidelines recommend the reliance on multiple sources of information (e.g., Bornstein, 2016). Certainly, a comprehensive interview is necessary, with a comprehensive structured interview such as the Structured Clinical Interview for *DSM–IV* Axis II Disorders (First, Gibbon, Spitzer, Williams, & Benjamin, 1997) adding to the interview's reliability. In addition, the Minnesota Multiphasic Personality Inventory—2—Restructured Form (MMPI–2–RF; Ben-Porath & Tellegen, 2008), a widely used multi-scale personality inventory, was included to broaden the sources of information as well as to increase reliability.

Anne was unable to provide an interpretable MMPI–2–RF profile, which was indicative of overreporting extreme negative emotionality, not uncommon given her history, but using a structured interview assisted in gathering some of the following information. She displayed both impulsivity and considerable persistent and long-standing affective instability. She presented as overly distressed and gave verbal reports of "overwhelming" anxiety, stress, self-loathing, and "miserable" mood. She also consistently displayed intense and uncontrollable anger with frequent verbal and occasional physical abuse toward her children, as well as a general suspiciousness toward others. With respect to impulsivity, she reported sexual promiscuity, binge drinking, and impulsive spending, as well as shoplifting when she was younger. Furthermore, Anne reported a history of unstable relationships characterized by sexual violence, physical violence, or an "on-and-off" nature, with a predilection toward extremes of valuation and devaluation (e.g., falling in love easily and also "hating" others). Furthermore, she displayed uncertainty about her identity and a history of pursuing multiple "on-and-off" vocational roles, educational pursuits, and mental health supports. She also reported recurrent suicidal thoughts (e.g., persistent thoughts of death) and self-harming behaviors (e.g., self-starvation and one previous known suicide attempt). Finally, she exhibited chronic feelings of emptiness, feeling like "there is nothing there."

Diagnosis Using the ICD–10–CM

Anne exhibits a number of symptoms possibly reflective of several mental disorders that are worthy of consideration. Given her history of significant trauma and emotional dysregulation and serious hypervigilance, at least partly in response to such trauma, Posttraumatic stress disorder (F43.1) is a viable candidate. Certainly, her level of emotional distress, with overwhelming anxiety and stress, combined with numerous traumatic events in her childhood, such as multiple episodes of sexual abuse or physical violence, should cause you to consider PTSD. However, there do not seem to be the recurring intrusive memories, reenactment, or even hypervigilance one typically sees in PTSD. There are also some symptoms that are not usually present in PTSD, such as self-loathing and extreme instability in interpersonal relationships. That the symptom picture is not entirely typical and that it is difficult to know whether the symptoms began within 6 months of the traumatic event(s), which occurred many years ago, probably rule out PTSD in this case.

Her extreme social anxiety, fear of criticism, and associated withdrawal could suggest a generalized Social phobia (F40.11). What is less consistent with a social phobia is her abuse toward her children and unstable relationships marked by suspiciousness and feelings of hatred, which include considerably more underlying aggression than is typically seen in a generalized social phobia, which derives more out of a fear of being criticized and viewed negatively by others.

Extreme negative emotionality, including miserable mood and self-loathing, suicidality, and chronic feelings of emptiness, also makes Anne a candidate for Major depressive disorder, recurrent (F33.1). People with major depression often experience negative emotions and strong feelings of inferiority. Again, relationships with others characterized by aggression are less common in depression, as opposed to feelings of personal inadequacy or even aggression toward oneself, making major depression a less likely diagnosis.

As you will see throughout the remainder of this formulation, it is our opinion that Anne's symptoms and behaviors are better accounted for by a chronic, inflexible, and maladaptive personality style in the form of a mixed personality disorder.[1] Let's start with the symptoms that lead you away from other diagnoses to a diagnosis of a personality disorder.

Many of Anne's symptoms seem to center on how she perceives herself in relation to others. She indicated persistent and pervasive feelings of tension and apprehension, given her proclivity to feel constantly stressed and overwhelmed, especially by social situations. She further indicated an unwillingness to get involved with others unless certain of being liked, restraint in intimate relationships, and a reluctance to confide in others because she reports fear of rejection. She is preoccupied with being criticized or rejected in social situations to the extent that she avoids such encounters. She exhibits inhibition in social relationships due to self-perception of inferiority and a pervasive self-perception of inferiority and hypersensitivity to criticism. In addition to fear of embarrassment and interpersonal rejection, Anne clearly demonstrated recurring suspicions that others would exploit or victimize her if given the opportunity (stating "it is safer to trust no one"). She indicated a long-standing history of "hating" others, being suspicious of their motives and feeling mistrustful toward people, and paranoid ideation of others' intentions and hidden meanings in their innocent remarks. Finally, she described holding grudges and having concerns of partner infidelity. Not surprisingly, these thoughts and feelings lead to considerable social avoidance.

This set of symptoms is most consistent with a persistent and pervasive pattern of behaviors that reflect an inflexible coping style and mode of relating to others, resulting in long-standing problems in social and vocational situations, along with subjective distress, all of which are essential characteristics in a personality disorder. Two personality disorders within the traditional diagnostic system are necessary to capture these

---

[1]Mixed personality disorder (F61.0) is included in ICD–10 but not in ICD–10–CM. We articulate the specific ICD–10–CM diagnoses later in the chapter.

social symptoms: Avoidant personality disorder (F60.6), which covers the anxiety and inadequacy she experiences in relationships, and Paranoid personality disorder (F60.0), which includes the suspiciousness and aggressiveness that are part of her relationships.

It has probably not escaped you that there is considerable overlap across the symptoms of these diagnoses—in particular, extreme dysfunction in interpersonal relationships, including an attempt to eschew close relationships—but also that the main strength of a categorical diagnosis system (ease of communication among health professionals) is completely diminished here, especially in light of major comorbidity (it is also noteworthy that Anne displays traits of two other personality disorders—Antisocial [F60.2; impulsivity and aggression] and Obsessive-compulsive [F60.5; rigidity and stubbornness]). That is, it takes four diagnostic categories to cover the various behaviors and emotions you have observed in Anne. What does a list of four diagnoses tell someone else about what is really going on with Anne? Could there be a more parsimonious and potentially empirically valid method of organizing this information?

ACTIVITY 14.2:

Before you continue reading, think about how you could better organize Anne's symptoms and traits according to a dimensional model. Describe where she falls on the impairment dimension discussed early in this chapter and how you (in your own words) would describe her (maladaptive) personality in a succinct manner without confinement to diagnostic categories.

A dimensional model of impairment and traits to characterize the personality style represents one potential solution. Is Anne impaired in functioning? Let's consider the evidence. Anne avoids social situations and is frequently angry and aggressive with others as a result of her inability to regulate her emotions. She always expects the worst in others and will attribute hostile intent in ambiguous circumstances. Moreover, she has substantial difficulty obtaining and maintaining employment. Finally, she is abusive toward her children and reported a significant lack of confidence in being able to appropriately care for them, to a degree that she allowed herself to be videotaped while stating she had abused them, hoping they would be removed from the home. As such, she demonstrates impairment in interpersonal, occupational, and legal domains. Using the personality disorder system that is proposed to be included in ICD–11, we would argue that she falls in the *severe* range of personality disorders.

Anne's symptoms and traits can be described in a fairly parsimonious manner from a personality trait perspective. She reaches highly maladaptive levels of negative affectivity and introversion. Indeed, she would be considered elevated on traits reflective of emotional instability (given her inability to regulate her emotions), anxiousness (owing to her intense, pervasive anxiety, especially about social interactions), separation insecurity (given her fear of rejection and abandonment), hostility (given her intense anger proneness and frustration intolerance), depressivity (due to her tendency to feel down, miserable, hopeless, and suicidal), and suspiciousness (owing to her paranoid ideation and interpersonal mistrust) from the negative affectivity domain. With respect to introversion, she would be very high on social withdrawal (given her tendency to socially isolate herself) and anhedonia (due to her inability to enjoy things in her environment and her chronic feelings of emptiness). Anne would also be considered to have moderate levels of impulsivity and psychoticism (due to her dissociative tendencies).

Thus, the proposed model for the ICD–11, which features an impairment model (Anne is severely impaired) and a parsimonious description based on a dimensional trait model, captures the full range of personality pathology (Anne is very high on negative affectivity and introversion). A clinically useful diagnosis can be made without the need to fit the person into personality disorder categories of questionable validity (Tyrer et al., 2015).

Ethical Considerations—Protecting Your Patient

> **ACTIVITY 14.3:**
>
> Given the introduction to this case, what are some ethical dilemmas you might encounter? Are you worried about the well-being of Anne's children? If so, is there anything you can do to ensure their safety without causing harm to Anne?

There are two main ethical issues you should consider. First, Anne reported (while videotaped during her initial session) that she becomes frustrated and angry to a point that she physically abuses her children. Psychologists are legally mandated to report to a designated authority when there is sufficient reason to believe that children have been exposed, or are in imminent danger of being exposed, to abuse or neglect; this should be unambiguously covered in the informed consent process. In such cases, you have to balance adhering to your ethical responsibility of maintaining confidentiality with minimizing harm to others and following the law yourself. This is also a risk management issue. Should harm come to the children and there was no report that could have led to their protection, you could be held liable. Sometimes, as in this case, clients reveal that they were so demoralized and overwhelmed that they feared for their children's safety in their company, and they had therefore manipulated the situation knowing quite well what the outcome would be. It is important that in these situations, you continue to monitor for potential indicators or current or imminent risk for abuse.

A second major (and related) issue is the risk for self-harm. In Anne's case, given the extent and frequency of her abuse toward her children and her expressed concern about being able to care for them, you decide that contacting Child Protective Services (CPS) is required. Even though Anne previously expressed a desire for her children to be removed from her home, she became extremely distressed and made suicidal references at the prospect of CPS's involvement. She had already described herself as constantly being preoccupied with death, and given her state of helplessness and hopelessness, suicide risk would be considered high. Again, the balance between adhering to differing ethical and legal obligations must be considered. As an initial step, an informal suicide risk determination should be conducted to determine the probability of self-harm; this would include an assessment of intent to commit suicide, articulation of any plans, and the level of direct means to carry out an attempt. Verbal or written safety plans (or both) are a good start to help clients develop more adaptive responses to suicidal ideation. If you have less confidence that this intervention would have a positive effect, emergency services (or hospitalization) should be considered.

A third issue is whether you want to provide services to someone as vulnerable, and yet inflexible, and with as many challenges as Anne. You have a right to decide which particular skills and areas of expertise you want to develop once you are in practice. At the same time, you do not have an ethical right to deny certain people services based on specific factors, such as those that are protected by federal law (American Psychological Association [APA; 2017] *Ethical Principles of Psychologists and Code of Conduct* [APA Ethics Code; Standard 3.01, Unfair Discrimination]). You will have to decide whether there is, in addition, an ethical imperative for you to deliver services to underserved and vulnerable populations, such as this case represents (see APA [2017] Ethics Code, Principle E: Respect for People's Rights and Dignity; and Canadian Psychological Association [CPA; 2017] Code of Ethics, Standard I, Values II, IV).

Risk Management—Protecting Your Patient, Protecting Yourself

ACTIVITY 14.4:

What risks could you encounter with a client like Anne who has problems with emotional regulation and instability? What can you do to protect yourself if Anne becomes hostile and resistant to treatment while still ensuring her well-being?

If you decide to establish a professional relationship with a person like Anne, being intentional and conscious of the ways you need to protect yourself is particularly important. A first important step is to be very clear with Anne about the role you will play and what your treatment with her will look like. This is a form of expectation management. It is important to be clear, right from the very beginning, about how far you will go and what you will do. That is, it is important to define your boundaries clearly. Further, it is important that you adhere carefully to those boundaries. Anne's mode of relating to others is likely to be inconsistent and inflexible, but this also means that she is likely fairly skilled at getting others to react to her in ways that either increase or decrease her anxiety. People who know her are likely to experience her behaviors as manipulative. Thus, it might be easy to give in to some of her requests—or demands—as a way of managing your own anxiety. Once one starts down that path, the risks mount. Some professionals get into considerable difficulty with boundary violations that evolve from a starting point of trying to be helpful with positive intentions.

Because people like Anne can be especially challenging, it is essential to have a group of colleagues who can act both as a support system and as a sounding board to make sure that what you are doing is appropriate and is not starting down a slippery slope of boundary violations. As discussed in Chapter 15 of this volume, such interaction with a group of professionals is recommended as an essential component of dialectical behavior therapy (DBT).

Disposition

ACTIVITY 14.5:

Anne clearly presents with a very complex symptom picture. What would you recommend for her treatment? What goals might you and Anne prioritize? Would you focus on any particular aspects of her personality or behaviors?

Given the severity of Anne's personality pathology, this will be a difficult case for any treatment provider. Certainly, Anne could benefit from intense individual psychotherapy focused on developing better emotional regulation skills, coping skills, self-esteem, and interpersonal relationships. A DBT approach (see Chapter 15, this volume) is empirically supported (e.g., Neacsiu, Eberle, Kramer, Wiesmann, & Linehan, 2014) and would be preferred because it encompasses so many strategies to minimize harm to self and others, mindfulness skills, cognitive behavioral strategies, social skills training, and ongoing support. However, DBT is a specialized form of treatment that is not always available in its full form in smaller communities. Therefore, given that many of Anne's feelings and behaviors can be traced back to maladaptive cognitive schemas, a cognitive behavioral approach could also be used should DBT not be accessible (e.g., Stoffers et al., 2012). Anne's impairment is, to a large degree, a dysfunction of coping. She is a person who has developed a set of coping mechanisms that do not work very effectively for her, so she continues to experience considerable emotional distress. Her coping style does not work very well for those around her either, such that others find her behaviors aversive. The goals of any type of therapy will be to help her develop more effective behavioral and emotional skills so that she can learn to respond to the challenges she faces in more effective ways.

In light of the severe nature of this particular case, psychotherapy should be provided by a licensed mental health professional competent to treat personality disorders. In addition, we strongly recommend that Anne undergo a careful evaluation for psychotropic medication (particularly for her high levels of affective dysregulation) by a psychiatrist to determine whether such additional treatment is warranted. In the end, regardless of treatment approach, it is unlikely that Anne's personality will be dramatically changed. Rather, the goal will be for her to develop sufficient coping skills to change her behaviors to become more adaptive when encountering stressful situations, despite her personality propensities.

References

American Psychiatric Association. (2013). *Diagnostic and statistical manual of mental disorders* (5th ed.). Washington, DC: Author.

American Psychological Association. (2017). *Ethical principles of psychologists and code of conduct* (2002, Amended June 1, 2010 and January 1, 2017). Retrieved from http://www.apa.org/ethics/code/index.aspx

Ben-Porath, Y., & Tellegen, A. (2008). *MMPI–2–RF: Manual for administration and scoring*. Minneapolis: University of Minnesota Press.

Bornstein, R. F. (2016). Evidence-based psychological assessment. *Journal of Personality Assessment, 3*, 1–11. http://dx.doi.org/10.1080/00223891.2016.1236343

Canadian Psychological Association. (2017). *Canadian code of ethics for psychologists* (4th ed.). Retrieved from http://www.cpa.ca/docs/File/Ethics/CPA_Code_2017_4thEd.pdf

Crawford, M. J., Koldobsky, N., Mulder, R., & Tyrer, P. (2011). Classifying personality disorder according to severity. *Journal of Personality Disorders, 25*, 321–330. http://dx.doi.org/10.1521/pedi.2011.25.3.321

First, M. B., Gibbon, M., Spitzer, R. L., Williams, J. B. W., & Benjamin, L. S. (1997). *Structured Clinical Interview for* DSM–IV *Axis II Disorders (SCID-II)*. Washington, DC: American Psychiatric Press.

Krueger, R. F., Hopwood, C. J., Wright, A., & Markon, K. (2014). DSM–5 and the path toward empirically based and clinically useful conceptualization of personality and psychopathology. *Clinical Psychology: Science and Practice, 21*, 245–261. http://dx.doi.org/10.1111/cpsp.12073

Krueger, R. F., & Markon, K. E. (2014). The role of the DSM–5 personality trait model in moving toward a quantitative and empirically based approach to classifying personality and psychopathology. *Annual Review of Clinical Psychology, 10*, 477–501. http://dx.doi.org/10.1146/annurev-clinpsy-032813-153732

Livesley, J. (2012). Tradition versus empiricism in the current DSM–5 proposal for revising the classification of personality disorders. *Criminal Behaviour and Mental Health, 22*, 81–90. http://dx.doi.org/10.1002/cbm.1826

Neacsiu, A. D., Eberle, J. W., Kramer, R., Wiesmann, T., & Linehan, M. M. (2014). Dialectical behavior therapy skills for transdiagnostic emotion dysregulation: A pilot randomized controlled trial. *Behaviour Research and Therapy, 59*, 40–51. http://dx.doi.org/10.1016/j.brat.2014.05.005

Skodol, A. E. (2012). Personality disorders in DSM–5. *Annual Review of Clinical Psychology, 8*, 317–344. http://dx.doi.org/10.1146/annurev-clinpsy-032511-143131

Stoffers, J. M., Völlm, B. A., Rücker, G., Timmer, A., Huband, N., & Lieb, K. (2012). Psychological therapies for people with borderline personality disorder. *Cochrane Database of Systematic Reviews, 8*, CD005652.

Tyrer, P. (2013). The classification of personality disorders in ICD–11: Implications for forensic psychiatry. *Criminal Behaviour and Mental Health, 23*, 1–5. http://dx.doi.org/10.1002/cbm.1850

Tyrer, P., Crawford, M., Sanatinia, R., Tyrer, H., Cooper, S., Muller-Pollard, C., . . . Weich, S. (2014). Preliminary studies of the ICD–11 classification of personality disorder in practice. *Personality and Mental Health, 8*, 254–263. Advance online publication. http://dx.doi.org/10.1002/pmh.1275

Tyrer, P., Reed, G. M., & Crawford, M. J. (2015). Classification, assessment, prevalence, and effect of personality disorder. *The Lancet, 385*, 717–726. http://dx.doi.org/10.1016/S0140-6736(14)61995-4

Widiger, T. A. (2011). The *DSM–5* dimensional model of personality disorder: Rationale and empirical support. *Journal of Personality Disorders, 25*, 222–234. http://dx.doi.org/10.1521/pedi.2011.25.2.222

Widiger, T. A., & Trull, T. J. (2007). Plate tectonics in the classification of personality disorder: Shifting to a dimensional model. *American Psychologist, 62*, 71–83. http://dx.doi.org/10.1037/0003-066X.62.2.71

World Health Organization. (1993). *ICD–10 classification of mental and behavioural disorders: Clinical descriptions and diagnostic guidelines.* Retrieved from http://www.who.int/classifications/icd/en/bluebook.pdf

Joyce P. Yang and Marsha M. Linehan

F60.3 Borderline Personality Disorder

15

Borderline personality disorder (BPD) is a serious disorder characterized by a pervasive pattern of dysregulation and instability across all domains of functioning. Individuals with BPD have difficulty with emotion regulation and often exhibit suicidal and nonsuicidal self-injurious (NSSI) behaviors. Approximately 10% of individuals with BPD commit suicide (Linehan, Rizvi, Welch, & Page, 2000). The prevalence of BPD in the general population is estimated to be around 1% to 2%, indicating that it is one of the more common personality disorders (Lenzenweger, Lane, Loranger, & Kessler, 2007; Torgersen, Kringlen, & Cramer, 2001). At the same time, clinicians often hesitate to treat clients diagnosed with BPD due to the challenging interpersonal behaviors, as well as potential increased risk.

The Case

As a therapist on a dialectical behavioral therapy (DBT) team, you have been referred a 20-year-old, Asian American woman, recently discharged from an inpatient psychiatry unit following a suicide attempt by lithium overdose. The client, Jenny, describes her attempt as occurring during a period of many stressors, especially final exams at her technical college and her

http://dx.doi.org/10.1037/0000069-016
An ICD–10–CM Casebook and Workbook for Students: Psychological and Behavioral Conditions, J. B. Schaffer and E. Rodolfa (Editors)

father's recent serious cancer diagnosis. She reports that on the day of her attempt, she felt a sense of chaotic agitation and an intense urge to do something to get out of the pain she was experiencing. She consumed a large quantity of alcohol (she is typically a nondrinker) and took all of the psychotropic medication she had on hand (a potentially lethal dose of lithium). She says she had not planned this act ahead of time. Rather, she acted impulsively in an attempt to do anything possible to reduce her distress. Her roommate found her in the bathroom and called 911. After receiving care in the hospital emergency department, she stayed in an inpatient psychiatric ward for 2 weeks, until she was discharged upon stabilization. Jenny presents to treatment indicating that she ultimately wanted to live but was experiencing suicidal and self-harm urges daily, as well as a great deal of emotional misery (which includes feelings such as shame, sadness, and hopelessness that she finds difficult to tolerate). She describes two previous suicide attempts during high school and technical college, both drug overdoses. She had experienced ambivalence both times, indicating the desire to escape, although not necessarily the urge to die; in her words, "If I ended up dead, in order to not feel the distress any more, that's okay." She contends that her thoughts about suicide were not as much about wanting to die, but more about wanting to escape the current pain she was feeling. She also had a long history of NSSI, including cutting along her arms and thighs. Upon entering treatment, Jenny commits to attempting to stay alive for 1 month in order to try the therapy.

In monitoring Jenny's suicidality (see also Chapter 6 in this casebook), it would be critical to assess *lethality*, which is the degree to which her chosen means have the capacity to lead to death (e.g., a gun would be high lethality; taking five Tylenol would likely be low lethality). Another important factor is *imminence*, the degree of immediacy of the patient's plan (e.g., "I am going to do this as soon as I leave this therapy session" would be high imminence, whereas "One day I might take action" would be lower imminence). Further, assessing *access to means* is helpful to have some understanding of whether a patient is able to carry out the suicide plan. For example, if a patient's plan is to overdose on prescription medication, but she has no prescriptions and does not know anybody who has any, then there is no access to preferred means. However, if the plan involves hanging using a belt and she has a closet full of belts at home, then ready access to means would be available. In addition, understanding whether the patient's desire is to die, to escape, to cry for help, or to access specific types of support (e.g., hospitalization) is useful in conceptualizing the function of the attempt.

When Jenny was approximately five years old, she had about three experiences involving an aunt roughly handling and cleaning her sexual organs, engaging in physical punishment, and verbally berating her in the process. She currently has flashbacks and memories of these events, which are associated with intense emotional misery, as well as increased suicide and self-harm urges. Jenny reported that she told her mother about the incidents, but her mother did not take them seriously, nor did she engage in any actions as a result. She described her relationship with her parents as inconsistent—her basic needs were met, but she experienced consistent invalidation of her emotions, with her mother in particular telling her to "just handle it" or that she was being "too sensitive" whenever she experienced negative emotions.

Jenny has dispositional anxiety and possibly biological sensitivity to negative emotion. Particularly when vulnerable (e.g., during periods of menstrual pain or high stress), she has difficulty tolerating emotions of shame, anger at self, or sadness, and she engages in maladaptive behavior such as suicide/self-harm planning and binging/purging. She has struggled with alternately restricting and binging and purging behaviors for many years. She typically binges and purges impulsively when emotionally distressed, which leads to additional feelings of guilt and shame, as well as subsequent food restriction the following day in an attempt to "make up" for the binging and purging. A day of restriction is then often followed by waking up in the middle of the night to binge, which she reports occurs in a "dreamlike" or unaware state.

Jenny currently spends a great deal of time thinking about suicide, including making plans for ways to die, thinking about means and how to procure lethal methods, and ruminating on what being dead would be like. Her thinking about self-harm follows a similar pattern.

Jenny reports that while she does care for her parents a great deal, and feels bound to and responsible for them, she also wishes that her relationship with them could be more consistent. She describes typically feeling like she shifts between being disconnected and connected to them, as she alternates between thinking they should have protected her from the traumatic experiences with her aunt to thinking that it was her own fault, not her parents'. She experiences a similar back and forth shift in connection with her friends, as she alternates between feeling let down by them and accepting that all people are fallible. She finds herself wanting to avoid getting too close to people due to fear of being abandoned by them, yet experiencing strong desires to be intimately connected to people around her. These contradictory thoughts and the subsequent inconsistency in her desires and identity affect many aspects of her life. As a result of the unstable values, she reports chronically feeling empty inside and emotionally dysregulated.

During your intake interview with Jenny, you view her as highly compliant. She is agreeable and forthcoming and expresses a genuine desire and hope to build a life she experiences as worth living. She seems motivated to put effort into her treatment and is willing to complete any homework you assign to her. Nevertheless, you are worried that Jenny is losing hope, as her emotional misery and suicide and self-harm urges continue to remain very high.

Assessment Using the ICD–10–CM

ACTIVITY 15.1:

What other assessment would you would want to conduct to gain a more complete understanding of Jenny? Which of her behaviors and attitudes would you prioritize in your initial assessment?

Thorough and accurate assessment is critical for successful treatment. Indeed, the majority of therapeutic errors or failures in therapy can be conceptualized as errors in assessment. You recognize, given the complexity of Jenny's case, that assessment will be an ongoing process that overlaps with the beginning of treatment. To understand fully her intense emotional misery and suicide and self-harm urges, clear and detailed *behavioral chain analyses* are necessary. Behavioral chain analyses involve defining the target (undesired) behavior and understanding all of the links leading up to the engagement in the behavior, beginning with the prompting event. Because Jenny has not acted on her suicide and self-harm urges for a number of weeks, the primary target behavior you are interested in understanding is thinking about and planning for suicide and self-harm. The chain analyses revealed the following links:

1. Her proximal vulnerability factors, which are factors in the immediate past, such as situations that happened during the day that make her vulnerable to intense emotions, include physical, especially menstrual, pain. Her distal vulnerability factors, which are factors in the more distant past that make her vulnerable, include biological sensitivity to emotion and periods of higher stress (e.g., final exams).

2. The prompting events include all precipitants that elicit intense emotions of shame, anger, and sadness, encompassing any sex-related stimuli (ranging from male friends making physical contact with her to hearing the words and content related to sex or sexual abuse), stressors such as academic assignments or exams, and binging/purging behaviors.

3. The links in the chain after the prompting event are (a) feeling intense, typically co-occurring emotions of shame, anger, and sadness; (b) thoughts of worthlessness, being bad and disgusting; (c) additional thoughts that are either "I should punish myself" or "I just need this to stop."

4. These lead to the target behavior of thinking and ruminating on self-harm or suicide ideations in order to escape the situation or punish herself.

5. The maintaining consequences of the target behavior are that Jenny experiences short-term relief from negative emotion because suicide/self-harm planning serves an escape function. This brief respite from the aversive experience of negative emotion means that her target behavior is negatively reinforced, that is, the aversive stimulus is eliminated and the relief causes her target behavior to be more likely to occur over time. (For further information on this process, see Mowrer, 1947.)

6. Although the target behavior of suicide/self-harm planning is reinforced in the short term, it leads to emotional misery shortly thereafter, as she experiences even more negative emotions as a result of thinking about suicide and self-harm, thereby perpetuating a vicious cycle.

ICD–10–CM Diagnosis

ACTIVITY 15.2:

What are the possible ICD–10–CM diagnoses for Jenny, including her primary diagnosis and any comorbid diagnoses (i.e., disorders that co-occur)? Considering the number of symptoms that Jenny reports and that they could point to a wide array of potential diagnoses, why would you select one diagnosis over another?

From the case description so far, it is clear that Jenny experiences many distressing psychological symptoms and may meet criteria for several disorders. The main psychological symptoms Jenny has reported are (a) pervasive and increasing emotional dysregulation, where she experiences strong emotions ranging from sadness to shame, worry/anxiety, and anger that she has difficulty understanding, tolerating, and coping with, and which permeate all areas of her life; (b) persistent suicide and self-harm planning; (c) chronic feelings of emptiness; (d) unstable and inconsistent relationships with family and friends; (e) unclear values and desires; and (f) restricting, binging, and purging behaviors.

The Blue Book, the accompanying manual concerning clinical descriptions and diagnostic guidelines for mental health disorders for *the ICD–10 Classification of Mental and Behavioural Disorders* (WHO, 1993), states that precedence can be given either to the diagnosis that necessitates the current admission to care (i.e., the symptoms that resulted in a patient's current treatment) or a "lifetime" diagnosis (one that better describes a patient's problems in living across the board; p. 12). Thus, one might debate between Major depressive disorder, recurrent (F33.x), which would be consistent with her emotion-related symptoms (symptoms a–e above), or focus on her emotion-related symptoms using a conceptualization of a "lifetime" diagnosis, which would point in the direction of a personality disorder.

One could start with a consideration of her strong emotions of sadness and shame, as well as suicide and self-harm planning, which are in line with a Major depressive disorder, recurrent (F33.x) diagnosis. At the same time, however, she has other symptoms that are better encompassed by the Borderline personality disorder (F60.3) diagnosis, such as intense negative emotions of anger, chronic feelings of emptiness, unstable and inconsistent relationships with family and friends, and unclear values and desires. Given the pervasive nature of her emotion dysregulation, which is not a typical symptom of Major depressive disorder, recurrent (F33.x; a diagnosis that focuses more on the length of time symptoms have been present than on the pervasiveness of those symptoms), her symptoms may be better accounted for by a "lifetime" diagnosis of Borderline personality disorder (F60.3). The underlying problem for many of Jenny's problematic behaviors, such as suicide and self-harm planning, is her difficulty in tolerating strong negative emotions. As she experiences intense negative emotions, because she feels like she cannot control or tolerate them, she has a strong urge to escape them, and therefore engages in destructive behaviors. This emotion dysregulation, which is a central feature of Jenny's presentation, is the core problem of Borderline personality disorder (F60.3). Keep in mind that the pervasive nature of the emotion dysregulation of Borderline personality disorder (F60.3) means that other comorbid (co-occurring) diagnoses and problems in living are very common. Studies report that among a population of individuals with BPD, between 60% and 96% also met criteria for a mood or anxiety disorder (Grant et al., 2008; Zanarini et al., 1998).

Restricting, binging, and purging are disordered eating behaviors. It may be difficult to differentiate between F50.0x Anorexia nervosa and F50.2 Bulimia nervosa, as restriction, binging, and purging can be components of both disorders. However, as Jenny is of normal height and weight, without amenorrhea, and her periods of restriction follow her binge and purge episodes, F50.2 Bulimia nervosa is likely the more appropriate secondary diagnosis. Hence, you diagnose Jenny has having F60.3 Borderline personality disorder as the primary diagnosis and F50.2 Bulimia nervosa, as a secondary diagnosis.

Ethical Considerations— Protecting Your Patient

ACTIVITY 15.3:

What are the specific ethical concerns with a person who presents with intense emotional distress and a history of self-harm? Given the complexity of this case, what could you do if you are unsure of how best to meet Jenny's needs?

In order to best protect the patient, therapist competence is highly important (*Ethical Principles of Psychologists and Code of Conduct* [APA Ethics Code], Standard 2.01, Boundaries of Competence; APA, 2017). Therapist competence is often defined in part by the extent to which a therapist is able to deliver a treatment to a specific standard (Fairburn & Cooper, 2011). Additionally, a key component of protecting the patient is the delivery of an empirically supported treatment (APA Ethics Code, Standard 2.04, Bases for Scientific and Professional Judgments), given that only empirically supported treatments by definition have scientific evidence indicating their effectiveness and efficacy. DBT has the most empirical support of all treatments for BPD, and at present is considered the frontline treatment for the disorder (Neacsiu & Linehan, 2014).

One of the major considerations leading mental health professionals to hesitate to treat individuals with BPD is fear of inability to adequately manage suicide risk (Neacsiu & Linehan, 2014). Should a provider be competent in treating suicide but choose not to do so due to the potential complications or risk associated with suicidal patients, it may be useful to consider the fundamental principle of justice in the APA Ethics Code (Principle D). Specifically, as Principle D: Justice highlights the importance of fairness in entitling all individuals access to and benefit from the contributions of psychology, an examination of whether psychologists are biased against suicidal patients, and how that intersects with the ethical principles guiding our field, may be warranted. Similarly, should it become reasonably clear that the patient is no longer benefiting from the treatment, according to the APA Ethics Code, Standard 10.10, Terminating Therapy, alternatives should be considered, as is the case with all psychological therapies.

One unique component of DBT is the consultation team, which comprises all clinicians who work together in the clinic to provide treatment. Consultation teams include the primary therapists as well as skills group leaders, who provide support to each other to maintain motivation for delivering effective treatment and enhance each other's clinical skills. Full DBT applied to fidelity involves this "therapy for the therapists" (Linehan, 1993, 2014) component in order to increase therapist adherence to the treatment and reduce burnout. Importantly, informed consent must be obtained from patients prior to participating in DBT, acknowledging that confidentiality extends to the team level, beyond the individual therapist. This clarification is useful for both increasing confidence that the clinician will be well supported and accountable in treatment delivery, as well as providing the patient with critical information about the treatment being initiated.

Risk Management—Protecting Your Patient, Protecting Yourself

ACTIVITY 15.4:

What specific risks do you foresee in working with Jenny? How can you protect yourself and your client if you become anxious and overwhelmed?

Similar to the discussion above about the ethics of protecting the patient, the primary protective factor for a therapist is providing evidence-based practice to fidelity (APA Ethics Code, Principle B: Fidelity and Responsibility). A competent DBT-trained therapist, in conjunction with a consultation team, is armed with the best known tools to date. Utilizing the most empirically supported treatment is the most scientifically sound, as well as self-protective, method to address the client's diagnosis. DBT requires that therapists are part of a DBT consultation team, which functions as support and guidance for the therapist, given the recognition that effective treatment of BPD is very stressful and adhering to the DBT therapeutic framework can be challenging. The consultation team exists to increase therapist adherence to DBT principles and in turn to help the therapist provide the best treatment possible.

Another critical component of risk management is diligent written documentation of the therapeutic process, including noting which evidence-based strategy was used for what and why. Each time it is warranted, a thorough suicide risk assessment (e.g., Linehan, 2009) should be conducted and adequately documented as part of the therapy record. Clear and thorough documentation of clinical contact is one of the most important ways of protecting yourself.

A final consideration for your protection is careful adherence to your own boundaries (APA Ethics Code, Standard 2.06, Personal Problems and Conflicts) in therapy in order to decrease the likelihood of therapist burnout—and violation of professional ethics. Therapy-interfering behaviors of the therapist are also targets for consideration in DBT. These include your own anxiety or emotional responses that may interfere with your ability to act in the client's best interest; addressing these emotions thoroughly will ensure the best provision of treatment possible, which in turn is the ultimate protection for you and your client. Another critical function of the DBT team is to help DBT therapists manage burnout with teamwork, group supervision, and opportunities to practice mindfulness skills (Perseius, Kåver, Ekdahl, Asberg, & Samuelsson, 2007; Shapiro, Brown, & Biegel, 2007).

Disposition

> **ACTIVITY 15.5:**
>
> Jenny's hope for the future is slowly decreasing as she continues to feel significant emotional misery and depression. What would you do to help Jenny cope with her emotions and avoid self-harm?

Using the treatment with the most compelling research evidence is a critical component when considering the safety and ethics of protecting the patient, as is taking seriously the ethical obligation of beneficence and nonmaleficence (APA Ethics Code, Principle A: Beneficence and Nonmaleficence). You have been treating Jenny for about 4 months using DBT (for detailed information about the treatment, see Linehan, 1993, 2014; for research on its efficacy, see Barnicot et al., 2012; Linehan et al., 2006; Linehan, Heard, & Armstrong, 1993; Mehlum et al., 2014; Turner, 2000).

Following the clear protocols for suicide risk management, you target life-threatening behaviors as the top treatment priority. Additionally, you encourage Jenny to use 24-hour telephone consultation calls encompassed in the treatment, allowing her to obtain crisis intervention and skills generalization between sessions.

You and Jenny have collaboratively articulated her goals in therapy as follows:

1. Stay alive and abstain from NSSI.
2. Target behaviors that interfere with quality of life: depression, binging/purging, handling stress more effectively.
3. Strengthen her relationships with friends and parents, operationally defined as more stability, thus maintain feeling connected to them, rather than continuously shifting between connection and disconnection.

Jenny renews her commitment to staying alive, one month at a time. She continues to report very intense suicide and self-harm urges on a weekly basis; through the use of crisis phone-coaching and distress tolerance skills, she has not acted on her urges. At the same time, she is growing increasingly hopeless, as each day feels like a struggle simply to stay alive and hold fast to her therapy commitment not to die. Due to Jenny's high suicide and self-harm urges, the majority of each session and all phone calls are spent on trying to keep her alive. You and Jenny spend each hour collaboratively working together to remove means for suicide, generate crisis plans, troubleshoot barriers, engender hope, recommit to treatment, and learn distraction skills to get through crisis moments, but with only limited success.

Your DBT team members, with fresh eyes on the case, understand Jenny's overall case conceptualization as follows: There are many prompting events or triggers that lead to her experiencing negative emotion (e.g., sadness); due to her inability to tolerate the negative emotions, she engages in avoid/escape behaviors such as binging and purging, as well as suicide and self-harm planning. These very behaviors designed to help escape negative emotion, however, end up prompting more negative emotion (e.g., shame, feelings of worthlessness), which sets the cycle in motion again. Your team members hypothesize that you have made a mistake that many therapists make, particularly when fearful of suicide risk—that is, in trying to keep the patient alive (the number one priority goal), you have confused the objective with how to get there. Specifically, you have focused on helping Jenny stay alive by abstaining from committing suicide, rather than helping Jenny stay alive by building a life experienced as worth living. As a result, therapy to date has focused solely on inhibiting suicidal and self-harm behaviors, with the majority of session and telephone coaching time talking about suicide and crisis planning. In other words, you focused on keeping the client alive, rather than on the core problem of what has to change in order for her to want to stay alive.

While previously you had focused on inhibiting actual suicide and self-harm behaviors, your DBT consultation team suggests that a way to break this cycle is inhibiting the *planning* behavior itself. They see that thinking about and planning for suicide and self-harm is functioning as an escape, as they explain that each repetition of a problematic behavior solidifies it as a coping mechanism in Jenny's behavioral repertoire. Indeed, thinking about suicide gets reinforced because the very process of thinking can often bring short-term relief (Brown, Comtois, & Linehan, 2002), which over time makes suicidal ideation even more entrenched and leads to long-term emotional misery.

The team's invaluable consultation is particularly helpful as you think in the context of operant conditioning (Skinner, 1976). It is important to understand that using distress tolerance skills *prior* to suicidal ideation, in order not to engage in planning behaviors, helps avoid perpetuating the cycle that is negatively reinforced each time. Recall that negative reinforcement in suicidal ideation occurs for many clients because thinking about suicide provides temporary relief (elimination of an aversive stimulus) from excruciating negative emotion (Mowrer, 1947). In other words, instructing clients to decrease the "air time" that suicide planning gets in their minds can be helpful. Concurrently working on mindfulness of current emotion (Linehan, 1993) and other emotion-regulation skills (Linehan, 2014) to increase the capacity to experience and tolerate negative emotions, without feeling the urge to have to escape them, is a critical goal in therapy for clients with BPD.

References

American Psychological Association. (2017). *Ethical principles of psychologists and code of conduct* (2002, Amended June 1, 2010 and January 1, 2017). Retrieved from http://www.apa.org/ethics/code/ethics-code-2017.pdf

Barnicot, K., Katsakou, C., Bhatti, N., Savill, M., Fearns, N., & Priebe, S. (2012). Factors predicting the outcome of psychotherapy for borderline personality disorder: A systematic review. *Clinical Psychology Review, 32,* 400–412. http://dx.doi.org/10.1016/j.cpr.2012.04.004

Brown, M. Z., Comtois, K. A., & Linehan, M. M. (2002). Reasons for suicide attempts and nonsuicidal self-injury in women with borderline personality disorder. *Journal of Abnormal Psychology, 111,* 198–202. http://dx.doi.org/10.1037/0021-843X.111.1.198

Fairburn, C. G., & Cooper, Z. (2011). Therapist competence, therapy quality, and therapist training. *Behaviour Research and Therapy, 49*(6–7), 373–378. http://dx.doi.org/10.1016/j.brat.2011.03.005

Grant, B. F., Chou, S. P., Goldstein, R. B., Huang, B., Stinson, F. S., Saha, T. D., . . . Ruan, W. J. (2008). Prevalence, correlates, disability, and comorbidity of *DSM–IV* borderline personality disorder: Results from the Wave 2 National Epidemiologic Survey on Alcohol and Related Conditions. *The Journal of Clinical Psychiatry, 69,* 533–545. http://dx.doi.org/10.4088/JCP.v69n0404

Lenzenweger, M. F., Lane, M. C., Loranger, A. W., & Kessler, R. C. (2007). *DSM–IV* personality disorders in the national comorbidity survey replication. *Biological Psychiatry, 62,* 553–564. http://dx.doi.org/10.1016/j.biopsych.2006.09.019

Linehan, M. M. (1993). *Cognitive–behavioral treatment of borderline personality disorder.* New York, NY: Guilford Press.

Linehan, M. M. (2009). *The University of Washington risk assessment and management protocol: UWRAMP.* Unpublished manuscript, University of Washington. http://depts.washington.edu/brtc/files/UWRAMP.pdf

Linehan, M. M. (2014). *DBT skills training manual.* New York, NY: Guilford Press.

Linehan, M. M., Comtois, K. A., Murray, A. M., Brown, M. Z., Gallop, R. J., Heard, H. L., . . . Lindenboim, N. (2006). Two-year randomized controlled trial and follow-up of dialectical behavior therapy vs therapy by experts for suicidal behaviors and borderline personality disorder. *Archives of General Psychiatry, 63,* 757–766. http://dx.doi.org/10.1001/archpsyc.63.7.757

Linehan, M. M., Heard, H. L., & Armstrong, H. E. (1993). Naturalistic follow-up of a behavioral treatment for chronically parasuicidal borderline patients. *Archives of General Psychiatry, 50,* 971–974. http://dx.doi.org/10.1001/archpsyc.1993.01820240055007

Linehan, M. M., Rizvi, S. L., Welch, S. S., & Page, B. (2000). Psychiatric aspects of suicidal behavior: Personality disorders. In K. Hawton & K. van Heeringen (Eds.), *The international handbook of suicide and attempted suicide* (pp. 147–178). http://dx.doi.org/10.1002/9780470698976.ch10

Mehlum, L., Tørmoen, A. J., Ramberg, M., Haga, E., Diep, L. M., Laberg, S., . . . Grøholt, B. (2014). Dialectical behavior therapy for adolescents with repeated suicidal and self-harming behavior: A randomized trial. *Journal of the American Academy of Child & Adolescent Psychiatry, 53,* 1082–1091. http://dx.doi.org/10.1016/j.jaac.2014.07.003

Mowrer, O. H. (1947). On the dual nature of learning: A re-interpretation of "conditioning" and "problem solving." *Harvard Educational Review, 17,* 102–148.

Neacsiu, A. D., & Linehan, M. M. (2014). Borderline personality disorder. In D. Barlow (Ed.), *Clinical handbook of psychological disorders* (5th ed.; pp. 491–507). New York, NY: Guilford Press.

Perseius, K. I., Kåver, A., Ekdahl, S., Asberg, M., & Samuelsson, M. (2007). Stress and burnout in psychiatric professionals when starting to use dialectical behavioural therapy in the work with young self-harming women showing borderline personality symptoms. *Journal of Psychiatric and Mental Health Nursing, 14,* 635–643. http://dx.doi.org/10.1111/j.1365-2850.2007.01146.x

Shapiro, S. L., Brown, K. W., & Biegel, G. M. (2007). Teaching self-care to caregivers: Effects of mindfulness-based stress reduction on the mental health of therapists in training. *Training and Education in Professional Psychology, 1,* 105–115. http://dx.doi.org/10.1037/1931-3918.1.2.105

Skinner, B. F. (1976). *About behaviorism.* New York, NY: Random House.

Torgersen, S., Kringlen, E., & Cramer, V. (2001). The prevalence of personality disorders in a community sample. *Archives of General Psychiatry, 58,* 590–596. http://dx.doi.org/10.1001/archpsyc.58.6.590

Turner, R. M. (2000). Naturalistic evaluation of dialectical behavior therapy-oriented treatment for borderline personality disorder. *Cognitive and Behavioral Practice, 7,* 413–419. http://dx.doi.org/10.1016/S1077-7229(00)80052-8

World Health Organization. (1993). *The ICD–10 classification of mental and behavioural disorders: Clinical descriptions and diagnostic guidelines.* Retrieved from http://www.who.int/classifications/icd/en/bluebook.pdf

Zanarini, M. C., Frankenburg, F. R., Dubo, E. D., Sickel, A. E., Trikha, A., Levin, A., & Reynolds, V. (1998). Axis I comorbidity of borderline personality disorder. *The American Journal of Psychiatry, 155,* 1733–1739. http://dx.doi.org/10.1176/ajp.155.12.1733

Beth Limberg, Raquel M. Peña, Brooke Davidson,
and Christina B. Yeagley

F90.0 Attention-Deficit Hyperactivity Disorder

16

A ttention-deficit hyperactivity disorder (ADHD) has the potential to be one of the most misdiagnosed disorders in childhood, being both over-diagnosed in boys as an explanation for behavior that can be active or even disruptive in a classroom setting and underdiagnosed in girls for whom daydreaming rather than attending to the teacher can be a symptom of ADHD. Based on the National Survey of Children's Health, one in 11 school-age children in the United States received an ADHD diagnosis by 2011, as reported by parents. As many as one in five high school boys and one in 11 high school girls had been diagnosed. On average, prevalence rates for ADHD have been increasing approximately 5% per year (Visser et al., 2014).

The ICD–10–CM (World Health Organization, 1993) identifies three presentations of ADHD: (a) Predominantly inattentive type (F90.0), (b) Pre-dominantly hyperactive type (F90.1), and (c) Combined type (F90.2). The ICD–10–CM provides Other (F90.8) and Unspecified (F90.9) types for less common presentations of ADHD. Consistent across all subtypes are difficulties with focus and paying attention, executive functioning (e.g., struggles with sequencing and planning, poor organizational skills), and emotional regula-tion (e.g., poor frustration tolerance, emotional reactivity; Barkley, 2014). The differences between subtypes are complex. Hyperactive and inattentive

http://dx.doi.org/10.1037/0000069-017
An ICD–10–CM Casebook and Workbook for Students: Psychological and Behavioral Conditions, J. B. Schaffer and E. Rodolfa (Editors)

types, for example, differ in patterns of comorbidities, responses to medication and underlying neurobiological problems (Diamond, 2005). Inattentive and combined types are also dissimilar, differing in type of attention deficit, gender ratio, developmental course, pattern of comorbidity, response to pharmacological treatment, and behavioral manifestation of executive function (Capdevila-Brophy et al., 2014). For example, the core cognitive deficits associated with Predominantly inattentive type include poor working memory and slow reaction times or processing speed (Diamond, 2005), attentional impairments that may be accounted for by sluggish or inhibited cognitive style as opposed to distractibility to external stimuli, as is central in the Combined type (Capdevila-Brophy et al., 2014). On the other hand, Hyperactive types have a deficit in response inhibition, manifesting as hyperactive and impulsive behavior (Diamond, 2005).

Gender differences related to ADHD are significant. While boys with ADHD are at higher risk of behavior problems, girls typically present with less overtly disruptive symptoms, such as forgetfulness, disorganization, low self-esteem, and anxiety. Possibly because of stereotyped gender expectations ("girls daydream") and the inattentive presentation typical in girls (rather than hyperactive), ADHD is often underdiagnosed in girls, or at best, diagnosed years later than in boys, despite a similar age of onset. ADHD symptoms tend to worsen in girls during adolescence, at which time they generally present as functional impairments such as academic deficits, depression, eating disorders, and addictions. Often these comorbid disorders are diagnosed in girls long before ADHD is assessed because of the less overt symptom presentation in ADHD. (For more information on gender differences, see Barkley, 2014; Nussbaum, 2012.)

ADHD is currently understood to be a highly heritable disorder with strong genetic underpinnings (Rende, 2014). Thinking about ADHD as a genetically influenced or biological disorder contributes to our assessment strategies; specifically, we assess for symptoms across time and across settings. However, there is also a complex interplay between genetics and the environment. We recognize that the environment contributes to the development and presentation of ADHD, and this contributes to our assessment and treatment strategies.

The Case

Alex is a fourth-grade, bilingual, and bicultural boy living in an ethnically and linguistically diverse community. He was referred to you for assessment by his teacher, who reports that he is "not doing as well as he could be." Although Alex maintained acceptable grades through third grade, he is now struggling to keep up with his peers, especially in math and reading. Alex's teacher reports that he is fidgety, emotionally reactive, and impulsive. He can be hard to redirect, he "invades the space" of his peers and his teachers, and, at times, he is experienced as antagonistic. Alex is observed to "dally," especially when it is time to transition to a new activity.

Given the opportunity, Alex chooses to play with younger children. Despite his academic and behavioral challenges, his teachers like him, often saying that he "has potential."

Alex is the second of three children of Santiago, a 35-year-old Mexican American businessman, and Janice, a 34-year-old retail manager of German–Irish descent. Both parents work full-time outside of the home. Santiago's job frequently requires him to be on the road for 2 or 3 days at a time, although he Skypes nightly. The parents identify their family as middle class, with "enough" money and with access to education, medical, faith-based, and recreational resources. Both parents attended college, but did not graduate, and both completed vocation-specific training. Santiago and Janice have been married for 13 years, and all three children are biological. Both parents are invested in their children's well-being and success.

Santiago and Janice report no family history of diagnosed mental illness or learning disabilities, although neither parent nor an aunt had much interest in school as children. Both parents, however, believe that education is important to their children's future and report that initially they attributed Alex's energy, lack of attention, and social "klutziness" to being a boy.

Janice and Santiago report that Alex demonstrated a typical developmental trajectory and that his medical history has been unremarkable except for a number of ear infections (H65.0x) when he was a toddler. They report that Alex was always moving as a young child and that at times they grew tired of his tantrums. Still, his difficult behaviors were offset by his enthusiasm, so they were not concerned. Before Alex was in school, he attended a local day care center, where teachers described him as "full of energy" and "all boy," and sometimes as a "handful."

Family strengths include loving and supportive parent–child relationships, adequate resources, and positive and helpful relationships with a broad extended family. Alex reports that he is good at soccer (his parents confirm this) and that he has a good friend who is also on his team. He reports that his favorite subject is science, although he struggles when he is assigned to be the note-taker for his group.

Assessment Using the ICD–10–CM

ACTIVITY 16.1:

Based on the concerns expressed about Alex, what additional assessment strategies would help you make a diagnosis? How could your assessment account for overlapping symptoms that apply to diagnoses other than ADHD?

ADHD is more challenging to diagnose than it might seem. Behavioral symptom checklists suggest that a child who is fidgety, hypermotoric, inattentive, or distractible has ADHD, but in fact, these symptoms can be caused by any number of conditions or disorders. Further complicating the picture, ADHD can be comorbid with a number of conditions or disorders, especially other neurodevelopmental disorders. Careful attention to symptoms, situational variables, and life experiences will help you properly identify the root of these behaviors. (See Barkley, 2014, as a recommended text for a comprehensive review of diagnostic issues.) Assessment is best completed within a multimodal, multidisciplinary framework, with a thorough clinical interview being central to the accuracy of your assessment and diagnosis. For structured methods of interviewing in ADHD, consult Barkley (2014). Further, Barkley suggested checklists that cover a broader spectrum of diagnostic symptoms in order to address concerns regarding overlapping symptoms and comorbid disorders rather than checklists specifically focused on ADHD (i.e., Behavior Assessment System for Children—2 [BASC–2; Reynolds & Kamphaus, 2015]; Child Behavior Checklist [CBCL; Achenbach, 2001]).

Diagnosis Using the ICD–10–CM

ACTIVITY 16.2:

What are the potential diagnoses that would fit Alex's presentation? Why would you rule out other possible disorders as the primary diagnosis? How would you integrate information from Alex's parents and teachers into your diagnosis? Are there others you might consult with for additional information?

SENSORY PROCESSING DISORDER

Although sensory processing disorder (SPD) is not well described in the ICD–10–CM, it remains an important disorder to rule out when diagnosing ADHD. In the literature (Postert, Averbeck-Holocher, Achtergarde, Müller, & Furniss, 2012; Yochman, Alon-Beery, Sribman, & Parush, 2013), SPD is characterized by difficulties in recognizing, regulating, and interpreting sensory stimuli at a level that severely impacts the child's ability to participate in daily activities. Children with sensory processing difficulties can present in a variety of ways, many of which are similar to ADHD, including difficulty falling or staying asleep, exhibiting high energy levels, poor personal space boundaries, and poor impulse control. A child who is underresponsive to sensory stimuli may appear inattentive. A child who is overresponsive to sensory stimuli can appear hyperactive.

Research demonstrates that, despite similarities in clinical presentation, SPD and ADHD are indeed separate disorders with unique symptom profiles (Yochman et al., 2013). For example, difficulties in self-care routines in children with SPD are often the result of a distress about or inability in completing the routines, while in children with ADHD, they are the result of problems with organization and distractibility. To complicate your assessment, comorbidity between ADHD and SPD is high, with some research suggesting that as many as half of children with ADHD exhibit behaviors related to sensory processing difficulties (Yochman et al., 2013).

As mentioned earlier, SPD is not well described in the ICD–10–CM, which often deals with broad, general diagnostic categories. Other disorders of psychological development (F88) can be used for SPD, but when using this code, you must also note whether there are developmental delays. Because SPD can have multiple etiologies, it may be appropriate to use diagnoses that reflect a specific etiology. A case that presents with symptoms of SPD will require a careful matching of the specific presenting symptoms and the various diagnostic options in the ICD–10–CM. You will want to work closely with the child's medical team, physician, occupational therapist, speech therapist, and, perhaps, neuropsychologist, to determine the ICD–10–CM coding that best reflects the child's sensory challenges.

PERVASIVE DEVELOPMENTAL DISORDERS (F84.X)

Pervasive developmental disorders (PDDs) are characterized by impairments in three main areas: (a) social functioning, (b) communication, and (c) restricted/repetitive behaviors. Children with PDD demonstrate problems with executive functioning that can lead to difficulties with attention. There is also a tendency for children with PDD to be over- or underresponsive to sensory stimulation, and these sensory challenges can demonstrate themselves in impulsive behaviors. Challenges with language processing and communication, often present in children with PDD, may lead the child to appear aloof and interfere with the child's ability to attend to and follow directions, much like the "inattentiveness" noted in children with ADHD inattentive type. The impairments in social functioning of children with PDD (e.g., difficulties reading social cues, following social rules, and relating to same-age peers) can present in similar ways to the social impairments in children with ADHD. The social challenges and delays experienced by children with PDD, however, are primary diagnostic indicators of the disorder, while in ADHD the social challenges are often secondary to impulsivity and not always significant. Finally, a child with PDD may exhibit stereotyped/repetitive behaviors, behaviors rarely seen in children with ADHD.

RECEPTIVE (F80.2) AND EXPRESSIVE (F80.1) LANGUAGE DISORDERS

Receptive language disorders are diagnosed when a child's ability to understand (receive) language falls below what is expected based on his or her developmental age. Expressive language disorders are characterized by difficulty expressing thoughts and feelings using words, despite language comprehension abilities that fall within normal limits. When receptive language difficulties are present, children may exhibit behavioral challenges that are similar to those with ADHD, such as difficulty following directions (here, due to slow language processing or a lack of understanding language rather than poor working memory or problems with executive functioning). Children with receptive language disorder may have trouble sitting still in the classroom because they have difficulty processing the language-based instruction, whereas children with ADHD tend to be fidgety as a result of behavioral disinhibition.

Both children with receptive and expressive language disorders may appear impulsive because they do not have the language necessary to communicate with others. Similar behaviors in children with ADHD are more likely a result of behavioral disinhibition or difficulty planning.

READING DISORDER (F81.0)

Although reading difficulties are not considered a primary deficit in ADHD, reading and listening comprehension are notably problematic for many children with ADHD (Flake, Lorch, & Milich, 2007; Flory et al., 2006); little is known, however, about the specific nature of these difficulties (Miller et al., 2013). Since working memory deficits are associated with ADHD (Capdevila-Brophy et al., 2014), it is hypothesized that difficulties with comprehension in children with ADHD are related to their inability to hold previously presented ideas while integrating new ideas. Children with ADHD may devote an exorbitant amount of cognitive resources to sustaining attention and consequently may be left with fewer cognitive resources for comprehension tasks such as connecting ideas and forming a coherent understanding of the story (Miller et al., 2013). ADHD and reading disorders are frequently comorbid, and both have strong, possibly overlapping, genetic influences (Rende, 2014).

DEPRESSION (F32.X–F34.X)

In children, symptoms of depression can present similarly to symptoms of ADHD. Depressed mood can present as emotional reactivity and irritability (Blackman, Ostrander, & Herman, 2005). Psychomotor changes (especially agitation), changes in sleep patterns or weight, and diminished ability to concentrate or think can also mimic ADHD symptoms. Depression can also contribute to a level of detachment from the outside world that could be mistaken for the distractibility or "zoning out" present in ADHD. Onset of depression can occur at any age, but the likelihood increases with the onset of puberty; depression frequently occurs in a cyclical pattern with periods of improvement interspersed with periods of worsening symptoms. ADHD, on the other hand, tends to present in early school years and be more consistent across time and settings.

Comorbidity is an important consideration. Daviss (2008) found that depression occurs in children with ADHD at a significantly higher rate than in children without ADHD. Additionally, children with both ADHD and depression are at greater risk of long-term impairment and suicide than children with either disorder alone.

ANXIETY (F41.X)

Anxiety disorders in children can also be mistaken for ADHD. Difficulty paying attention and focusing, impulsivity, difficulty with self-control, and hyperactivity may look, on the surface, like ADHD; however, for children with an anxiety disorder such symptoms are typically behavioral manifestations of their preoccupation with excessive worry, fears, and tension. Frequently, anxiety in children is accompanied by a heightened fight-or-flight response, with physical symptoms such as muscle tension, stomachache, headache, nausea, and vomiting. Finally, the symptoms of children with anxiety disorders often develop (or worsen) following a significant life stressor (e.g., death of relative or pet, change of school, parental or family discord, a recent move). As with depression, the genetic influence in anxiety disorders is often revealed in a family history of mood or anxiety disorders.

SEVERE STRESS (F43.X)

Trauma can manifest with some symptoms similar to ADHD; the cognitive processes behind the symptoms, however, may be more unique to the child's traumatic experiences and directly follow the traumatic event. For example, children who have experienced severe stress may appear emotionally reactive due to hypervigilance or may appear easily distracted because they are experiencing intrusive and upsetting thoughts. Difficulty focusing on tasks or staying organized, as well as impulsivity, can also reflect a posttraumatic response.

Differentiating ADHD from trauma is further complicated by increased rates of comorbidity (American Academy of Pediatrics [AAP], 2014). Brown et al. (2017) investigated the relationships between ADHD and adverse childhood experiences, including poverty, divorce, death of a parent or guardian, domestic violence, parental substance abuse or incarceration, familial mental illness, and discrimination, and found that 17% of children diagnosed with ADHD had four or more adverse childhood experiences compared with 6% of children without ADHD.

In the interview with the child and caregivers, often you must listen for what is not said, as parents may or may not associate their child's behavior with trauma, such as food insecurity or community violence, or may be reluctant to admit to it, as in the case of sexual abuse.

OPPOSITIONAL DEFIANT DISORDER (F91.3), CONDUCT DISORDER (F91.X), AND REACTIVE ATTACHMENT DISORDER (F94.1–F94.2)

These disorders must be considered within a careful developmental and diagnostic framework. Young children are naturally oppositional. School-age children with impulse control issues can be oppositional and will likely make poor behavioral choices. Clinicians should take care to evaluate for ADHD and the other disorders before labeling children with conduct- and attachment-related disorders that are often ill understood and therefore overly pathologized (see Fraser & Wray, 2008; Noordermeer et al., 2017).

Given Alex's developmental and psychosocial history, you can almost immediately rule out PDD. Family and medical histories are negative for general risk factors for PDD, and although Alex's parents did discuss impulsivity and social challenges, they did not describe the qualitatively different social engagement and nonreciprocal or stereotypic communication patterns typical in PDD; nor did they describe repetitive or stereotypic behavior patterns. With no evidence of the most common neurodevelopmental risk factors or early sensory indicators for sensory processing difficulties, you also rule out SPD. Finally, you rule out trauma, as neither the clinical interview with Alex's parents nor the review of intake paperwork (which includes a checklist of challenging experiences) revealed trauma, even considering the special attention you gave to Alex's early years (as his symptoms date back to toddlerhood).

Since language processing disorders and reading disorders are frequently comorbid with ADHD, it is important for you to identify whether Alex meets criteria for multiple diagnoses or if perhaps a language processing disorder or reading disorder better accounts for the challenges that he is experiencing at home and in school. A review of Alex's history is not definitive. Repeated ear infections as a young child and tantruming (beyond what is expected developmentally) are consistent with speech delays and language disorders. Reports of disinterest in school in his mother, father, and aunt could indicate a family history of ADHD or of undiagnosed learning difficulties. Alex's behavior and academic difficulties could be accounted for by any of these conditions, although because his high energy and emotional reactivity (tantrums) predate his attendance in school, it is unlikely that his behavior and academic issues are explained solely by a reading disorder. Further assessment is indicated, as is consultation with a speech and language pathologist and the school resource specialist. Psychological assessment could include behavioral checklists for parents and teachers, specific tests for attention, language processing, and reading comprehension, or more comprehensive intelligence and achievement testing. Because Alex is bilingual, it will be important for you to interpret all assessment results in light of the current research on dual language learners (e.g., Hammer et al., 2014). It will be equally important to dispel the myths related to dual language learners and language processing disorders (e.g., the myth that dual language learners are slower to pick up language than monolingual learners, or that dual language learners with language processing disorders should focus on only one language; Kohnert, 2010).

Finally, Alex's teachers and parents report that he can be emotionally reactive, difficult to redirect, and slow to process information at school. These behaviors are consistent with the diagnostic criteria for depressive disorders in children; however, family history is negative for mood and anxiety disorders, and Alex's early presentation of symptoms is more reflective of the developmental trajectory of ADHD. Alex may be experiencing some anxiety regarding his father's frequent traveling, but the consistency of his behavior over time is more indicative of ADHD. Therefore, depression and anxiety can be ruled out as primary diagnoses. However, because of the frequent comorbidity seen with ADHD and depression, and because of the significant risk factors associated such comorbidity, you will continue to monitor for depression with periodic psychosocial assessments.

Because, on the basis of your initial assessment, Alex meets all of the requirements for Attention-deficit hyperactivity disorder, combined type (F90.2), and because you have been able to rule out other potential diagnoses, you diagnose Attention-deficit hyperactivity disorder, combined type (F90.2). You further document rule-outs for both language processing and reading disorders.

Ethical Considerations—Protecting Your Clients

ACTIVITY 16.3:

What specific ethical issues might you encounter when assessing Alex? Does the involvement of his parents raise any special issues?

Careful diagnostic assessment in children, especially with a complicated diagnostic picture, requires multidimensional and multidisciplinary evaluation. With parental consent (see the American Psychological Association [APA; 2017] *Ethical Principles of Psychologists and Code of Conduct* [APA Ethics Code], Standard 9.03, Informed Consent in Assessments), you seek to gather information from as many sources as possible. Sources of information may or may not include clinical interviews and brief diagnostic screening tests with parents, children, teachers, and day care providers, and review of medical, educational, and legal records. Multiple sources of information from multiple domains provide sufficient bases for an appropriate diagnosis (APA Ethics Code, Standard 9.01, Bases for Assessments).

Ongoing consultation and collaboration with allied professionals (e.g., teachers, resource specialists, speech and language pathologists, occupational therapists, psychologists, physicians and nurses) will help you understand when to refer for additional assessment (APA Ethics Code, Standard 3.09, Cooperation With Other Professionals). You don't want to run the risk of assuming that all behavior is rooted in mental health, when in fact, an alternative condition may more appropriately explain the behavior. At the same time, remain grounded in your own scope of practice (APA Ethics Code, Standard 2.01, Boundaries of Competence). Possessing knowledge of another's practice is not the same as possessing the skill to do what an allied professional does.

Finally, all work with children and families involves the management of multiple therapeutic relationships (with the child, with the parent, between child and parent; see APA Ethics Code, Standard 10.02, Therapy Involving Couples or Families). When conducting assessments, you should clarify early and often how data will be gathered, from whom, and who will have access to what information. Parents and children may not understand what information they control, what they can share, and when they have the right to refuse to share (and with whom).

Risk Management—Protecting Your Client, Protecting Yourself

ACTIVITY 16.4:

What risk factors might you consider when working with Alex and his family? What are the limitations of your role as a psychologist when working with a child and his or her parents? What steps can you take to protect your practice?

Research on child development and child pathology (especially brain development and genetic–environment interaction) is published at a remarkable rate. To provide effective treatment, it is important to maintain a working knowledge of this literature so that your assessment and diagnosis remains current (APA Ethics Code, Standard 2.03, Maintaining Competence). The American Academy of Pediatrics (2011), for example, recommends behavioral therapy as the first line of treatment for preschoolers and medication and behavioral therapy combined for school-age children and adolescents. Thorough assessment leads to an accurate diagnosis that guides treatment recommendations. As such, assessment includes understanding what the parents and child want or expect from treatment, both specifically (What does the family want from you?) and more broadly (What does the family believe about mental health and mental health services?), so that the family is confident in responding to your recommendations (APA Ethics Code, Standard 2.01b). When considering treatment related to ADHD, for example, medication is often recommended. This recommendation may be met with relief or with resistance, often based in the parents' beliefs about medication. These beliefs may be based in cultural or social expectations (e.g., my child just needs to behave, medication will serve as an excuse for bad behavior), medication myths (e.g., if my child is on medication, he or she will never learn to behave, because medication will serve as a crutch), fears (e.g., if my child takes medication, it means that I've failed as a parent), or inaccurate or incomplete information (e.g., taking psychostimulants will lead my child down the path of later substance abuse). There is, in fact, limited long-term research on the interplay between medication and the developing brain (Singh & Chang, 2012). Knowing whether to refer parents to their child's pediatrician or to a child psychiatrist may be guided by knowing the basics about what the experts know and recommend. Knowing your role and staying within the bounds of your competence will be crucial.

Disposition

ACTIVITY 16.5:

Given the complications, what might you include in Alex's treatment plan? How could his parents be involved in this treatment plan? Are there any particular strategies you would teach them?

The results of your assessment, and the ensuing diagnosis, guide you as you determine how much attention to devote to any particular system or intervention strategy and how to prioritize interventions. A multidimensional, systems approach is recommended when working with children diagnosed with ADHD and their families (AAP, 2011), and as such, intervention is often appropriate in multiple settings (e.g., clinical office, home, school, community). Given Alex's presentation, work in both the family and the school system is indicated. Because of his age and the primacy of peer relationships, you prioritize cognitive and behavioral social strategies to help Alex develop and maintain friendships. Cognitive and behavioral strategies are also helpful in teaching children to focus and slow down to make thoughtful decisions (Barkley, 2014) and to develop skills pertinent to maintaining social relationships and academic achievement. As treatment progresses, you can use emotional approaches to support self-understanding and self-esteem. Remember to keep an eye out for depression or anxiety that may develop secondary to ADHD or other life events.

You also provide psychoeducation to Alex's parents (and to Alex) on the diagnosis of ADHD and recommended treatments, as well as specific behavior management strategies for Santiago and Janice to use in the home (Barkley, 2014). While waiting for the results of the assessments regarding language processing and reading disorders, you can introduce the concept of providing instructions and reminders using multiple modalities (e.g., supplementing verbal directions with visual cues). Especially helpful for children with language processing difficulties, these strategies are also effective for children with ADHD. As your treatment progresses, you will likely provide support for caring for a child with special needs (e.g., responding to potential experiences of guilt or parent-blaming, responding to the needs of the other children in the family).

You may be asked by Alex's parents to help with decisions related to interacting with school and medical personnel. You can offer strategies for collaborating with teachers and for engaging academic resource supports. Both at home and at school, certain environmental interventions can support the growth and success of children with ADHD (Barkley, 2014). Home and classroom organization, removal of clutter, and visual scheduling systems are just a few techniques that help children with ADHD stay organized. Alternating movement activities with attention-demanding activities can also be effective, as well as identifying the child's most productive times of day and matching academic demands accordingly. These strategies, originally employed by adults, can be taught to children as they grow older so that they can manage themselves more effectively (see also Monastra, 2014, 2016).

Finally, consider the needs and strengths of the individual child, the parents, and the family, remembering that relationships are paramount. You may use relational interventions with Alex and his family to repair relationship hurts, to create (or support) a compassionate narrative about Alex, his parents, and ADHD, and to establish realistic expectations. Remember to consider the systems with which Alex and his family interact (e.g., educational, medical, social services, legal, faith communities, cultural groups). You are prudent to consider also the broader, metasystems that influence children and families (e.g., community, racial and ethnic affiliation, socioeconomic status, disability, immigration status, etc.) and the experiences that Alex's family has had with these metasystems (e.g., privilege, oppression/discrimination).

References

Achenbach, T. (2001). *Child behavior checklist—Cross informant version.* Burlington, VT: Author.

American Academy of Pediatrics. (2011). ADHD: Clinical practice guideline for the diagnosis, evaluation, and treatment of attention-deficit/hyperactivity disorder in children and adolescents. *Pediatrics, 128*(5), 1–16. http://dx.doi.org/10.1542/peds.2011-2654

American Academy of Pediatrics. (2014). *Study finds ADHD and trauma often go hand in hand.* Retrieved from https://www.aap.org/en-us/about-the-aap/aap-press-room/pages/Study-Finds-ADHD-and-Trauma-Often-go-Hand-in-Hand.aspx

American Psychological Association. (2017). *Ethical principles of psychologists and code of conduct* (2002, Amended June 1, 2010 and January 1, 2017). Retrieved from http://www.apa.org/ethics/code/index.aspx

Barkley, R. (2014). *Attention-deficit hyperactivity disorder: A handbook for diagnosis and treatment.* New York, NY: Guilford Press.

Blackman, G. L., Ostrander, R., & Herman, K. C. (2005). Children with ADHD and depression: A multisource, multimethod assessment of clinical, social, and academic functioning. *Journal of Attention Disorders, 8,* 195–207. http://dx.doi.org/10.1177/1087054705278777

Brown, N. M., Brown, S. N., Briggs, R. D., Germán, M., Belamarich, P. F., & Oyeku, S. O. (2017). Associations between adverse childhood experiences and ADHD: Analysis of the 2011 National Survey of Children's Health. *Academic Pediatrics, 17,* 349–355. http://dx.doi.org/10.1016/j.acap.2016.08.013

Capdevila-Brophy, C., Artigas-Pallarés, J., Navarro-Pastor, J. B., García-Nonell, K., Rigau-Ratera, E., & Obiols, J. E. (2014). ADHD predominantly inattentive subtype with high sluggish cognitive tempo: A new clinical entity? *Journal of Attention Disorders, 18,* 607–616. http://dx.doi.org/10.1177/1087054712445483

Daviss, W. B. (2008). A review of co-morbid depression in pediatric ADHD: Etiology, phenomenology, and treatment. *Journal of Child and Adolescent Psychopharmacology, 18,* 565–571. http://dx.doi.org/10.1089/cap.2008.032

Diamond, A. (2005). Attention-deficit disorder (attention-deficit/hyperactivity disorder without hyperactivity): A neurobiologically and behaviorally distinct disorder from attention-deficit/hyperactivity disorder (with hyperactivity). *Development and Psychopathology, 17*(3), 807–825. http://dx.doi.org/10.1017/S0954579405050388

Flake, R. A., Lorch, E. P., & Milich, R. (2007). The effects of thematic importance on story recall among children with attention deficit hyperactivity disorder and comparison children. *Journal of Abnormal Child Psychology, 35*(1), 43–53. http://dx.doi.org/10.1007/s10802-006-9078-z

Flory, K., Milich, R., Lorch, E. P., Hayden, A. N., Strange, C., & Welsh, R. (2006). Online story comprehension among children with ADHD: Which core deficits are involved? *Journal of Abnormal Child Psychology, 34,* 850–862. http://dx.doi.org/10.1007/s10802-006-9070-7

Fraser, A., & Wray, J. (2008). Oppositional defiant disorder. *Australian Family Physician, 37,* 402–405. Retrieved from http://www.racgp.org.au/afpbackissues/2008/200806/200806fraser.pdf

Hammer, C. S., Hoff, E., Uchikoshi, Y., Gillanders, C., Castro, D., & Sandilos, L. E. (2014). The language and literacy development of young dual language learners: A critical review. *Early Childhood Research Quarterly, 29,* 715–733. http://dx.doi.org/ 10.1016/j.ecresq.2014.05.008

Kohnert, K. (2010). Bilingual children with primary language impairment: Issues, evidence and implications for clinical actions. *Journal of Communication Disorders, 43,* 456–473. http://dx.doi.org/10.1016/j.jcomdis.2010.02.002

Miller, A. C., Keenan, J. M., Betjemann, R. S., Willcutt, E. G., Pennington, B. F., & Olson, R. K. (2013). Reading comprehension in children with ADHD: Cognitive underpinnings of the centrality deficit. *Journal of Abnormal Child Psychology, 41,* 473–483. http://dx.doi.org/10.1007/s10802-012-9686-8

Monastra, V. (2014). *Parenting children with ADHD: 10 lessons that medicine cannot teach.* Washington, DC: American Psychological Association.

Monastra, V. (2016). *Teaching life skills to children and teens with ADHD.* Washington, DC: American Psychological Association.

Noordermeer, S. D. S., Luman, M., Weeda, W. D., Buitelaar, J. K., Richards, J. S., Hartman, C. A., . . . Oosterlaan, J. (2017). Risk factors for comorbid oppositional defiant disorder in attention-deficit/hyperactivity disorder. *European Child & Adolescent Psychiatry, 26,* 1155–1164. http://dx.doi.org/10.1007/s00787-017-0972-4

Nussbaum, N. L. (2012). ADHD and female specific concerns: A review of the literature and clinical implications. *Journal of Attention Disorders, 16*(2), 87–100. http:// dx.doi.org/10.1177/1087054711416909

Postert, C., Averbeck-Holocher, M., Achtergarde, S., Müller, J. M., & Furniss, T. (2012). Regulatory disorders in early childhood: Correlates in child behavior, parent–child relationship, and parental mental health. *Infant Mental Health Journal, 33,* 173–186. http://dx.doi.org/10.1002/imhj.20338

Rende, R. (2014). *Psychosocial interventions for genetically influenced problems in childhood and adolescence* (pp. 45–68). http://dx.doi.org/10.1002/9781118948187.ch03

Reynolds, C., & Kamphaus, R. (2015). *Behavioral Assessment System for Children* (3rd ed.; BASC–3). New York, NY: Pearson Education.

Singh, M. K., & Chang, K. D. (2012). The neural effects of psychotropic medications in children and adolescents. *Child and Adolescent Psychiatric Clinics of North America, 21,* 753–771. http://dx.doi.org/10.1016/j.chc.2012.07.010

Visser, S., Danielson, M., Bitsko, R., Holbrook, J. R., Kogan, M. D., Ghandour, R. M., . . . Blumberg, S. J. (2014). Trends in the parent-report of health care provider-diagnosed and medicated attention-deficit/hyperactivity disorder: United States, 2003–2011. *Journal of the American Academy of Child and Adolescent Psychiatry, 53*(1), 34–46. http:// dx.doi.org/10.1016/j.jaac.2013.09.001

World Health Organization. (1993). *The ICD–10 classification of mental and behavioural disorders: Clinical descriptions and diagnostic guidelines.* Retrieved from http://www. who.int/classifications/icd/en/bluebook.pdf

Yochman, A., Alon-Beery, O., Sribman, A., & Parush, S. (2013). Differential diagnosis of sensory modulation disorder (SMD) and attention deficit hyperactivity disorder (ADHD): Participation, sensation, and attention. *Frontiers in Human Neuroscience, 7,* 862. Advance online publication. http://dx.doi.org/10.3389/fnhum.2013.00862

Index

About the Editors

Jack B. Schaffer, PhD, now retired, spent 17 years in independent practice and 16 years as a faculty member in two medical schools and a professional school. His private practice specialized in clinical and neuropsychological assessments and psychotherapy with adults and families. He received his doctorate in clinical psychology from the University of North Dakota and is certified by the American Board of Professional Psychology in clinical psychology and clinical health psychology. He is a fellow and past president of the Association of State and Provincial Psychology Boards and a past chair of the State of Minnesota Board of Psychology. He currently serves on the American Psychological Association's Commission on Accreditation. Dr. Schaffer's professional interests include psychological assessment, defining and assessing professional competence, and ethical and legal issues. He enjoys woodworking, bicycling, and spending time with his wife, his two children, and four grandchildren.

Emil Rodolfa, PhD, is a professor of psychology at Alliant International University's California School of Professional Psychology (CSPP) in Sacramento. He received his doctorate from Texas A&M University and was training director and director of the University of California Counseling and Psychological Services before joining the faculty at CSPP. He is the founding editor of *Training and Education in Professional Psychology* and was associate editor of *Professional Psychology Research and Practice*. Dr. Rodolfa is a fellow of the American Psychological Association, a fellow and past president of the Association of State and Provincial Psychology Boards, a board member emeritus and past chair of the Association of Psychology Postdoctoral and Internship Centers, and a past president of the State of California Board of Psychology. His professional interests include defining and assessing professional competence, ethical and legal issues, supervision and training, college student mental health, and the assessment and treatment of anxiety and depression. He enjoys spending time with his family, playing horseshoes, and barbecuing (some might call it grilling) at his cabin in the mountains.